Praise for
THE ANTHROPOCENE REVIEWED

#1 *New York Times* Bestseller
#1 *Wall Street Journal* Bestseller
#1 Indie Bestseller
***USA Today* Bestseller**
International Bestseller

GOODREADS CHOICE NONFICTION BOOK OF THE YEAR

"Essential to the human conversation. John Green whispered the truth of humanity onto the page, and as with all good secrets, you'll need to lean in closely to hear." —*Library Journal,* starred review

"*The Anthropocene Reviewed* is the perfect book to read whenever you need a reminder of what it is to feel small and human, in the best possible way."
—*San Francisco Chronicle*

"Charming, curious, and heartfelt. Each essay feels like its own adventure on a journey toward understanding our world and humanity's impact on it."
—*NPR,* Best Books of the Year

"Moving, entertaining and mind-expanding. . . . Green has a Gladwell-esque ability to explain complex phenomena and his sense of humor and eye for life's absurdities bring lightness to difficult and sometimes harrowing topics."
—*The Irish Times*

"Green's style is akin to that of someone like Susan Orlean, combining deeply personal anecdotes with fascinating facts. . . . The result is like falling into a Wikipedia hole if the entries were written as a form of therapy."
—A.V. Club

"Green's intellectual curiosity, sense of humor, vulnerability, and philosophical questioning are both interesting and inspiring." —*The Harvard Press*

"Poignant and reassuring. . . . A reminder that even with everything going on in the world, we can still find joy in little things. Humans have an incredible capacity to love, and this book is proof that no matter how big or small, there is so much in this world to love." —*Business Insider*

"Green searches for joy—large and small—in human nature."
—*Parade Magazine,* Best Books of the Year

"Each short review is rich with meaning and filled with surprises and together, they amount to a resonant paean to hard-won hope."
—*Publishers Weekly*, starred review

"Each of the entries is a small gem, polished to near perfection. . . .
What unites them is Green's uncanny ability to structure each piece
as both a critique of human foibles and an embracing of them."
—*Shelf Awareness*, starred review

"There is something of the sermon in Green's essays as he mixes curiosity
and erudition with confession, compassion, and wit, searching for illuminating life lessons amid life's dark chaos. His particular mix of irony and sincerity enables him to embrace both the sublime and the ridiculous." —*Booklist*

"Green's empathy and sense of humor shine through." —*Indianapolis Monthly*

"Lyrical and beautiful, funny and hopeful, intricate and entertaining
all at once. Beautifully written." —*Shondaland*

"These personal essays explore humanity in every detail
from funny and small to complex and powerful."
—Isaac Fitzgerald, TODAY Show Summer Reading Recommendations

"In his novels, John Green conjures richly imagined, heartfelt drama that
lovingly explores the human condition. With *The Anthropocene Reviewed*,
John pulls off the same magic trick while writing about the largest ball of
paint. . . and it is glorious. Every page is full of insight. I loved it."
—Roman Mars, creator and host of *99% Invisible*

"*The Anthropocene Reviewed* somehow satisfies all the contradictory demands
I have for a book right now: it stimulates my brain while getting me out
of my head while taking me to faraway places while grounding me in the
wonders of my everyday. I'm so glad it's here. I need it." —Anna Sale, host
of *Death, Sex & Money* and author of *Let's Talk About Hard Things*

"If loving something out loud takes courage, and I think it does, John Green
is Evel Knievel and *The Anthropocene Reviewed* is a series of ever-more-impressive motorcycle jumps." —Latif Nasser, co-host of *Radiolab*

THE
ANTHROPOCENE
REVIEWED

THE
ANTHROPOCENE
REVIEWED

Essays on a Human-Centered Planet

by John Green

DUTTON

DUTTON

An imprint of Penguin Random House LLC
penguinrandomhouse.com

Previously published as a Dutton hardcover in May 2021
First Dutton trade paperback printing: March 2023
Copyright © 2021 by John Green
Additional content for this edition copyright © 2023 by John Green

Dutton trade paperback ISBN: 9780525555247
International edition ISBN: 9780525556558

Printed in the United States of America
2nd Printing

Edited by Julie Strauss-Gabel
Book design by Anna Booth
Text set in Bembo MT Pro

I have to confess I'm not a huge fan of copyright pages in general with their small type, obtuse verbiage, and morally charged legalese. I do appreciate, though, that copyright pages identify the book's font, as above. Designer Anna Booth set this book in Bembo MT Pro. Bembo was released in 1929 by the Monotype Corporation, but it is based on a design first cut in 1495 by Francesco Griffo, who worked for the famed Venetian printer Aldus Manutius. The first printing press arrived in Venice in 1469; within thirty years, there were more than four hundred presses, printing everything from Greek classics to travelogues. The typeface Bembo is based on was first used to print Pietro Bembo's short memoir of visiting Mt. Etna. Robert Slimbach has called Griffo's font design an "ideal balance of beauty and functionality," and although I'm no font designer, I agree. I give Bembo MT Pro four and a half stars.

To my friends, colleagues, and fellow travelers
Rosianna Halse Rojas and Stan Muller

CONTENTS

THE ANTHROPOCENE REVIEWED

This page is known to publishers and bookbinders as the "half-title page," because it lists the title but not the author name or subtitle. The half title once served a real function in the printing and bookbinding process, but these days it is mostly ornamental. I've always felt like half-title pages are a bit gratuitous. By the time I've arrived here as a reader, I already know the title of the book, and if I need to be reminded, it's perpetually available to me on the book's front cover. But, then again, in an age of screen reading, I suppose every facet of bookmaking is anachronistic, and I do deeply love the feel of paper, and the sight of print, so I'll give half-title pages two and a half stars.

INTRODUCTION

MY NOVEL *TURTLES ALL THE WAY DOWN* was published in October of 2017, and after spending that month on tour for the book, I came home to Indianapolis and blazed a trail between my children's tree house and the little room where my wife and I often work, a room that depending on your worldview is either an office or a shed.

This was not a metaphorical trail. It was an actual trail in the woods, and to make it I cleared dozens of the prolific and invasive honeysuckle trees that choke much of Central Indiana, and I dug up the English ivy that had taken over, and then I covered the path in wood chips and lined it with bricks. I worked on the path ten or twelve hours a day, five or six days a week, for a month. When I finally finished, I timed myself walking along the path from our office to the tree house. Fifty-eight seconds. It took me a month to build a fifty-eight-second walk in the woods.

A week after finishing the path, I was searching through a drawer for some ChapStick when all at once and without any warning, my balance failed. The world began to roll and spin. I was suddenly a very small boat in very high seas. My eyes shivered in their sockets, and I began vomiting. I was rushed to the hospital, and for weeks afterward, the world spun and spun. Eventually I was diagnosed with labyrinthitis, a disease of the inner ear with a wonderfully resonant name that is nonetheless an unambiguously one-star experience.

Recovery from labyrinthitis meant weeks in bed, unable to read or watch TV or play with my kids. I had only my thoughts—at times drifting through a drowsy sky, at other times panicking me with their insistence and omnipresence. During these long, still days, my mind traveled all over, roaming through the past.

The writer Allegra Goodman was once asked, "Whom would you like to write your life story?" She answered, "I seem to be writing it myself, but since I'm a novelist, it's all in code." For me, it had started to feel like some people thought they knew the code. They would assume I shared the worldviews of a book's protagonists, or they'd ask me questions as if I *were* the protagonist. One famous interviewer asked me if I also, like the narrator of *Turtles All the Way Down*, experience panic attacks while kissing.

I had invited such questions by having a public life as a mentally ill person, but still, talking so much about myself in the context of fiction became exhausting for me, and a little destabilizing. I told the interviewer that no, I do not have anxiety around kissing, but I do experience panic attacks, and they are intensely frightening. As I talked, I felt distant from myself—like my self wasn't really mine, but instead something I was selling or at the very least renting out in exchange for good press.

As I recovered from labyrinthitis, I realized I didn't want to write in code anymore.

In 2000, I worked for a few months as a student chaplain at a children's hospital. I was enrolled in divinity school and planning to become an Episcopal minister, but my time at the hospital disavowed me of those plans. I couldn't handle the devastation I saw there. I still can't handle it. Instead of going to divinity school, I moved to Chicago and worked as a typist for temp agencies until eventually landing a job doing data entry for *Booklist* magazine, a biweekly book review journal.

A few months later, I got my first chance to review a book after an editor asked me if I liked romance novels. I told her I loved them, and she gave me a novel set in seventeenth-century London. Over the next five years, I reviewed hundreds of books for *Booklist*—from picture books about the Buddha to poetry collections—and in the process, I became fascinated by the format of the review. *Booklist* reviews were limited to 175 words, which meant each sentence must work multiple jobs. Every review had to introduce a book while also analyzing it. Your compliments needed to live right alongside your concerns.

At *Booklist*, reviews do not include ratings on a five-star scale. Why would they? In 175 words, one can communicate far more to potential readers than any single data point ever could. The five-star scale has only been used in critical analysis for the past few decades. While it was occasionally applied to film criticism as early as the 1950s, the five-star scale wasn't used to rate hotels until 1979, and it wasn't widely used to rate books until Amazon introduced user reviews.

The five-star scale doesn't really exist for humans; it exists for data aggregation systems, which is why it did not become standard until the internet era. Making conclusions about a book's quality from a 175-word review is hard work for artificial intelligences, whereas star ratings are ideal for them.

———

It's tempting to make labyrinthitis a metaphor: My life lacked balance and so I was devastated by a balance disorder. I spent a month drawing a straight line of a trail only to be told that life is never simple paths—only dizzying labyrinths folding in on themselves. Even now I'm structuring this introduction like a maze, coming back to places I thought I'd left.

But this symbolization of disease is exactly what I've tried to write against in my novels *Turtles All the Way Down* and *The Fault in Our Stars*, where I hope at least OCD and cancer are portrayed not as battles to be won or as symbolic manifestations of character flaws or whatever, but as illnesses to be lived with as well as one can. I did not get labyrinthitis because the universe wanted to teach me a lesson about balance. So I tried to live with it as well as I could. Within six weeks, I was mostly better, but I still experience bouts of vertigo, and they are terrifying. I know now with a viscerality I didn't before that consciousness is temporary and precarious. It's not a metaphor to say that human life is a balancing act.

As I got better, I wondered what I would do with the rest of my life. I went back to making a video every Tuesday and a weekly podcast with my brother, but I wasn't writing. That fall and winter was the longest I'd gone without trying to write for an audience since I was fourteen years old. I suppose I missed writing, but in the way you miss someone you used to love.

———————

I left *Booklist* and Chicago in 2005, because my wife, Sarah, got into graduate school in New York. When she finished her degree, we moved to Indianapolis, where Sarah worked for the Indianapolis Museum of Art as a curator of contemporary art. We have lived here ever since.

I read so much at *Booklist* that I can't remember when I first came across the word *Anthropocene*, but it must have been around 2002. The Anthropocene is a proposed term for the current geologic age, in which humans have profoundly reshaped the planet and its biodiversity. Nothing is more human than aggrandizing humans, but we are a hugely powerful force on Earth in the twenty-first century.

My brother, Hank, who started out his professional life as a biochemist, once explained it to me like this: As a person, he told me, your biggest problem is other people. You are vulnerable to people, and reliant upon them. But imagine instead that you are a twenty-first-century river, or desert, or polar bear. Your biggest problem *is still people*. You are still vulnerable to them, and reliant upon them.

Hank had been with me on the book tour that fall of 2017, and to pass the time on long drives between cities, we'd try to one-up each other with absurd Google user reviews for the places we drove past. A user named Lucas, for example, gave Badlands National Park one star. "Not enough mountain," he reported.

In the years since I'd been a book reviewer, everyone had become a reviewer, and everything had become a subject for reviews. The five-star scale was applied not just to books and films but to public restrooms and wedding photographers. The medication I take to treat my obsessive-compulsive disorder has more than 1,100 ratings at Drugs.com, with an average score of 3.8. A scene in the movie adaptation of my book *The Fault in Our Stars* was filmed on a bench in Amsterdam; that bench now has hundreds of Google reviews. (My favorite, a three-star review, reads in its entirety: "It is a bench.")

As Hank and I marveled at the sudden everywhereness of reviewing on a five-star scale, I told him that years earlier, I'd had an idea to write a review of Canada geese.

Hank said, "The Anthropocene . . . REVIEWED."

I'd actually written a few of the reviews back in 2014—the one about Canada geese, and also one on Diet Dr Pepper. In early 2018, I sent those reviews to Sarah and asked for her thoughts.

When I reviewed books, "I" was never in the review. I imagined myself as a disinterested observer writing from outside. My early reviews of Diet Dr Pepper and Canada geese were similarly written in the nonfictional version of third-person omniscient narration. After Sarah read them, she pointed out that in the Anthropocene, there are no disinterested observers; there are only participants. She explained that

when people write reviews, they are really writing a kind of memoir—here's what *my* experience was eating at this restaurant or getting
my hair cut at this barbershop. I'd written 1,500 words about Diet Dr
Pepper without once mentioning my abiding and deeply personal love
of Diet Dr Pepper.

Around the same time, as I began to regain my sense of balance,
I reread the work of my friend and mentor Amy Krouse Rosenthal,
who'd died a few months earlier. She'd once written, "For anyone trying
to discern what to do w/ their life: PAY ATTENTION TO WHAT
YOU PAY ATTENTION TO. That's pretty much all the info u need."
My attention had become so fractured, and my world had become so
loud, that I wasn't paying attention to what I was paying attention to.
But when I put myself into the reviews as Sarah suggested, I felt like for
the first time in years, I was at least trying to pay attention to what I pay
attention to.

———————

This book started out as a podcast, where I tried to chart some of the
contradictions of human life as I experience it—how we can be so com-
passionate and so cruel, so persistent and so quick to despair. Above all,
I wanted to understand the contradiction of human power: We are at
once far too powerful and not nearly powerful enough. We are powerful enough to radically reshape Earth's climate and biodiversity, but not
powerful enough to choose *how* we reshape them. We are so powerful
that we have escaped our planet's atmosphere. But we are not powerful
enough to save those we love from suffering.

I also wanted to write about some of the places where my small life
runs into the large forces of the Anthropocene. In early 2020, after two
years of writing the podcast, an exceptionally large force appeared in the
form of a novel coronavirus. I began then to write about the only thing
I could write about. Amid the crisis—and writing to you from April of

2021, I am still amid it—I find much to fear and lament. But I also see humans working together to share and distribute what we collectively learn, and I see people working together to care for the sick and vulnerable. Even separated, we are bound up in each other. As Sarah told me, there are no observers; only participants.

————————

At the end of his life, the great picture book author and illustrator Maurice Sendak said on the NPR show *Fresh Air*, "I cry a lot because I miss people. I cry a lot because they die, and I can't stop them. They leave me, and I love them more."

He said, "I'm finding out as I'm aging that I'm in love with the world."

It has taken me all my life up to now to fall in love with the world, but I've started to feel it the last couple of years. To fall in love with the world isn't to ignore or overlook suffering, both human and otherwise. For me anyway, to fall in love with the world is to look up at the night sky and feel your mind swim before the beauty and the distance of the stars. It is to hold your children while they cry, to watch as the sycamore trees leaf out in June. When my breastbone starts to hurt, and my throat tightens, and tears well in my eyes, I want to look away from feeling. I want to deflect with irony, or anything else that will keep me from feeling directly. We all know how loving ends. But I want to fall in love with the world anyway, to let it crack me open. I want to feel what there is to feel while I am here.

Sendak ended that interview with the last words he ever said in public: "Live your life. Live your life. Live your life."

Here is my attempt to do so.

"YOU'LL NEVER WALK ALONE"

IT IS MAY OF 2020, and I do not have a brain well suited to this.

I find more and more that I refer to it as "it" and "this" without naming or needing to name, because we are sharing the rare human experience so ubiquitous that the pronouns require no antecedent. Horror and suffering abound in every direction, and I want writing to be a break from it. Still, it makes its way in—like light through window blinds, like floodwater through shut doors.

I suppose you are reading this in my future. Maybe you are reading in a future so distant from my present that "this" is over. I know it will never fully end—the next normal will be different from the last one. But there will be a next normal, and I hope you are living in it, and I hope I am living in it with you.

In the meantime, I have to live in this, and find comfort where I can. For me, lately, comfort has meant a show tune.

In 1909, the Hungarian writer Ferenc Molnár debuted his new play, *Liliom*, in Budapest. In the play, Liliom, a troubled and periodically violent young carousel barker, falls in love with a woman named Julie. When Julie becomes pregnant, Liliom attempts a robbery to support his burgeoning family, but the robbery is a disaster, and Liliom dies. He ends up in purgatory for sixteen years, after which he is allowed a single day to visit his now-teenaged daughter, Louise.

Liliom flopped in Budapest, but Molnár was not a playwright who suffered from a shortage of self-belief. He continued mounting productions around Europe and then eventually in the U.S., where a 1921 translation of the play attracted good reviews and moderate box office success.

The composer Giacomo Puccini tried to adapt *Liliom* into an opera, but Molnár refused to sell him the rights, because he wanted "*Liliom* to be remembered as a play by Molnár, not as an opera by Puccini." Instead, Molnár sold the rights to Richard Rodgers and Oscar Hammerstein, the musical theater duo who were fresh off the success of *Oklahoma!* In doing so, Molnár ensured that *Liliom* would be remembered almost entirely as a musical by Rodgers and Hammerstein, retitled *Carousel*, which premiered in 1945.

In the musical, Rodgers and Hammerstein's song "You'll Never Walk Alone" is sung twice—first to encourage the newly widowed Julie after her husband's death, and then by Louise's classmates years later, at a graduation ceremony. Louise doesn't want to join in the song—she's too upset—but even though her father is now invisible to her, Louise can feel his presence and encouragement, and so eventually she starts to sing.

The lyrics of "You'll Never Walk Alone" contain only the most obvious imagery: The song tells us to "walk on through the wind and through the rain," which is not a particularly clever evocation of a storm. We are also told to "walk on with hope in your heart," which feels aggressively trite. And it reports that "at the end of the storm, there's a golden sky and the sweet silver song of a lark." But in reality, at the end of the storm, there are tree branches strewn everywhere, and downed power lines, and flooded rivers.

And yet, the song works for me. Maybe it's the repetition of the words "walk on." I think two of the fundamental facts of being a person are 1. We must go on, and 2. None of us ever walks alone. We may *feel* alone (in fact, we *will* feel alone), but even in the crushing grind of isolation, we aren't alone. Like Louise at her graduation, those who are distant or even gone are still with us, still encouraging us to walk on.

The song has been covered by everyone from Frank Sinatra to Johnny Cash to Aretha Franklin. But the most famous cover came in 1963 from Gerry and the Pacemakers, a band that, like the Beatles, was from Liverpool, managed by Brian Epstein, and recorded by George Martin. In keeping with their band name, the Pacemakers changed the meter of the song, increasing the tempo, giving the dirge a bit of pep, and their version became a #1 hit in the UK.

Fans of Liverpool Football Club almost immediately began to sing the song together during games. That summer, Liverpool's legendary manager Bill Shankly told the Pacemakers' lead singer, Gerry Marsden, "Gerry, my son, I have given you a football team, and you have given us a song."

Today, "You'll Never Walk Alone" is etched in wrought iron above the gates of Anfield, Liverpool's stadium. Liverpool's famous Danish defender Daniel Agger has YNWA tattooed on the knuckles of his right hand. I've been a Liverpool fan for decades,[1] and for me the song is so linked to the club that when I hear the opening notes, I think of all the times I've sung it with other fans—sometimes in exaltation, often in lamentation.

When Bill Shankly died in 1981, Gerry Marsden sang "You'll Never Walk Alone" at the memorial service—as it has been sung at many funerals for many Liverpool supporters. The miracle of "You'll Never Walk Alone" for me is how well it works as a funeral song, and as a high school

---

1.   Why? When I was twelve, I was on my middle school soccer team. I was awful, of course, and rarely played. We had one good player on our team, a guy named James. James was from England, and he told us that in England, there were professional soccer teams, and thousands of fans would stand together, shoulder to shoulder, and sing all through the games. He told us that the best team in England was Liverpool. And I believed him.

graduation song, and as a we-just-beat-Barcelona-in-the-Champions-League song. As former Liverpool player and manager Kenny Dalglish said, "It covers adversity and sadness and it covers the success." It's a song about sticking together even when your dreams are tossed and blown. It's a song about both the storm and the golden sky.

At first blush, it may seem odd that the world's most popular football song comes from musical theater. But football *is* theater, and fans make it musical theater. The anthem of West Ham United is called "I'm Forever Blowing Bubbles," and at the start of each game, you'll see thousands of grown adults blowing bubbles from the stands as they sing, "I'm forever blowing bubbles, pretty bubbles in the air / They fly so high, nearly reach the sky / Then like my dreams, they fade and die." Manchester United fans refashioned Julia Ward Howe's U.S. Civil War anthem "Battle Hymn of the Republic" into the song "Glory, Glory Man United." Manchester City fans sing "Blue Moon," a 1934 Rodgers and Hart number.

All these songs are made great by the communities singing them. They are assertions of unity in sorrow and unity in triumph: Whether the bubble is flying or bursting, we sing together.

"You'll Never Walk Alone" is cheesy, but it's not wrong. The song doesn't claim the world is a just or happy place. It just asks us to walk on with hope in our hearts. And like Louise at the end of *Carousel*, even if you don't really believe in the golden sky or the sweet silver song of the lark when you start singing, you believe it a little more when you finish.

In March 2020, a video made the rounds online in which a group of British paramedics sang "You'll Never Walk Alone" through a glass wall to coworkers on the other side, who were in an intensive care unit. The paramedics were trying to encourage their colleagues. What a word that is, *en-courage*. Though our dreams be tossed and blown, still we sing ourselves and one another into courage.

I give "You'll Never Walk Alone" four and a half stars.

HUMANITY'S TEMPORAL RANGE

WHEN I WAS NINE OR TEN, I saw a planetarium show at the Orlando Science Center in which the host, with no apparent emotion in his voice, explained that in about a billion years, the sun will be 10 percent more luminescent than it is now, likely resulting in the runaway evaporation of Earth's oceans. In about four billion years, Earth's surface will become so hot that it will melt. In seven or eight billion years, the sun will be a red giant star, and it will expand until eventually our planet will be sucked into it, and any remaining Earthly evidence of what we thought or said or did will be absorbed into a burning sphere of plasma.

Thanks for visiting the Orlando Science Center. The exit is to your left.

It has taken me most of the last thirty-five years to recover from that presentation. I would later learn that many of the stars we see in the night sky are red giants, including Arcturus. Red giants are common. It is common for stars to grow larger and engulf their once-habitable solar systems. It's no wonder we worry about the end of the world. Worlds end all the time.

A 2012 survey conducted across twenty countries found wide variance in the percentage of people who believe humanity will end within their lifetimes. In France, 6 percent of those polled did; in the United States, 22 percent. This makes a kind of sense: France has been home to apocalyptic preachers—the bishop Martin of Tours, for instance, wrote "There is no doubt that the Antichrist has already been born." But that was back in the fourth century. American apocalypticism has a much more recent history, from Shaker predictions the world would end in 1794 to famed radio evangelist Harold Camping's calculations that the apocalypse was coming in 1994—and then, when that didn't happen, in 1995. Camping went on to announce that the end times would commence on May 21, 2011, after which would come "five months of fire, brimstone and plagues on Earth, with millions of people dying each day, culminating on October 21st, 2011 with the final destruction of the world." When none of this came to pass, Camping said, "We humbly acknowledge we were wrong about the timing," although for the record no individual ever humbly acknowledged anything while referring to themselves as "we." I'm reminded of something my religion professor Donald Rogan told me once: "Never predict the end of the world. You're almost certain to be wrong, and if you're right, no one will be around to congratulate you."

Camping's personal apocalypse arrived in 2013, when he died at the age of ninety-two. Part of our fears about *the* world ending must stem from the strange reality that for each of us *our* world will end, and soon. In that sense, maybe apocalyptic anxieties are a by-product of humanity's astonishing capacity for narcissism. How could the world possibly survive the death of its single most important inhabitant—me? But I think something else is at work. We know we will end in part because we know other species have ended.

"Modern humans," as we are called by paleontologists, have been around for about 250,000 years. This is our so-called "temporal range," the length of time we've been a species. Contemporary elephants are at least ten times older than us—their temporal range extends back to the Pliocene Epoch, which ended more than 2.5 million years ago. Alpacas have been around for something like 10 million years—forty times longer than us. The tuatara, a species of reptile that lives in New Zealand, first emerged around 240 million years ago. They've been here a thousand times longer than we have, since before Earth's supercontinent of Pangaea began to break apart.

We are younger than polar bears and coyotes and blue whales and camels. We are also far younger than many animals we drove to extinction, from the dodo to the giant sloth.

———

In the spring of 2020, a few weeks after the emergence of a novel coronavirus began to shut schools and clear out grocery stores in the U.S., someone sent me a collection they'd made of times I'd publicly mentioned my fear of an infectious disease pandemic. On the podcast *10 Things That Scare Me*, I'd listed near the top, "a global disease pandemic that will result in the breakdown of human norms." Years earlier, in a video about world history, I'd speculated about what might happen "if some superbug shows up tomorrow and it travels all these global trade routes." In 2019, I'd said on a podcast, "We all must prepare ourselves for the global pandemic we all know is coming." And yet, I did nothing to prepare. The future, even in its inevitabilities, always feels vague and nebulous to me—until it doesn't.

After my kids' school closed, and after I'd found a mask that I'd bought years earlier to minimize sawdust inhalation while building their tree house, but long before I understood the scope of the pandemic, I called my brother, Hank, and told him I was feeling frightened. Hank is the levelheaded one, the sane one, the calm one. He always has been. We have never let the fact of my being older get in the way of Hank being the wise older brother. Ever since we were little, one of the ways I've managed my anxiety is by looking to him. My brain cannot reliably report to me whether a perceived threat is really real, and so I look at Hank, and I see that he's not panicked, and I tell myself that I'm okay. If anything were *truly* wrong, Hank wouldn't be able to portray such calm confidence.

So I told Hank I was scared.

"The species will survive this," he answered, a little hitch in his voice.

"*The species will survive this?* That's all you've got for me???"

He paused. I could hear the tremble in his breath, the tremble he's been hearing in my breath our whole lives. "That's what I've got for you," he said after a moment.

I told Hank I'd bought sixty cans of Diet Dr Pepper, so that I could drink two for each day of the lockdown.

And only then could I hear the old smile, the my-older-brother-really-is-a-piece-of-work smile. "For someone who has spent four decades worrying about disease pandemics," he said, "you sure don't know how disease pandemics work."

One rule of retail marketing maintains that to maximize sales, businesses need to create a sense of urgency. *Mega-sale ends soon! Only a few tickets still available!* These commercial threats, especially in the age of e-commerce, are almost always a fiction. But they're effective, an echo of our apocalyptic visions: If we feel a sense of urgency about the human experiment, maybe we'll actually get to work, whether that's rushing to save souls before the Rapture or rushing to address climate change.

I try to remind myself that back in the fourth century, Martin of Tours's eschatological anxiety must have felt as real to him as my current anxiety feels to me. A thousand years ago, floods and plagues were seen as apocalyptic portents, because they were glimpses of a power far beyond our understanding. By the time I was growing up, amid the rise of computers and hydrogen bombs, Y2K and nuclear winter made for better apocalyptic worries. Today, these worries sometimes focus on artificial intelligence run amok, or on a species-crushing pandemic that we have proven ourselves thoroughly unprepared for, but most commonly my worry takes the form of climate anxiety, or eco-anxiety—terms that did not exist a few decades ago but are now widespread phenomena.

Humans are already an ecological catastrophe. In just 250,000 years, our behavior has led to the extinction of many species, and driven many more into steep decline. This is lamentable, and it is also increasingly needless. We probably didn't know what we were doing thousands of years ago as we hunted some large mammals to extinction. But we know what we're doing now. We know how to tread more lightly upon the earth. We could choose to use less energy, eat less meat, clear fewer forests. And we choose not to. As a result, for many forms of life, humanity *is* the apocalypse.

———————

There are worldviews that embrace cyclic cosmologies—Hindu eschatology, for instance, lays out a series of multibillion-year periods called kalpas during which the world goes through a cycle of formation, maintenance, and then decline. But in linear eschatologies, the end times for humanity are often referred to as "the end of the world," even though our departure from Earth will very probably not be the end of the world, nor will it be the end of life in the world.

Humans are a threat to our own species and to many others, but the planet will survive us. In fact, it may only take life on Earth a few million years to recover from us. Life has bounced back from far more serious shocks. Two hundred and fifty million years ago, during the Permian extinction, ocean surface waters likely reached 104 degrees Fahrenheit, or 40 degrees Celsius. Ninety-five percent of Earth's species went extinct, and for five million years afterward, Earth was a "dead zone" with little expansion of life.

Sixty-six million years ago, an asteroid impact caused a dust cloud so huge that darkness may have pervaded Earth for *two years*, virtually stopping photosynthesis and leading to the extinction of 75 percent of land animals. Measured against these disasters, we're just not that important. When Earth is done with us, it'll be like, "Well, that Human Pox wasn't great, but at least I didn't get Large Asteroid Syndrome."

The hard part, evolutionarily, was getting from prokaryotic cells to eukaryotic ones, and then getting from single-celled organisms to multicellular ones. Earth is around 4.5 billion years old, a timescale I simply cannot get my head around. Instead, let's imagine Earth's history as a calendar year, with the formation of Earth being January 1, and today being December 31 at 11:59 PM. The first life on Earth emerges around February 25. Photosynthetic organisms first appear in late March. Multicellular life doesn't appear until August or September. The first dinosaurs like eoraptor show up about 230 million years ago, or December 13 in our calendar year. The meteor impact that heralds the end of the dinosaurs happens around December 26. *Homo sapiens* aren't part of the story until December 31 at 11:48 PM.[2]

Put another way: It took Earth about three billion years to go from single-celled life to multicellular life. It took less than seventy million years to go from *Tyrannosaurus rex* to humans who can read and write and dig up fossils and approximate the timeline of life and worry about its ending. Unless we somehow manage to eliminate all multicellular life from the planet, Earth won't have to start all the way over, and it will be okay—at least until the oceans evaporate and the planet gets consumed by the sun.

But we'll be gone by then, as will our collective and collected

---

2.   Agriculture and large human communities and the building of monolithic structures all occur within the last minute of this calendar year. The Industrial Revolution, two world wars, the invention of basketball, recorded music, the electric dishwasher, and vehicles that travel faster than horses all happen in the last couple of seconds.

memory. I think part of what scares me about the end of humanity is the end of those memories. I believe that if a tree falls in the woods and no one is there to hear it, it does make a sound. But if no one is around to play Billie Holiday records, those songs really won't make a sound anymore. We've caused a lot of suffering, but we've also caused much else.

I know the world will survive us—and in some ways it will be *more* alive. More birdsong. More creatures roaming around. More plants cracking through our pavement, rewilding the planet we terraformed. I imagine coyotes sleeping in the ruins of the homes we built. I imagine our plastic still washing up on beaches hundreds of years after the last of us is gone. I imagine moths, having no artificial lights toward which to fly, turning back to the moon.

There is some comfort for me in knowing that life will go on even when we don't. But I would argue that when our light goes out, it will be Earth's greatest tragedy, because while I know humans are prone to grandiosity, I also think we are by far the most interesting thing that ever happened on Earth.

It's easy to forget how wondrous humans are, how strange and lovely. Through photography and art, each of us has seen things we'll never see—the surface of Mars, the bioluminescent fish of the deep ocean, a seventeenth-century girl with a pearl earring. Through empathy, we've felt things we might never have otherwise felt. Through the rich world of imagination, we've seen apocalypses large and small.

We're the only part of the known universe that knows it's in a universe. We know we are circling a star that will one day engulf us. We're the only species that knows it has a temporal range.

––––––––––

Complex organisms tend to have shorter temporal ranges than simple ones, and humanity faces tremendous challenges. We need to find a way to survive ourselves—to go on in a world where we are powerful enough to warm the entire planet but not powerful enough to stop warming it. We may even have to survive our own obsolescence as technology learns to do more of what we do better than we can do it. But we are better positioned to solve our biggest problems than we were one hundred or one thousand years ago. Humans have more collective brainpower than we've ever had, and more resources, and more knowledge collected by our ancestors.

We are also shockingly, stupidly persistent. Early humans probably used many strategies for hunting and fishing, but a common one was persistence hunting. In a persistence hunt, the predator relies on tracking prowess and sheer perseverance. We would follow prey for hours, and each time it would run away from us, we'd follow, and it would run away again, and we'd follow, and it would run away again, until finally the quarry became too exhausted to continue. That's how for tens of thousands of years we've been eating creatures faster and stronger than us.

We. Just. Keep. Going. We spread across seven continents, including one that is entirely too cold for us. We sailed across oceans toward land we couldn't see and couldn't have known we would find. One of my favorite words is *dogged*. I love dogged pursuits, and dogged efforts, and dogged determination. Don't get me wrong—dogs are indeed very dogged. But they ought to call it *humaned*. Humaned determination.

For most of my life, I've believed we're in the fourth quarter of human history, and perhaps even the last days of it. But lately, I've come to believe that such despair only worsens our already slim chance at long-term survival. We must fight like there is something to fight for, like we are something worth fighting for, because we are. And so I choose to believe that we are not approaching the apocalypse, that the end is not coming, and that we will find a way to survive the coming changes.

"Change," Octavia Butler wrote, "is the one unavoidable, irresistible, ongoing reality of the universe." And who am I to say we are done changing? Who am I to say that Butler was wrong when she wrote "The Destiny of Earthseed is to take root among the stars"? These days, I choose to believe that our persistence and our adaptability will allow us to keep changing with the universe for a very, very long time.

So far, at a paltry 250,000 years, it's hard to give humanity's temporal range more than one star. But while I initially found my brother's words distressing, these days I find myself repeating them, and believing them. He was right. He always is. The species will survive this, and much more to come.

And so in hope, and in expectation, I give our temporal range four stars.

HALLEY'S COMET

ONE OF THE ENDURING MYSTERIES of Halley's comet is that no-body knows how to spell its name, as the comet is named for an as-tronomer who spelled his own surname variously as Hailey, Halley, and Hawley. We think language moves around a lot these days, with the emergence of emojis and the shifting meaning of words like *literally*, but at least we know how to spell our own names. I'm going to call it Hal-ley's comet, with apologies to the Hawleys and Haileys among us.

It's the only periodic comet that can regularly be seen from Earth by the naked eye. Halley's comet takes between seventy-four and seventy-nine years to complete its highly elliptical orbit around the sun, and so once in a good human lifetime, Halley brightens the night sky for several weeks. Or twice in a human lifetime, if you schedule things well. The American writer Mark Twain, for instance, was born as the comet blazed above the Missouri sky. Seventy-four years later, he wrote, "I came in with Halley's Comet in 1835. It is coming again next year, and I expect to go out with it." And he did, dying in 1910 as Halley reap-peared. Twain had a hell of a gift for narrative structure, especially when it came to memoir.

Seventy-six years later, the comet returned in the late winter of

1986. I was eight. This apparition of the comet was, to quote Wikipedia, "the least favorable on record," with the comet much farther from Earth than usual. The comet's distance, combined with the tremendous growth of artificial light, meant that in many places Halley was invisible to the naked eye.

I was living in Orlando, Florida, a town that throws a lot of light up at the night sky, but on Halley's brightest weekend, my dad and I drove up to the Ocala National Forest, where our family owned a little cabin. At the tail end of what I still consider to be one of the best days of my life, I saw the comet through my dad's birding binoculars.

Humanity may have known that Halley was a repeating comet thousands of years ago. There is a reference in the Talmud to "a star that appears once in seventy years and makes the captains of ships err." But back then it was common for humans to forget over time what they had already learned. Maybe not only back then, come to think of it.

At any rate, Edmond[3] Halley noticed that the 1682 comet he observed seemed to have a similar orbit to comets that had been reported in 1607 and 1531. Fourteen years later, Halley was still thinking about the comet, writing to Isaac Newton, "I am more and more confirmed that we have seen that comett now three times since ye year 1531." Halley then predicted the comet would return in 1758. It did, and it has been named for him ever since.

Because we so often center history on the exploits and discoveries of individuals, it's easy to forget that broad systems and historical forces drive shifts in human understanding. While it is true, for example, that Halley correctly predicted the comet's return, his colleague and contemporary Robert Hooke had already expressed "a very new opinion" that some comets might be recurring. Even putting aside the Talmud's

---

3.   Or possibly Edmund.

possible awareness of periodic comets, other sky gazers were beginning to have similar ideas around the same time. Seventeenth-century Europe—with not just Newton and Hooke, but also Boyle and Galileo and Gascoigne and Pascal—saw so many important scientific and mathematical breakthroughs not because the people born in that time and place happened to be unusually smart, but because the analytic system of the scientific revolution was emerging, and because institutions like the Royal Society allowed well-educated elites to learn from one another more efficiently, and also because Europe was suddenly and unprecedentedly rich. It's no coincidence that the scientific revolution in Britain coincided with the rise of British participation in the Atlantic slave trade and the growing wealth being extracted from colonies and enslaved labor.

We must, then, try to remember Halley in context—not as a singular genius who emerged from a family of soap-boilers to discover a comet, but as a searching and broadly curious person who was also, like the rest of us, "a bubble on the tide of empire," as Robert Penn Warren memorably put it.

That noted, Halley was brilliant. Here's just one example of his use of lateral thinking, as discussed in John and Mary Gribbin's book *Out of the Shadow of a Giant*: When asked to work out the acreage of land in every English county, Halley "took a large map of England, and cut out the largest complete circle he could from the map." That circle equated to 69.33 miles in diameter. He then weighed both the circle and the complete map, concluding that since the map weighed four times more than the circle, the area of England was four times the area of the circle. His result was only 1 percent off from contemporary calculations.

Halley's polymathic curiosity makes his list of accomplishments read like they're out of a Jules Verne novel. He invented a kind of diving bell to go hunting for treasure in a sunken ship. He developed an early magnetic compass and made many important insights about Earth's magnetic

field. His writing on Earth's hydrological cycle was tremendously in-
fluential. He translated the Arab astronomer al-Battānī's tenth-century
observations about eclipses, using al-Battānī's work to establish that the
moon's orbit was speeding up. And he developed the first actuarial table,
paving the way for the emergence of life insurance.

Halley also personally funded the publication of Newton's three-
volume *Principia* because England's leading scientific institution, the
Royal Society, "rashly spent all its publishing budget on a history of fish,"
according to historian Julie Wakefield. Halley immediately understood
the significance of the *Principia*, which is considered among the most
important books in the history of science.[4] "Now we are truly admitted
as table-guests of the Gods," Halley said of the book. "No longer does
error oppress doubtful mankind with its darkness."

Of course, Halley's ideas didn't always hold up. Error still oppressed
doubtful humankind (and still does). For example, partly based on Newton's incorrect calculations of the moon's density, Halley argued there
was a second Earth inside of our Earth, with its own atmosphere and
possibly its own inhabitants.

———

By the time Halley's comet showed up in 1986, the scientific revolution's
approach to knowledge-building had proven so successful that even third
graders like me knew about the layers of the earth. That day in the Ocala
National Forest, my dad and I made a bench by nailing two-by-fours to
sections of tree trunk. It wasn't particularly challenging carpentry, but in
my memory, at least, it took us most of the day. Then we started a fire,

---

4.   In *Out of the Shadow of a Giant*, Mary Gribbin and John Gribbin argue that while the
Principia is of course important, it also relied upon—and at times outright stole—research
from others, especially Robert Hooke. They write, "The famous story of the falling apple
seen during the plague year of 1665 is a myth, invented by Newton to bolster his (false)
claim that he had the idea for a universal theory of gravity before Hooke." It's sort of comforting to know that even Isaac Newton exaggerated what he got done during his plague
year.

cooked some hot dogs, and waited for it to get properly dark—or as dark as Central Florida got in 1986.

I don't know how to explain to you how important that bench was to me, how much it mattered that my dad and I had made something together. But that night, we sat next to each other on our bench, which just barely fit the two of us, and we passed the binoculars back and forth, looking at Halley's comet, a white smudge in the blue-black sky.

My parents sold the cabin almost twenty years ago, but not long before they did, I spent a weekend there with Sarah. We'd just started dating. I walked her down to the bench, which was still there. Its fat legs were termite-ridden, and the two-by-fours were warped, but it still held our weight.

Halley's comet is not a monolithic spherical miniplanet flying through space, as I imagined it to be. Instead, it is many rocks that have coalesced into a peanut-shaped mass—a "dirty snowball," as the astronomer Fred Whipple put it. In total, Halley's dirty snowball of a nucleus is nine miles long and five miles wide, but its tail of ionized gas and dust particles can extend more than sixty million miles through space. In 837 CE, when the comet was much closer to Earth than usual, its tail stretched across more than half of our sky. In 1910, as Mark Twain lay dying, Earth actually passed through the comet's tail. People bought gas masks and anti-comet umbrellas to protect against the comet's gases.

In fact, though, Halley poses no threat to us. It's approximately the same size as the object that struck Earth sixty-six million years ago leading to the extinction of dinosaurs and many other species, but it's not on a collision course with Earth. That noted, Halley's comet will be more than five times closer to Earth in 2061 than it was in 1986. It'll be brighter in the night sky than Jupiter, or any star. I'll be eighty-three—if I'm lucky.

———

When you measure time in Halleys rather than years, history starts to look different. As the comet visited us in 1986, my dad brought home a personal computer—the first in our neighborhood. One Halley earlier, the first movie adaptation of *Frankenstein* was released. The Halley before that, Charles Darwin was aboard the HMS *Beagle*. The Halley before that, the United States wasn't a country. The Halley before that, Louis XIV ruled France.

Put another way: In 2021, we are five human lifetimes removed from the building of the Taj Mahal, and two lifetimes removed from the abolition of slavery in the United States. History, like human life, is at once incredibly fast and agonizingly slow.

———

Very little of the future is predictable. That uncertainty terrifies me, just as it terrified those before me. As John Gribbin and Mary Gribbin write, "Comets were the archetypal unpredictable phenomenon, appearing entirely without warning, rousing superstitious awe in the eighteenth century to an even greater extent than eclipses."

Of course, we still know almost nothing about what's coming—neither for us as individuals nor for us as a species. Perhaps that's why I find it so comforting that we do know when Halley will return, and that it will return, whether we are here to see it or not.

I give Halley's comet four and a half stars.

OUR CAPACITY FOR WONDER

TOWARD THE END of F. Scott Fitzgerald's novel *The Great Gatsby*, the narrator is sprawled out on a beach at night when he begins thinking about the moment Dutch sailors first saw what is now called New York. Fitzgerald writes, "For a transitory enchanted moment, man must have held his breath in the presence of this continent, compelled into an aesthetic contemplation he neither understood nor desired, face to face for the last time in history with something commensurate to his capacity for wonder." It's a hell of a sentence. A lot changed in *Gatsby* between the first manuscript and the finished book—in 1924, Fitzgerald's publisher actually had galleys printed of the novel, then called *Trimalchio*, before Fitzgerald revised extensively and changed the title to *The Great Gatsby*. But in all of the editing and cutting and rearranging, that particular sentence never changed. Well, except that in one draft Fitzgerald misspelled the word *aesthetic*—but who hasn't?

Gatsby took a circuitous route on its way to being one of the Great American Novels. The initial reviews weren't great, and the book was widely considered to be inferior to Fitzgerald's first novel, *This Side of Paradise*. In the *New York Herald*, Isabel Paterson wrote that *Gatsby* was "a book for the season only." H. L. Mencken called it, "obviously unimportant" in the *Chicago Tribune*. The *Dallas Morning News* was especially brutal, writing, "One finishes *The Great Gatsby* with a feeling of regret, not for the fate of the people in the book, but for Mr. Fitzgerald. When *This Side of Paradise* was published, Mr. Fitzgerald was hailed as a young man of promise . . . but the promise, like so many, seems likely to go unfulfilled." Yikes.

The novel sold modestly—not nearly as well as either of his previous books. By 1936, Fitzgerald's annual royalties from book sales amounted to around eighty dollars. That year, he published "The Crack-Up," a series of essays about his own physical and psychological collapse. "I began to realize that for two years my life had been a drawing on resources that I did not possess, that I had been mortgaging myself physically and spiritually up to the hilt." In the end, Fitzgerald would die just a few years later, at the age of 44, his books mostly forgotten.

But then, in 1942, the U.S. Council on Books in Wartime began sending books to American troops fighting in World War II. More than 150,000 copies of the Armed Services Edition of *Gatsby* were shipped overseas, and the book became a hit at last. Armed Services Editions were paperback books that fit into a soldier's pocket; they popularized several books now considered classics, including Betty Smith's *A Tree Grows in Brooklyn*. Smith's book was one of the few books by women included in the program; the vast majority were written by white men.

The Council on Books in Wartime's slogan was "Books are weapons in the war of ideas," which was the kind of slogan generals could get behind even if many of the books chosen, including *Gatsby*, weren't particularly patriotic. The program proved a tremendous success. One soldier told the *New York Times* that the books were "as popular as pin-up girls."

By 1960, *Gatsby* was selling fifty thousand copies a year; these days it sells over half a million copies a year, not least because it's difficult to escape high school English in the U.S. without being assigned the book.

It's short, reasonably accessible, and rather than being a book for "the season only," it has proven to be a book for all seasons.

Gatsby is a critique of the American Dream. The only people who end up rich or successful in the novel are the ones who start out that way. Almost everyone else ends up dead or destitute. And it's a critique of the kind of vapid capitalism that can't find anything more interesting to do with money than try to make more of it. The book lays bare the carelessness of the entitled rich—the kind of people who buy puppies but won't take care of dogs, or who purchase vast libraries of books but never read any of them.

And yet *Gatsby* is often read as a *celebration* of the horrifying excess of the Anthropocene's richer realms. Shortly after the book came out, Fitzgerald wrote to a friend, "Of all the reviews, even the most enthusiastic, not one had the slightest idea what the book was about."

Sometimes, that still feels true. To tell a story of my own horrifying excess, I once stayed at the famous Plaza Hotel in New York City and received a "free upgrade" to the Great Gatsby suite. The room was a study in visual overstimulation—sparkling silver wallpaper, ornate furniture, fake trophies and autographed footballs lining the mantel. The room seemed utterly unaware that, in the novel, Daisy and Tom Buchanan are the bad guys.

Eventually, in what may have been the most entitled moment of my life, I called and requested a room change because the ceaseless tinkling of the Gatsby Suite's massive crystal chandelier was disturbing my sleep. As I made that call, I could feel the eyes of Fitzgerald staring down at me.

But *Gatsby* lends itself to the confusion that Fitzgerald lamented. Yes, it is unwavering in its condemnation of American excess, but even so, the whole novel pulses with an intoxicatingly rhythmic prose. Just read the first sentence aloud: "In my younger and more vulnerable years, my father gave me some advice that I've been turning over in my mind ever since." You can damn near tap your foot to it. Or take this one:

"Gatsby turned out all right in the end; it is what preyed on Gatsby, what foul dust floated in the wake of his dreams that temporarily closed out my interest in the abortive sorrows and short-winded elations of men."

When words roll like that, it's hard not to enjoy the party, and for me that's the real genius of *Gatsby*. The book makes you feel for the entitled spoiled disgusting rich *and* the poor people living in the valley of ashes, and everyone in between. You know the parties are vapid and maybe even evil, but you still want to be invited. And so in bad times, *Gatsby* feels like a condemnation of the American idea, and in good times it feels like a celebration of that same idea. David Denby has written that the book has "become a kind of national scripture, recited happily or mournfully, as the occasion requires."

So it has become for that sentence near the book's end. "For a transitory enchanted moment, man must have held his breath in the presence of this continent, compelled into an aesthetic contemplation he neither understood nor desired, face to face for the last time in history with something commensurate to his capacity for wonder."

There's just the one problem with that line, which is that it's not true. It's not true that "man" held his breath in the presence of this continent, because if we are imagining "man" as all of humanity, then "man" had known about, and indeed lived in, the area for tens of thousands of years. In fact, the use of "man" in the sentence ends up telling us a lot about whom, precisely, the narrator thinks of as a person, and where the narrator centers their story.

That "last time in history" also proved wrong, of course. Within a few decades of *Gatsby*'s publication, human beings stepped foot on the moon. Not long after that, we sent a telescope into space that allowed us to glimpse what the universe looked like just after the Big Bang.

Maybe the novel knows this. It is, after all, a book about hearkening back to a past that never existed, trying to fix some single moment from the past into permanence, when the past is neither fixed nor fixable.

And so maybe the novel knows that hearkening back to these transitory enchanted moments is a doomed enterprise. Maybe the Plaza knew they were making a room about (and for) the baddies.

But I will confess this endless parsing of ambivalences and ironies exhausts me. Here's the plain truth, at least as it has been shown to me: We are never far from wonders. I remember when my son was about two, we were walking in the woods one November morning. We were along a ridge, looking down at a forest in the valley below, where a cold haze seemed to hug the forest floor. I kept trying to get my oblivious two-year-old to appreciate the landscape. At one point, I picked him up and pointed out toward the horizon and said, "Look at that, Henry, just look at it!" And he said, "Weaf!" I said, "What?" And again he said, "Weaf," and then reached out and grabbed a single brown oak leaf from the little tree next to us.

I wanted to explain to him that you can see a brown oak leaf anywhere in the eastern United States in November, that nothing in the forest was less interesting. But after watching him look at it, I began to look as well, and I soon realized it wasn't just a brown leaf. Its veins spidered out red and orange and yellow in a pattern too complex for my brain to synthesize, and the more I looked at that leaf with Henry, the more I was compelled into an aesthetic contemplation I neither understood nor desired, face-to-face with something commensurate to my capacity for wonder.

Marveling at the perfection of that leaf, I was reminded that aesthetic beauty is as much about how and whether you look as what you see. From the quark to the supernova, the wonders do not cease. It is our attentiveness that is in short supply, our ability and willingness to do the work that awe requires.

Still, I'm fond of our capacity for wonder. I give it three and a half stars.

LASCAUX CAVE PAINTINGS

IF YOU'VE EVER HAD OR BEEN A CHILD, you are probably already familiar with hand stencils. They were the first figurative art made by both my kids—somewhere between the ages of two and three, my children spread the fingers of one hand out across a piece of paper, and then with the help of a parent traced their five fingers. I remember my son's face as he lifted his hand and looked absolutely shocked to see the shape of his splayed fingers still on the paper, a semipermanent record of himself.

I am extremely happy that my children are no longer three, and yet to look at their little hands from those early artworks is to be inundated with a strange, soul-splitting joy. Those pictures remind me that my kids are not just growing up but also growing away from me, running toward their own lives. But *I* am applying that meaning to *their* hand stencils, and the complicated relationship between art and its viewers is never more fraught than when we look deeply into the past.

In September of 1940, an eighteen-year-old mechanic named Marcel Ravidat was walking in the southwestern French countryside, when his dog, Robot, disappeared down a hole. (Or so the story goes, anyway.[5]) When Robot returned, Ravidat thought the dog might've discovered a rumored secret passageway to the nearby Lascaux Manor.

And so a few days later, he returned with some rope and three friends—sixteen-year-old Georges Agniel, fifteen-year-old Jacques Marsal, and thirteen-year-old Simon Coencas. Georges was on summer vacation and would soon return to Paris for the school year. Jacques, like Marcel, was a local. And Simon, who was Jewish, had sought refuge with his family in the countryside amid the Nazi occupation of France.

That day, Agniel later remembered, "We descended with our oil lamps and went forward. There were no obstacles. We went through a room and then by the end we found ourselves in front of a wall and saw that it was full of drawings. We immediately understood we were in a prehistoric cave."

Simon Coencas recalled, "With my little gang . . . we were hoping to find a treasure. We found one, but not the one we thought."

In the cave, they discovered over nine hundred paintings of animals—horses, stags, bison, and also species that are now extinct, including a woolly rhinoceros. The paintings were astonishingly detailed and vivid, with red, yellow, and black paint made from pulverized minerals that were likely blown through a narrow tube—possibly a hollowed bone—onto the walls of the cave. It would eventually be established that these artworks were at least seventeen thousand years old. One of the boys recalled that in the flickering of their oil lamps, the figures seemed to be moving, and indeed, there is some evidence that the artists' drawing techniques were intended to convey a kind of flip-book animation by torchlight.[6]

---

5.   Ravidat told the version of the story with the dog, but his earliest version of the story did not feature the dog as a central character. Even when history is only a few decades old, it can be difficult to piece together. Nothing lies like memory.
6.   This is explored in wondrous detail in Werner Herzog's movie *Cave of Forgotten Dreams*, where I first learned of the Lascaux cave paintings.

Just days after the cave's discovery, Simon Coencas and his family, fearing the growing Nazi presence in the countryside, moved again—this time to Paris, where relatives had promised to help hide them. But the family was betrayed by a business partner, and Simon's parents were murdered by the Nazis. Simon was imprisoned for a time, but narrowly escaped the death camps and survived the rest of the war hiding in a tiny attic room with his siblings. He would not see his three friends from that Lascaux summer for forty-six years.

So there were four boys who discovered the cave, but only two who could remain there—Jacques and Marcel. They were both so profoundly moved by the paintings that all through that fall and winter, they camped outside the cave to protect it. They only left after a reinforced door was installed at the cave's entrance. In 1942, Jacques and Marcel joined the French Resistance together. Jacques was captured and sent to a prison camp, but both survived the war, and when they got home, they both immediately returned to the cave.

After World War II, the French government took ownership of the site, and the cave was opened to the public in 1948. Marcel and Jacques both served as tour guides. When Pablo Picasso saw the cave paintings on a visit that year, he reportedly said, "We have invented nothing."

The cave is not particularly large—only about ninety meters deep—but it contains nearly two thousand paintings. Aside from the animals, hundreds of abstract shapes are painted on the walls, most commonly red and black circles.

What might these symbols mean? We can't know. There are so many mysteries at Lascaux: Why, for instance, are there no paintings of reindeer, which we know were the primary source of food for the Paleolithic humans who lived in that cave? Why is the human form so rarely depicted?[7] Why are certain areas of the cave filled with images, including pictures on the ceiling that required the building of scaffolding to create, while other areas have only a few paintings? And were the paintings spiritual? *Here are our sacred animals.* Or were they practical? *Here is a guide to some of the animals that might kill you.*

At Lascaux, there are also some "negative hand stencils," as they are known to art historians. These paintings were created by pressing one hand with fingers splayed against the wall of the cave, and then blowing pigment, leaving the area around the hand painted. Similar hand stencils have been found in caves around the world. We've found memories of hands from up to forty thousand years ago from Indonesia to Australia to Africa to the Americas. These hand stencils remind us of how different life was in the distant past—amputations, likely from frostbite, were common in Europe, and so you often see negative hand stencils with three or four fingers. Life was difficult and often short: As many as a quarter of women died in childbirth, and around 50 percent of children did not live to the age of five.

But the hand stencils also remind us that humans of the past were as human as we are. Their hands were indistinguishable from ours. More than that, we know they were like us in other ways. These communities hunted and gathered, and there were no large caloric surpluses, so every healthy person would have had to contribute to the acquisition of food and water—and yet somehow, they still made time to create art, almost as if art isn't optional for humans.

We see all kinds of hands—child and adult—stenciled on cave walls around the world, but almost always the fingers are spread, like my kids'

---

7.   Barbara Ehrenreich, in her essay "The Humanoid Stain," proposes one reason why cave art might not have focused on humans: We weren't yet living on a human-centered planet. "The marginality of human figures in cave paintings suggests that, at least from a human point of view, the central drama of the Paleolithic went on between the various megafauna—carnivores and large herbivores." At any rate, there is only one human-like image at Lascaux—a sort of stick figure with long legs and what appears to be a bird's head.

hand stencils. I'm no Jungian, but it's fascinating and a little strange that so many Paleolithic humans, who couldn't possibly have had any contact with one another, created the same types of paintings using similar techniques—techniques that we are still using to paint hand stencils.

But then again, what the Lascaux art means to me is likely different from whatever it meant to the people who made it. The paeloanthropologist Genevieve von Petzinger has theorized that the abstract dots and squiggles found in cave paintings may have been an early form of written language, with a consistent set of meanings even across broad distances.

What was the motivation for the negative hand stencils? Perhaps they were part of religious rituals, or rites of passage. Some academics theorize that the hand stencils were part of hunting rituals. Or maybe the hand is just a convenient model situated at the end of the wrist. To me, though, the hand stencils say, "I was here." They say, "You are not new."

The Lascaux cave has been closed to the public for many years now—too many people breathing inside of it led to the growth of mold and lichens, which has damaged some of the art. Just the act of looking at something can ruin it, I guess. The cave's tour guide discoverers, Marcel Ravidat and Jacques Marsal, were among the first people to note the impact of contemporary humans on the ancient human art.

They were reunited with their codiscoverers Simon Coencas and Georges Agniel for the first time in 1986. After that, the "little gang" met regularly until one by one, they passed away. Simon Coencas was the last to die—in early 2020, at the age of ninety-three. So now the people who found Lascaux are gone, and Lascaux itself is sealed off from view, visited only by the scientists working to preserve it. But tourists can still visit imitation caves, called Lascaux II, Lascaux III, and Lascaux IV, in which the artwork has been meticulously re-created.

Humans making fake cave art to save real cave art may feel like Peak Anthropocene absurdity, but I confess I find it overwhelmingly hopeful that four kids and a dog named Robot discovered a cave containing seventeen-thousand-year-old handprints, that the two teenagers who could stay devoted themselves to the cave's protection, and that when humans became a danger to that cave's beauty, we agreed to stop going.

We might have graffitied over the paintings, or kept on visiting them until the black mold ate them away entirely. But we didn't. We let them live on by sealing them off.

The cave paintings at Lascaux exist. You cannot visit. You can go to the fake cave we've built, and see nearly identical hand stencils, but you will know: This is not the thing itself, but a shadow of it. This is a handprint, but not a hand. This is a memory that you cannot return to. And to me, that makes the cave very much like the past it represents.

I give the cave paintings at Lascaux four and a half stars.

SCRATCH 'N' SNIFF STICKERS

SMELL IS ONE OF THE LAST REALMS where virtual reality still feels deeply virtual. Recently, I found myself at a theme park riding a VR roller coaster that felt breath-stealingly real. It wasn't just that falling felt like falling and turning felt like turning; I even felt the mist on my face as I flew through ocean spray.

But that water did not *smell* like the ocean. It smelled like this room deodorizer I'd used in high school called "Spring Rain." "Spring Rain" didn't actually smell like spring rain any more than it smelled like the ocean, but the scent did somehow communicate moisture, so I can understand why it had been repurposed as ocean-y. Still, nobody who has ever smelled the salty din of a cresting wave could possibly mistake it for the scent being pumped into that VR experience, and the smell of "Spring Rain" wrenched my mind from its state of joyfully suspended disbelief. Suddenly, I was not on a flying tour of a heaving ocean but instead stuck inside a dark room with a bunch of strangers.

One of the things that makes smell so powerful, of course, is its connection to memory. Helen Keller wrote that smell is "a potent wizard that transports us across a thousand miles and all the years we have lived." The scent of artificial "Spring Rain" takes me back to an Alabama dorm room in 1993. The smell of actual spring rain, meanwhile, returns me to the drenching thunderstorms of my childhood in Central Florida.

Smell's radical specificity is part of what connects it so particularly to memory; it's also part of why imitation is so difficult, even when it comes to artificial odors. The scent of Chanel No. 5, for instance, is not patented, and doesn't need to be, because no one can re-create it. But I think there's something else at play with smells that try to mimic nature, which is that nothing in the real world ever smells quite like we imagine it should. Actual spring rain, for instance, seems like it ought to smell at once moist and crisp, like the artificial scent does. But in fact, springtime rain smells earthy and acidic.

Humans, meanwhile, smell like the exhalations of the bacteria that colonize us, a fact we go to extraordinary lengths to conceal, not only via soap and perfume, but also in how we collectively imagine the human scent. If you had an artificial intelligence read every novel ever written and then, based on those stories, guess the human odor, the AI would be spectacularly wrong. In our stories, people smell like vanilla, lavender, and sandalwood. The AI would presume we all smell not like the slowly decaying organic matter we are, but instead like newly mown grass and orange blossoms.

Which, incidentally, were two of the scratch 'n' sniff sticker scents from my childhood. Scratch 'n' sniff stickers were wildly popular in the 1980s, and I maintained a collection of them in a large pink sticker book. The stickers fascinated me—if you scratched or rubbed them, scent erupted without explanation. Like most virtual scents, scratch 'n' sniff smells tend to be rather imperfect simulacrums, which is why the stickers generally depicted the scent they were going for. The pizza-scented stickers were usually slices of pizza, and so on. But they really did smell—often quite overpoweringly.

The smells best captured by scratch 'n' sniff tend to be either aggressively artificial—cotton candy, for instance—or else straightforwardly chemical. A rotten eggsy odor is added to natural gas so that humans can smell a gas leak, and in 1987, the Baltimore Gas and Electric Company sent out scratch 'n' sniff cards to their customers that mimicked the odor so effectively that several hundred people called the fire department to report leaks. The cards were soon discontinued.

By the time I was ten or eleven, everyone had moved on from sticker collecting—everyone, that is, except for me. Even in middle school, I continued to surreptitiously collect stickers, especially scratch 'n' sniff ones, because they took me back to a time and place that felt safer. In sixth grade, I had one class in a trailer each day. Because of some scheduling error, the teacher of that class had to walk across the entire school to get to the trailer, which meant that for about five minutes, we students were all on our own. Many days, a group of kids would throw me to the ground and then grab me by my limbs and pull on me as hard as they could. They called this "the abominable snowman." Other times, garbage was poured on my head as I sat at my desk. Aside from the physical pain, it made me feel small and powerless. But I didn't really resist it, because many days it was the only time I had any social interaction. Even when there was wet garbage on my head, I tried to laugh, like I was in on the joke.

When my mom got home from work, she would ask me how school was. If I told the truth, she would hold me and comfort me, encouraging me that this was temporary, that life would get better. But most days I would lie and tell her that school was fine. I didn't want my hurt to travel through to her. On those days, I would go into my room and pull the pink sticker book out from my bookcase, and I would scratch the stickers, close my eyes, and inhale as deeply as I possibly could.

I had all the hits: Garfield eating chocolate, the lawn mower that smelled like grass, the taco that smelled like tacos. But I particularly loved the fruits—the cloyingly and otherworldly sweet distillations of raspberry and strawberry and banana. God, I loved scratch 'n' sniff bananas. They didn't smell like bananas, of course. They smelled like the Platonic ideal of bananas. If real bananas were a note played on a home piano, scratch 'n' sniff bananas were that same note played on a church's pipe organ.

Anyway, the weird part is not that I collected scratch 'n' sniff stickers until I was a teenager. The weird part is, I still have that sticker album. And the stickers, when scratched, still erupt with scent.

Scratch 'n' sniff stickers are created by a process called microencapsulation, which was originally developed in the 1960s for carbonless copy paper. When you fill out a white paper form and your pen imprints upon the pink and yellow sheets below, that's microencapsulation at work. Tiny droplets of liquid are encapsulated by a coating that protects those droplets until something decapsulates them. In copy paper, the pressure of a pen releases encapsulated ink. In scratch 'n' sniff stickers, scratching breaks open microcapsules containing scented oils.

Microencapsulation is used for all kinds of things these days—including time-released medication—and it has proven a useful technology in part because, depending on the coating used, microcapsules can last a while.

How long? Well, I know for a fact that scratch 'n' sniff stickers can survive for at least thirty-four years, because I just scratched a garbage can sticker I got when I was seven, and it still smells. Not like garbage, exactly, but like something.

The longevity of microcapsules offers a tantalizing possibility: that a smell might disappear from our world before the microencapsulated version of that smell disappears. The last time anyone smells a banana, it might be via a scratch 'n' sniff sticker, or some futuristic version of one.

This all makes me wonder what smells I've already missed out on. When thinking about the past, we tend to focus on the awful smells, which were apparently legion. Ancient writers often showcase an acute awareness of disgusting odors—the Roman poet Martial compares one person's scent to "a chicken putrefying in an aborted egg" and "a billy goat fresh from making love."

But there must also have been wonderful smells, many of which are gone now. Or at least gone for now. It's conceivable that they'll be back with us in scratch 'n' sniff form someday: In 2019, scientists at Harvard used DNA samples of an extinct species of Hawaiian mountain hibiscus to reconstitute the smell of its flower. But there's no real way to judge the scent's accuracy, since its antecedent is gone forever.

In fact, while I've been making distinctions between natural scents and artificial ones, at this point in our planet's story, many purportedly natural scents are already shaped by human intervention, including the banana. In the U.S. at least, there is only one banana cultivar in most grocery stories, the Cavendish banana, which didn't exist two hundred years ago and was not widely distributed until the 1950s.

I remember the smell of rain as acidic in part because rain in my childhood actually was more acidic than contemporary rain. Humans were pumping more sulfur dioxide into the atmosphere in the 1980s than they are today, which affects the pH of rain. In my part of the world, rain is still more acidic than it would be without human emissions, so I'm not even sure that I know the smell of "natural" rain.

The challenge for scratch 'n' sniff sticker makers isn't, in the end, to mimic the natural world, which doesn't really exist as a thing separate from humanity. The challenge is to imagine what combination of smells will make humans remember the smell of bananas, or ocean mist, or freshly mown grass. I wouldn't bet against us finding a way to artificialize scent effectively—God knows we've artificialized much else. But we haven't succeeded yet. When I open that ancient sticker book and scratch at the yellowing stickers curling at the edges, what I smell most is not pizza or chocolate, but my childhood.

I give scratch 'n' sniff stickers three and a half stars.

DIET DR PEPPER

THE STORY OF DR PEPPER BEGINS IN 1885, in Waco, Texas, where a pharmacist named Charles Alderton combined twenty-three syrup flavors to create a new kind of carbonated drink. Notably, Alderton sold the recipe for Dr Pepper after a few years because he wanted to pursue his passion, pharmaceutical chemistry. He worked at the drug company Eli Lilly before going back to his hometown to head up the laboratory at the Waco Drug Company.[8]

Alderton's soda probably would've remained a Texas-only phenomenon, eventually disappearing like so many other local soda flavors—the opera bouquet, the swizzle fizz, the almond sponge—had it not been for the dogged determination of Woodrow Wilson Clements, who preferred to be called "Foots," a nickname he picked up in high school due to his oddly shaped toes. Foots, the youngest of eight children, grew up in the tiny Alabama town of Windham Springs. He got a football

---

8. Dr Pepper is a drug, too, of course. Caffeine and sugar are two of the defining chemical compounds of the Anthropocene. Pepsi, Coca-Cola, root beer, and most other flavored sodas were invented either by chemists or pharmacists, and in the nineteenth century, there was no bright line between medicinal cocktails and recreational ones.

scholarship at the University of Alabama, where he was teammates with Bear Bryant.[9]

In 1935, when Foots was a senior in college, he started working as a Dr Pepper salesman. He retired fifty-one years later as CEO of a soft drink company worth over $400 million. By 2020, the Keurig Dr Pepper corporation, which owns, among many other brands, 7UP, RC Cola, and four different kinds of root beer, is valued at over $40 billion. Almost all of its products are some form of sweetened and/or caffeinated water.

Foots Clements succeeded because he understood precisely what made Dr Pepper significant. "I've always maintained," he said, "you cannot tell anyone what Dr Pepper tastes like because it's so different. It's not an apple; it's not an orange; it's not a strawberry; it's not a root beer; it's not even a cola." Cola, after all, is derived from kola nuts and vanilla, two real-world flavors. Sprite has that lemon-lime taste. Purple soda is ostensibly grape-flavored. But Dr Pepper has no natural-world analogue.

In fact, U.S. trademark courts have tackled this issue, categorizing Dr Pepper and its knockoffs as "pepper sodas," even though they contain no pepper, and the "pepper" in Dr Pepper refers not to the spice but either to someone's actual name or else to pep, the feeling that Dr[10] Pepper supposedly fills you with. It's the only category of soda not named for what it tastes like, which to my mind is precisely why Dr Pepper marks such an interesting and important moment in human history. It was an artificial drink that didn't taste *like* anything. It wasn't like an orange but better, or like a lime but sweet. In an interview, Charles Alderton once said that he wanted to create a soda that tasted

---

9.   Bear Bryant became a legendary football coach in Alabama—so legendary that when I attended high school outside of Birmingham in the 1990s, I knew three kids named Bryant and one kid named Bear.

10.   There is no period in the Dr of Dr Pepper. The company dropped it in the 1950s because the bubbly lettering at the time made "Dr. Pepper" look to many readers like "Dri Pepper," which sounds like maybe the worst soda imaginable.

like the soda fountain in Waco smelled—all those artificial flavors swirling together in the air. Dr Pepper is, in its very conception, unnatural. The creation of a chemist.

The first zero-calorie version of Dr Pepper was released in 1962. This initial "Dietetic Dr Pepper" was a failure, but Diet Dr Pepper became a huge success when it was reformulated in 1991 with a new artificial sweetener, aspartame. It also relaunched with a new advertising slogan. *Diet Dr Pepper: It tastes more like regular Dr Pepper.* Which it really does. Coke and Diet Coke are barely recognizable as relatives. If Coke is a golden eagle, Diet Coke is a hummingbird. But Dr Pepper and Diet Dr Pepper taste like each other, which is especially interesting since, as Foots Clements pointed out, neither of them tastes like anything else.

Now, many people find the artificiality of Diet Dr Pepper revolting. You often hear people say, "There are so many chemicals in it." Of course, there are also lots of chemicals in wine, or coffee, or air. The underlying concern, though, is a sensible one: Diet Dr Pepper is just *so* profoundly artificial. But that's why I love it. Diet Dr Pepper allows me to enjoy a relatively safe taste that was engineered for me. When I drink it, I think of the kids at that soda fountain in Waco, Texas, most of whom rarely knew the pleasures of an ice-cold drink of any kind, and how totally enjoyable those first Dr Peppers must've been.

Each time I drink Diet Dr Pepper, I am newly astonished. Look at what humans can do! They can make ice-cold, sugary-sweet, zero-calorie soda that tastes like everything and also like nothing. I don't labor under the delusion that Diet Dr Pepper is good for me, but, in moderation, it also probably isn't bad for me. Drinking too much Diet Dr Pepper can be bad for your teeth and may increase other health risks. But as Dr. Aaron Carroll puts it in his book *The Bad Food Bible*, "There's a potential—and, likely, very real—harm from consuming added sugar. There is likely none from artificial sweeteners."

So Diet Dr Pepper probably isn't a health risk for me. And yet I feel as if I'm committing a sin whenever I drink Diet Dr Pepper. Nothing that sweet can be truly virtuous. But it's an exceptionally minor vice, and for whatever reason, I've always felt like I *need* a vice. I don't know whether this feeling is universal, but I have some way-down vibrating part of my subconscious that needs to self-destruct, at least a little bit.

In my teens and early twenties, I smoked cigarettes compulsively, thirty or forty a day. The pleasure of smoking for me wasn't about a buzz; the pleasure came from the jolt of giving in to an unhealthy physical craving, which over time increased my physical cravings, which in turn increased the pleasure of giving in to them. I haven't smoked in more than fifteen years, but I don't think I ever quite escaped that cycle. There remains a yearning within my subconscious that cries out for a sacrifice, and so I offer up a faint shadow of a proper vice and drink Diet Dr Pepper, the soda that tastes more like the Anthropocene than any other.

After going through dozens of slogans through the decades—Dr Pepper billed itself as "tasting like liquid sunshine," as the "Pepper picker-upper," as the "most original soft drink ever"—these days the company's slogan is more to the point. They call it "the one you crave."

I give Diet Dr Pepper four stars.

VELOCIRAPTORS

UNTIL 1990, when Michael Crichton's novel *Jurassic Park* was published, velociraptors were not particularly well-known dinosaurs. The book, about a theme park containing dinosaurs created from cloned DNA samples, became a runaway bestseller. Three years later, Steven Spielberg's film adaptation brought the novel's dinosaurs to awe-inspiring life with computer-generated animations the likes of which moviegoers had never seen. Even decades later, *Jurassic Park*'s dinosaurs still look astonishingly lifelike, including the velociraptors, which are portrayed as scaly creatures, about six feet in height, from present-day Montana. In the film franchise, they are not just vicious but also terrifyingly intelligent. In *Jurassic Park III*, a character claims that velociraptors are "smarter than dolphins, smarter than primates." In the movies, they figure out how to open a door—in fact, the first time I remember hearing my brother, Hank, curse came as we were watching *Jurassic Park*. When the velociraptors turned the door handle, I heard my ten-year-old brother mutter, "Oh, *shit*."

Crichton's velociraptors are the kind of scary, intimidating animal you might want to name, say, a professional sports franchise after, and indeed, when the National Basketball Association expanded into Canada in 1995, Toronto chose the Raptors as its team name. Today, the velociraptor stands alongside *T. rex* and stegosaurus as among the best-known dinosaurs, even though the actual creatures that lived in the late Cretaceous period some seventy million years ago have almost nothing in common with the velociraptors of our contemporary imagination.

For starters, velociraptors did not live in what is now Montana; they lived in what is now Mongolia and China, hence the scientific name, *Velociraptor mongoliensis.* While they were smart for dinosaurs, they were not smarter than dolphins or primates; they were probably closer to chickens or possums. And they were not six feet tall; they were about the size of a contemporary turkey, but with a long tail that could stretch for over three feet. They are estimated to have weighed less than thirty-five pounds, so it's difficult to imagine one killing a human. In fact, they were probably mostly scavengers, eating meat from already dead carcasses.

Furthermore, velociraptors were not scaly but feathered. We know this because researchers found quill knobs on a velociraptor's forearm in 2007. But even in Crichton's day, most paleontologists thought velociraptors and other members of the Dromaeosauridae family were feathered. Although velociraptors are not believed to have flown, their ancestors probably did. Mark Norell of the American Museum of Natural History put it this way: "The more we learn about these animals, the more we find out that there is basically no difference between birds and their closely related dinosaur ancestors like velociraptor. Both have wishbones, brooded their nests, possess hollow bones, and were covered in feathers. If animals like velociraptor were alive today, our first impression would be that they were just very unusual looking birds." Indeed, as a guide recently pointed out to me at the Houston Museum of Natural Science, pictures of birds without feathers look a lot like pictures of dinosaurs.

Velociraptors probably did sometimes hunt. A famous fossil discovered in 1971 in Mongolia preserved a velociraptor locked in battle with a pig-sized dinosaur called protoceratops. The velociraptor appears to have had one of its sickle-shaped claws embedded in the neck of the protoceratops, which was biting down on the velociraptor's arm when they were both suddenly buried in sand, perhaps due to a collapsing sand dune. But we don't know how often velociraptors hunted, or how successfully, or whether they hunted in packs.

Crichton based his velociraptors on a different dinosaur, the deinonychus, which did live in present-day Montana and was the approximate size and shape of *Jurassic Park*'s velociraptors. Crichton took the name "velociraptor" because he thought it was "more dramatic," which presumably is also why the theme park is called Jurassic Park even though most of the dinosaurs in the park did not live in the Jurassic age, which ended one hundred and forty-five million years ago, but instead in the Cretaceous age, which ended sixty-six million years ago with the extinction event that resulted in the disappearance of around three-quarters of all plant and animal species on Earth, including all large species of what we now consider dinosaurs.

And so our image of velociraptors says more about us than it does about them. Really, even what we do know, or think we know, about dinosaurs is endlessly shaped by assumptions and presuppositions, some of which will eventually prove incorrect. In ancient China, dinosaur fossils were believed to be dragon bones. In 1676, the first dinosaur bone to be described by European scientists, a piece of thigh bone from a Megalosaurus, was thought to have come from the kind of giants depicted in the Bible.[11]

Megalosaurus was first described in a scientific journal in 1824, around the time the paleontologist Mary Ann Mantell discovered the first known fossils of an iguanodon. The *Tyrannosaurus rex* wasn't named until 1905. The first velociraptor fossil was discovered in 1924.

---

11.   That bone, incidentally, was named *Scrotum humanum*, which is a reasonable description of its approximate shape.

Scientists have been debating for more than a century whether the long-necked brontosaurus of the Jurassic age even existed or is just a misidentified apatosaurus. The brontosaurus was real in the late nineteenth century, only to become a fiction for much of the twentieth, only to become real again in the last few years. History is new. Prehistory is newer. And paleontology is newer still.

But the weird thing to me about velociraptors is that even though I know they were feathered scavengers about the size of a swan, when I imagine them, I can't help but see the raptors of *Jurassic Park*. Knowing the facts doesn't help me picture the truth. That's the wonder and terror of computer-generated images for me: If they look real, my brain isn't nearly sophisticated enough to understand they are not. We've long known that images are unreliable—Kafka wrote that "nothing is as deceptive as a photograph"—and yet I still can't help but believe them.

Like the velociraptor, I have a large brain for my geologic age, but maybe not large enough to survive effectively in the world where I find myself. My eyes still believe what they see, long after visual information stops being reliable. Still, I'm fond of raptors—both the ones I've seen that never existed, and the ones that existed but I've never seen.

I give velociraptors three stars.

CANADA GEESE

THE CANADA GOOSE is a brown-bodied, black-necked, honking waterfowl that has recently become ubiquitous in suburban North America, Europe, and New Zealand. With a song like a dying balloon and a penchant for attacking humans, the Canada goose is hard to love. But then again, so are most of us.[12]

These days, the world contains between four and six million Canada geese, although from where I'm sitting in Indianapolis, that estimate feels low, as there appear to be four to six million of them currently residing in my backyard. Regardless, global Canada goose populations are growing, but they were once exceptionally rare. In fact, the subspecies you're most likely to see in parks and retention ponds, the giant Canada goose, was believed to be extinct early in the twentieth century due to year-round, unrestricted hunting.

Canada geese were particularly susceptible to so-called "live decoys." Hunters captured geese, rendered them flightless, and kept them in ponds or fields. The call of these captured geese then attracted flocks

---

12.   You may wonder, as I have, whether U.S. ornithologists assigned "Canada" to the goose's name for the same reason the Italians called syphilis "the French disease," while the Poles called it "the German disease" and the Russians called it "the Polish disease." The answer is no. Taxonomists first observed the geese in Canada.

of wild ones, which could be shot. Hunters often doted on their live decoys. A hunter named Philip Habermann wrote, "Watching and listening to the decoys work was akin to the pleasure of hunting with a fine dog," a reminder that humans have long drawn strange lines between pet and prey.

But in 1935, live decoys were made illegal, and goose populations began to recover—very slowly at first, and then spectacularly.

In mid-January 1962, Harold C. Hanson was among the ornithologists who sought to band, weigh, and measure some Minnesota geese. "On that memorable day," he would later write, "the temperature held around zero and a strong wind blew but this only added zest to the enterprise." The geese they weighed were so huge that they thought the scales must be off, but no: It turned out the giant Canada goose had survived. These days, there are over one hundred thousand giant Canada geese in Minnesota. Non-native populations of the geese have exploded from Australia to Scandinavia. In Britain, the Canada goose population has risen by a factor of at least twenty in the past sixty years.

This success is partly down to those laws protecting the birds, but also because in the past several decades, humans have rendered *lots* of land perfect for geese. Heavily landscaped suburbs, riverside parks, and golf courses with water features are absolutely ideal living conditions for them. Canada geese especially love eating seeds from the *Poa pratensis* plant, which is the most abundant agricultural crop in the United States. Also known as Kentucky bluegrass, we grow *Poa pratensis* in parks and in our front yards, and since the plant is of limited utility to humans,[13] geese must feel like we plant it just for them. One ornithologist observed, "Goslings and adults were found to show a marked preference for *Poa pratensis* from about 36 hours after hatching."

Geese also enjoy rural fields near rivers and lakes, but the ratio of city geese to country geese in the United States is actually quite similar to the

13.   See p. 165

human ratio. At any given time, about 80 percent of American humans are in or near urban areas. For Canada geese, it's about 75 percent.

In fact, the more you look, the more connections you find between Canada geese and people. Our population has also increased dramatically in the past several decades—there were just over two billion people on Earth in 1935, when live goose decoys were made illegal in the U.S. In 2021, there are more than seven billion people. Like humans, Canada geese usually mate for life, although sometimes unhappily. Like us, the success of their species has affected their habitats: A single Canada goose can produce up to one hundred pounds of excrement per year, which has led to unsafe *E. coli* levels in lakes and ponds where they gather. And like us, geese have few natural predators. If they die by violence, it is almost always human violence. Just like us.

But even though Canada geese are perfectly adapted to the human-dominated planet, they seem to feel nothing but disdain for actual humans. Geese honk and strut and bite to keep people away, even though they're thriving because of our artificial lakes and manicured lawns. In turn, many of us have come to resent Canada geese as a pest animal. I know I do.

But they also allow me to feel like there's still some proper nature in my highly sanitized, biologically monotonous suburban life. Even if geese have become mundane, there remains something awe-inspiring about seeing them fly overhead in a perfect V formation. As one enthusiast put it, the Canada goose "excites the imagination and quickens the heartbeat." More than pigeons or mice or rats, geese still feel wild to me.

I suppose it's a kind of symbiotic relationship in which neither party much likes the other, which reminds me: Just before graduating from college, my girlfriend and I were on our way to pick up some groceries in her ancient blue sedan when she asked me what my biggest fear was.

"Abandonment," I said. I was worried the end of college would spell the end of our relationship, and I wanted her to reassure me, to tell me that I need not fear being alone, because she would always be there, and etc. But she wasn't the sort of person to make false promises, and most promises featuring the word "always" are unkeepable. Everything ends, or at least everything humans have thus far observed ends.

Anyway, after I said abandonment, she just nodded, and then I filled the awkward silence by asking her what her biggest fear was.

"Geese," she answered.

And who can blame her? In 2009, it was a flock of Canada geese that flew into the engines of US Airways Flight 1549, forcing Captain Sully Sullenberger to splash-land the aircraft on the Hudson River. In 2014, a Canadian cyclist spent a week in the hospital after being attacked by a Canada goose.

You can do something about abandonment. You can construct a stronger independent self, for instance, or build a broader network of meaningful relationships so your psychological well-being isn't wholly reliant upon one person. But you, as an individual, can't do much about the Canada goose.

And that seems to me one of the great oddities of the Anthropocene. For better or worse, land has become ours. It is ours to cultivate, to shape, even ours to protect. We are so much the dominant creature on this planet that we essentially decide which species live and which die, which grow in numbers like the Canada goose, and which decline like its cousin the spoon-billed sandpiper. But as an individual, I don't feel that power. I can't decide whether a species lives or dies. I can't even get my kids to eat breakfast.

In the daily grind of a human life, there's a lawn to mow, soccer practices to drive to, a mortgage to pay. And so I go on living the way I feel like people always have, the way that seems like the right way, or even the only way. I mow the lawn of *Poa pratensis* as if lawns are natural, when in fact we didn't invent the suburban American lawn until one hundred and sixty years ago. And I drive to soccer practice, even though that was impossible one hundred and sixty years ago—not only because there were no cars, but also because soccer hadn't been invented. And I pay the mortgage, even though mortgages as we understand them today weren't widely available until the 1930s. So much of what feels inevitably, inescapably human to me is in fact very, very new, including the everywhereness of the Canada goose. So I feel unsettled about the Canada goose—both as a species and as a symbol. In a way, it has become my biggest fear.

The goose isn't to blame, of course, but still: I can only give Canada geese two stars.

TEDDY BEARS

THE ENGLISH WORD *BEAR* comes to us from a Germanic root, *bero*, meaning "the brown one" or "the brown thing." In some Scandinavian languages, the word for bear derives from the phrase "honey eaters." Many linguists believe these names are substitutes, created because speaking or writing the actual word for bear was considered taboo. As those in the wizarding world of Harry Potter were taught never to say "Voldemort," northern Europeans often did not say their actual word for bear, perhaps because it was believed saying the bear's true name could summon one. In any case, this taboo was so effective that today we are left with only the replacement word for bear—essentially, we call them "You Know Who."

Even so, we've long posed a much greater threat to bears than they have to us. For centuries, Europeans tormented bears in a practice known as bearbaiting. Bears would be chained to a pole and then attacked by dogs until they were injured or killed, or they'd be placed into a ring with a bull for a fight to the death. England's royals loved this stuff: Henry VIII had a bear pit made at the Palace of Whitehall.

References to bearbaiting even show up in Shakespeare, when Macbeth laments that his enemies "have tied me to a stake; I cannot fly, / But, bear-like, I must fight the course." This is an especially interesting passage since by Shakespeare's time, bears had been extinct in Britain for perhaps a thousand years, likely due to overhunting by humans. To fight the course "bear-like" couldn't refer to bear behaviors in the natural world, only to the violence bears suffered and meted out in a human-choreographed spectacle.

Although plenty of people recognized bearbaiting as a "rude and dirty pastime," as the diarist John Evelyn put it, the objections to it weren't usually about animal cruelty. "The Puritan hated bearbaiting, not because it gave pain to the bear, but because it gave pleasure to the spectators," wrote Thomas Babington Macaulay.

It would be inaccurate, then, to claim our dominion over bears is a wholly recent phenomenon. Still, it's a bit odd that our children now commonly cuddle with a stuffed version of an animal we used to be afraid to call by name.

———————

Here's the story of the teddy bear as it is usually told: In November of 1902, U.S. President Teddy Roosevelt went bear hunting in Mississippi, which was an extremely Teddy Roosevelt thing to do. The hunting party's dogs chased a bear for hours before Roosevelt gave up and returned to camp for some lunch.

Roosevelt's hunting guide that day, a man named Holt Collier, continued to track the bear with his dogs as the president ate lunch. Collier had been born enslaved in Mississippi, and after Emancipation became one of the world's most accomplished horse riders. (He also killed over three thousand bears in his lifetime.) While Roosevelt was away, Collier's dogs cornered the bear. Collier blew a bugle to alert the president, but before Roosevelt returned, Collier had to club the bear with a rifle butt because it was mauling one of his dogs.

By the time the president arrived on the scene, the bear was tied to a tree and semiconscious. Roosevelt refused to shoot it, feeling it would be unsportsmanlike. Word of the president's compassion spread throughout the country, especially after a cartoon in the *Washington Post* by Clifford Berryman illustrated the event. In the cartoon, the bear is reimagined as an innocent cub with a round face and large eyes looking toward Roosevelt with meek desperation.

Morris and Rose Michtom, Russian immigrants living in Brooklyn, saw that cartoon and were inspired to create a stuffed version of the cartoon cub they called "Teddy's Bear." The bear was placed in the window of their candy shop and became an immediate hit. Curiously, a German firm independently produced a similar teddy bear around the same time, and both companies ended up becoming hugely successful. The German manufacturer, Steiff, had been founded a couple decades earlier by Margarete Steiff, and her nephew Richard designed the Steiff teddy bear. By 1907, they were selling nearly a million of them per year. That same year, back in Brooklyn, the Michtoms used their teddy bear sales to found the company Ideal Toys, which went on to manufacture a huge array of popular twentieth-century playthings, from the game Mouse Trap to the Rubik's Cube.

The typical contemporary teddy bear looks approximately like the 1902 ones did—brown body, dark eyes, a round face, a cute little nose. When I was a kid, a talking teddy bear named Teddy Ruxpin became popular, but what I loved about teddy bears was their silence. They didn't ask anything of me, or judge me for my emotional outbursts. One of my most vivid childhood memories is of my tenth birthday. I retreated to my room after an exhausting party and cuddled up with a teddy bear, but I found that it didn't really work anymore, that whatever had once soothed me about this soft and silent creature no longer did. I remember thinking that I would never be a kid again, not really, which was the first time I can recall feeling that intense longing for the you to whom you can never return. Sarah Dessen once wrote that home is "not a place, but a moment." Home is a teddy bear, but only a certain teddy bear at a certain time.

The bears of our imagination have become increasingly sweet and cuddly since the debut of the teddy bear. Winnie-the-Pooh first arrived in 1926; Paddington Bear in 1958. The Care Bears showed up in 1981 as the ultimate unthreatening ursine friends. Characters like Funshine Bear and Love-A-Lot Bear starred in aggressively saccharine picture books with titles like *Caring Is What Counts* and *Your Best Wishes Can Come True.*

In the broader world, at least those of us living in cities began to see bears as we thought Roosevelt had seen them—creatures to be pitied and preserved. If I forget to turn off the lights when leaving a room, my daughter will often shout, "Dad, the polar bears!" because she has been taught that minimizing our electricity usage can shrink our carbon footprint and thereby preserve the habitat of polar bears. She's not afraid of polar bears; she's afraid of their extinction. The animals that once terrorized us, and that we long terrorized, are now often viewed as weak and vulnerable. The mighty bear has become, like so many creatures on Earth, dependent upon us. Their survival is contingent upon our wisdom and compassion—just as that bear in Mississippi needed Roosevelt to be kind.

In that sense, the teddy bear is a reminder of the astonishing power of contemporary humanity. It's hard to understand how dominant our species has become, but I sometimes find it helpful to consider it purely in terms of mass: The total combined weight of all living humans currently on Earth is around three hundred and eighty-five million tons. That is the so-called biomass of our species. The biomass of our livestock—sheep, chickens, cows, and so on—is around eight hundred million tons. And the combined biomass of every other mammal and bird on Earth is less than one hundred million tons. All the whales and tigers and monkeys and deer and bears and, yes, even Canada geese—together, they weigh less than a third of what we weigh.[14]

For many species of large animals in the twenty-first century, the single most important determinant of survival is whether their existence is useful to humans. But if you can't be of utility to people, the second best thing you can be is cute. You need an expressive face, ideally some large eyes. Your babies need to remind us of our babies. Something about you must make us feel guilty for eliminating you from the planet.

Can cuteness save a species? I'm dubious. The part of the teddy bear origin story that often doesn't get told is that right after Roosevelt sportingly refused to kill the bear, he ordered a member of his hunting party to slit its throat, so as to put the bear out of its misery. No bears were saved that day. And now there are fewer than fifty bears left in Mississippi. Global sales of teddy bears, meanwhile, have never been higher.

I give the teddy bear two and a half stars.

---

14.   We are all dwarfed by bacteria, though. According to one recent estimate, the biomass of bacteria is about thirty-five times larger than the combined biomass of all animals.

THE HALL OF PRESIDENTS

I GREW UP IN ORLANDO, FLORIDA, about fifteen miles away from the world's most-visited theme park, Walt Disney World's Magic Kingdom. When I was a kid, Orlando was such a tourist city that whenever you flew out of the airport, a message played saying, "We hope you enjoyed your visit." In response, my parents would always sigh, and then mutter, "We live here."

I first visited the Magic Kingdom in 1981, when I was four and it was ten. I loved the park back then. I remember meeting Goofy and allowing myself to believe it was actually Goofy. I remember getting scared on the Snow White ride, and feeling big because I could ride Thunder Mountain, and I remember being so tired at the end of the day that I'd fall asleep with my face pressed against the glass of our Volkswagen Rabbit.

But then I got older. As a teenager, I began to define myself primarily by what I disliked, and my loathes were legion. I hated children's books, the music of Mariah Carey, suburban architecture, and shopping malls. But most of all, I hated Disney World. My friends and I had a word for the artificiality and corporatized fantasy of pop music and theme parks and cheerful movies: We called all of it "plastic." The TV show *Full House* was plastic. The Cure's new stuff was kind of plastic. And Disney World? God, Disney World was so plastic.

This period of my life coincided with a terrible blessing. My mother won a community service award, and the award came with four free annual passes to Disney. That summer, I was fourteen, and my family dragged me to Disney World All. The. Time.

I realize I'm probably not garnering much sympathy with my sorrowful tale of getting into Disney World for free dozens of times in one summer. But fourteen-year-old me hated it. For one thing, Disney World was always hot, and in 1992, I had a semireligious allegiance to wearing a trench coat, which did not pair well with the pounding and oppressive swamp heat of Central Florida summers. The coat was meant to protect me from the world, not the weather, and in that respect it succeeded. Still, I was always sweating, and I must've been quite a sight to my fellow theme park visitors—a rail-thin child with a hunter-green coat to my knees, droplets of sweat erupting from every facial pore.

But of course I wanted those people to be freaked out by me, because I was freaked out by them. I was repulsed by the idea that they were giving money to a corporation in order to escape their horrible, miserable lives that were horrible and miserable in part because our corporate overlords controlled all the means of production.

At any rate, I had to survive many long summer days at Disney World. I usually started out sitting on a bench near the entrance to the park, scrawling snippets of stories into a yellow legal pad, and then eventually the day would get unbearably warm, and I'd make my way to the Hall of Presidents, which was one of the least crowded and best air-conditioned attractions at the Magic Kingdom. For the remainder of the day, I'd return to the Hall of Presidents show over and over, writing in that legal pad all the while. I began the first short story I ever finished while sitting through the Hall of Presidents show. The story was about a crazed anthropologist who kidnaps a family of hunter-gatherers and takes them to Disney World.[15]

The Hall of Presidents was an opening-day attraction at the Magic Kingdom, and it has been a constant presence since the park opened in 1971. In a building modeled after Independence Hall in Philadelphia, where the U.S. Constitution was debated, visitors first enter a waiting room, which features busts of several presidents and also a bust of the Disney Company's founder, Walt Disney, who is identified as "An American Original."

Since there is almost never a wait for the Hall of Presidents, you soon enter the main theater, whereupon you are told that the attraction is dedicated to the memory of Walt Disney. This always struck me as a bit excessive, not only because Disney's sculpted head appears in the waiting room but also because the entire park is named after him. After Disney thanks Disney, there's a movie about American history before the screen eventually ascends to reveal the stars of the show—life-size animatronic re-creations of every American president. The animatronics are at once creepily lifelike and terrifyingly robotic—a proper descent into the uncanny valley. As my daughter, then four years old, said when we visited the Hall of Presidents, "Those are NOT humans."

Only a couple of the presidents actually speak. Animatronic Abraham Lincoln stands and recites the Gettysburg Address, and since the early 1990s, the animatronic current president has made a speech at the end of the show, using their own voice. When we visited in 2018, animatronic Donald Trump uttered a few sentences, including, "Above all, to be an American is to be an optimist," which is just a fundamental misunderstanding of how citizenship gets conferred in nation-states.

---

15.   I lost the story shortly after finishing it. In my memory, the story had real promise, and for many years I believed that if I could just find that story, I would discover that my next book was already half-written, and I'd only need to tighten up the plot a little and expand a few of the characters. Then a few years back, my dad found a copy of the story and sent it to me, and of course it is terrible and lacks a single redeeming quality.

The Hall of Presidents doesn't ignore the various horrors of American history, but it's also an unapologetically patriotic celebration of the United States and its presidents. In fact, one of the last lines of the show is, "Our presidency is no longer just an idea. It is an idea with a proud history." And I would argue it *is* an idea with a proud history. But it is also an idea with many other histories—a shameful history, an oppressive history, and a violent history, among others. One of the challenges of contemporary life for me is determining how those histories can coexist without negating each other, but the Hall of Presidents doesn't really ask them to coexist. Instead, it imagines a triumphalist view of American history: *Sure, we had some failures, but thankfully we solved them with our relentless optimism, and just look at us now.*

Two of the Anthropocene's major institutions are the nation-state and the limited liability corporation, both of which are real and powerful—and on some level made-up. The United States isn't real the way a river is real, nor is the Walt Disney Company. They are both ideas we believe in. Yes, the United States has laws and treaties and a constitution and so on, but none of that prevents a country from splitting apart or even disappearing. From the neoclassical architecture that attempts to give the U.S. a sense of permanence[16] to the faces on our money, America has to continually convince its citizens that it is real, and good, and worthy of allegiance.

Which is not so different from the work that the Walt Disney Company tries to do by revering its founding father and focusing on its rich history. Both the nation and the corporation can only exist if at least some people believe in them. And in that sense, they really are kinds of magic kingdoms.

As a teen, I liked to imagine what life might be like if we all stopped

---

16.   *We're not a two-hundred-year-old nation; we're an extension of the Greek Republic and therefore thousands of years old!*

believing in these constructs. What would happen if we abandoned the idea of the U.S. Constitution being the ruling document of our nation, or the idea of nation-states altogether? Perhaps it is a symptom of middle age that I now want to imagine better nation-states (and better-regulated private corporations) rather than leaving behind these ideas. But we cannot do the hard work of imagining a better world into existence unless we reckon honestly with what governments and corporations want us to believe, and why they want us to believe it.

Until then, the Hall of Presidents will always feel a little plastic to me. I give it two stars.

AIR-CONDITIONING

OVER THE LAST HUNDRED YEARS, the weather for humans has gotten considerably hotter, not just because of global warming, but also because of where we are choosing to live. In the United States, for instance, the three states with the largest population gains in the past century—Nevada, Florida, and Arizona—are also among the warmest states. This trend is perhaps best exemplified by the U.S.'s fifth largest city, Phoenix, Arizona, which had a population of 5,544 people in 1900. In 2021, Phoenix was home to around 1.7 million people. The average high temperature in August is 103 degrees Fahrenheit, and yet they have a professional ice hockey team, the Arizona Coyotes. Until 1996, the Coyotes were known as the Jets, and they were based in Winnipeg, Manitoba, where the weather is considerably cooler, but the NHL followed the money and the people toward the equator.

One of the reasons for this huge shift in human geography is the miracle of air-conditioning, which allows people to control the temperature of their interior spaces. Air-conditioning has deeply reshaped human life in rich countries—from small things, like the declining percentage of time that windows are open in buildings, to large things, like the availability of medication. Insulin, many antibiotics, nitroglycerin, and lots of other drugs are heat sensitive and can lose their efficacy if not stored at so-called "room temperature," which is defined as between 68 and 77 degrees Fahrenheit, temperatures that no rooms in summertime Phoenix could have hoped to achieve before air-conditioning. Climate-controlled drug storage remains one of the big challenges for healthcare systems in poor countries, where many health facilities have no electricity.

Even the reading experience you're having right now is contingent upon air-conditioning—this book was printed in an air-conditioned facility.[17] In fact, air-conditioning was *invented* for a facility not too dissimilar from the one that printed this book. In 1902, a young engineer named Willis Carrier was tasked with solving a problem in Buffalo, New York: A printing company's magazine pages were warping due to summertime humidity. Carrier created a device that essentially reversed the process of electric heating, running air through cold coils instead of hot ones. This reduced humidity, but it also had the useful side effect of decreasing indoor temperatures. Carrier went on to make more inquiries into what he called "treating air," and the company he cofounded, the Carrier Corporation, remains one of the largest air-conditioning manufacturers in the world.

Heat has long been a worry for humans. In ancient Egypt, houses were cooled by hanging reeds from windows and trickling water down them. Then, as now, controlling indoor temperatures wasn't only about comfort and convenience, because heat can kill humans. In an essay with the catchy title "An Account of the Extraordinary Heat of the Weather in July 1757, and the Effects of It," the English physician John Huxham wrote that heat caused "sudden and violent pains of the head, and vertigo, profuse sweats, great debility and depression of the spirits." He also noted that the urine of heat wave victims was "high-colored and in small quantity."

---

17.   If you're reading an e-book or listening to this book, the same is true, because in both cases, the book is likely stored in the cloud, or else was at one point, and the cloud is not really a cloud; it is a huge array of linked servers that almost never overheat or corrode, because they are kept artificially dry and cool via air-conditioning.

In many countries today, including the United States, heat waves cause more deaths than lightning, tornadoes, hurricanes, floods, and earthquakes combined. A 2003 European heat wave that was concentrated in France led to the deaths of over seventy thousand people. Deadly heat waves from Australia to Algeria and from Canada to Argentina have been common throughout history, but one of the weirdnesses of the Anthropocene is that in the wealthier parts of the world, heat is now more of a health problem in mild climates than in hot ones. Over the past twenty years, people living in usually cool central France, where home AC is uncommon, have been far more likely to die from heat waves than people living in usually sweltering Phoenix, where over 90 percent of households have at least some form of air-conditioning.

There is another peculiarity of modern air-conditioning: cooling the indoors warms the outdoors. Most of the energy that powers air-conditioning systems comes from fossil fuels, the use of which warms the planet, which over time will necessitate more and more conditioning of air. According to the International Energy Agency, air-conditioning and electric fans combined already account for around 10 percent of all global electricity usage, and they expect AC usage will more than triple over the next thirty years. Like most other energy-intensive innovations, AC primarily benefits people in rich communities, while the consequences of climate change are borne disproportionately by people in impoverished communities.

Climate change is probably the biggest shared challenge facing twenty-first-century humans, and I fear future generations will judge us harshly for our failure to do much about it. They will likely learn in their history classes—correctly—that as a species, we knew carbon emissions were affecting the planet's climate back in the 1970s. And they will learn—correctly—about the efforts in the 1980s and 1990s to limit carbon emissions, efforts that ultimately failed for complicated and multifaceted reasons that I assume the history classes of the future will have successfully boiled down into a single narrative. And I suspect that our choices will seem unforgivable and even unfathomable to the people reading those history books. "It is fortunate," Charles Dudley Warner wrote more than a century ago, "that each generation does not comprehend its own ignorance. We are thus enabled to call our ancestors barbarous."[18]

Even as we are beginning to experience the consequences of climate change, we are struggling to mount a global human response to this global problem caused by humans. Some of that is down to public misinformation and the widespread distrust of expertise. Some of it is because climate change feels like an important problem but not an urgent one. The wildfires that have become more common must be put out today. It is much harder for us to make the big changes that would, over generations, decrease the probability of those fires.

But I think it is also hard for us to confront human-caused climate change because the most privileged among us, the people who consume the most energy, can separate ourselves from the weather. I am certainly one such person. I am insulated from the weather by my house and its conditioned air. I eat strawberries in January. When it is raining, I can go inside. When it is dark, I can turn on lights. It is easy for me to feel like climate is mostly an outside phenomenon, whereas I am mostly an inside phenomenon.

But that's all a misconception. I am utterly, wholly dependent on what I imagine as the outside world. I am contingent upon it. For humans, there is ultimately no way out of the obligations and limitations of nature. We *are* nature. And so, like history, the climate is both something that happens to us and something we make.

---

18. Warner is remembered for one other quote. He was the first person known to make a version of the joke, "Everybody talks about the weather, but nobody ever does anything about it." But of course, we are doing something about the weather.

Here in Indianapolis, high temperatures reach above 90 degrees Fahrenheit only about thirteen days per year, and yet most of our homes and office buildings are air-conditioned. This is in part because architecture has changed dramatically in the last fifty years, especially when it comes to commercial buildings, to assume the existence of air-conditioning. But AC is also becoming more common because more of us expect to be able to control our interior environments. When I'm outside, if I can adjust my wardrobe a bit, I feel entirely comfortable if the temperature is anywhere between 55 and 85 degrees Fahrenheit. But inside, my comfort zone drops dramatically, down to a couple of degrees. I loathe sweating while sitting inside, as I often did when I lived in an un-air-conditioned apartment in Chicago. I find it equally uncomfortable to feel goose bumps of chill indoors. Like an expensive painting or a fragile orchid, I thrive only in extremely specific conditions.

I am not alone in this respect. A Cornell University study in 2004 found that office temperatures affect workplace productivity. When temperatures were increased from 68 degrees Fahrenheit to 77, typing output rose by 150 percent and error frequency dropped by 44 percent. This is no small matter—the author of the study said it suggested "raising the temperature to a more comfortable thermal zone saves employers about two dollars per worker, per hour." Why, then, are so many summertime office environments so cool when it is both more expensive and less efficient to keep summertime temperatures low? Perhaps because the definition of "room temperature" has historically been established by analyzing the temperature preferences of forty-year-old, 154-pound men wearing business suits. Studies have consistently found that on average women prefer warmer indoor temperatures.

But when people point out the bias of AC settings in office buildings—especially when women point it out—they've often been mocked for being overly sensitive. After the journalist Taylor Lorenz tweeted that office air-conditioning systems are sexist, a blog in the *Atlantic* wrote, "To think the temperature in a building is sexist is absurd." But it's not absurd. What's absurd is reducing workplace productivity by using precious fossil fuels to excessively cool an office building so that men wearing ornamental jackets will feel more comfortable.

I need to get used to feeling a bit warmer. It's the only future for us. When I was a kid in Florida, it seemed natural to me to grab a sweatshirt before heading to the movie theater. Air-conditioning, like so much else in the Anthropocene, was a kind of background hum that reshaped my life without my ever thinking about it. But writing to you from the early hours of 2021, entering a movie theater at all feels wildly unnatural. What's "natural" for humans is always changing.

I am immensely grateful for air-conditioning. It makes human life far better. But we need to broaden our definition of what constitutes climate control, and quickly.

I give air-conditioning three stars.

STAPHYLOCOCCUS AUREUS

YEARS AGO, I acquired an infection in my left eye socket caused by the bacteria *Staphylococcus aureus*. My vision clouded, and my eye swelled shut. I ended up hospitalized for over a week.

Had I experienced the same infection anytime in history before 1940, I would've likely lost not just my eye but my life. Then again, I probably wouldn't have lived long enough to acquire orbital cellulitis, because I would've died of the staph infections I had in childhood.

When I was in the hospital, the infectious disease doctors made me feel very special. One told me, "You are colonized by some fascinatingly aggressive staph." Only about 20 percent of humans are persistently colonized with *Staphylococcus aureus*—the precise reasons why are not yet clear—and I am apparently one of them. Those of us who carry the bacteria all the time are more likely to experience staph infections. After marveling at my particular staph colony, the doctor told me I wouldn't believe the petri dishes if I saw them, and then called my continued existence a real testament to modern medicine.

Which I suppose it is. For people like myself, colonized by fascinatingly aggressive bacteria, there can be no hearkening back wistfully to past golden ages, because in all those pasts I would be thoroughly dead.

In 1941, Boston City Hospital reported an 82 percent fatality rate for staph infections.

I remember as a child hearing phrases like "Only the strong survive" and "survival of the fittest" and feeling terrified, because I knew I was neither strong nor fit. I didn't yet understand that when humanity protects the frail among us, and works to ensure their survival, the human project as a whole gets stronger.

Because staph often infects open wounds, it has been especially deadly during war. Near the beginning of World War I, the English poet Rupert Brooke famously wrote, "If I should die, think only this of me: / That there's some corner of a foreign field / That is for ever England." Brooke would indeed die in the war, in the winter of 1915—not in some corner of a foreign field, but on a hospital boat, where he was killed by a bacterial infection.

By then, there were thousands of doctors treating the war's wounded and ill. Among them was a seventy-one-year-old Scottish surgeon, Alexander Ogston, who decades earlier had discovered and named *Staphylococcus*.

Ogston was a huge fan of Joseph Lister, whose observations about postsurgical infection led to the use of carbolic acid and other sterilization techniques. These drastically increased surgical survival rates. Ogston wrote to Lister in 1883, "You have changed surgery . . . from being a hazardous lottery into a safe and soundly based science," which was only a bit of an exaggeration. Before antiseptics, Ogston wrote, "After every operation we used to await with trembling the dreaded third day, when sepsis set in." One of Ogston's colleagues, a nurse who worked with him at the Aberdeen Royal Infirmary, declined surgery for a strangulated hernia, choosing death, "for she had never seen a case which was operated on recover."

After visiting Lister and observing complex knee surgeries healing without infection, Ogston returned to the hospital in Aberdeen and tore down the sign above the operating room that read, "Prepare to meet thy God." No longer would surgery be a last-ditch, desperate effort.

Ogston was so obsessed with Lister's carbolic acid spray that his students wrote a poem about it, which reads in part:

> *And we learned the thing of the future*
> *Was using unlimited spray.*
> *The spray, the spray, the antiseptic spray*
> *A.O. would shower it morning, night and day*
> *For every sort of scratch*
> *Where others would attach*
> *A sticking plaster patch*
> *He gave the spray.*

Ogston's first wife, Mary Jane, died after childbirth a few years before these revelations, at the age of twenty-five. There's no record of her cause of death, but most maternal deaths at the time were caused by postpartum infection, often due to *Staphylococcus aureus*. And Ogston had seen hundreds of his patients die of postsurgical infection.

No wonder, then, that he was obsessed with antiseptic protocols. Still, he wanted to understand not just how to prevent infection, but also what precisely was causing it. By the late 1870s, many discoveries were being made by surgeons and researchers about various bacteria and their role in infection, but *Staphylococcus* was not identified until Ogston lanced a pus-filled, abscessed leg wound belonging to one James Davidson.

Under the microscope, Davidson's abscess was brimming with life. Ogston wrote, "My delight may be conceived when there were revealed to me beautiful tangles, tufts and chains of round organisms in great numbers."

Ogston named these tufts and chains *Staphylococcus*, from the Greek word for bunches of grapes. And they do often look like grape bunches—plump spheres gathered together in tight clusters. But Ogston wasn't content with just seeing bacteria. "Obviously," he wrote, "the first step to be taken was to make sure the organisms found in Mr. Davidson's pus were not there by chance." So Ogston set up a laboratory in the shed behind his home and began trying to grow colonies of staph, eventually succeeding by using a chicken egg as the medium. He then injected the bacteria into guinea pigs and mice, which became violently ill. Ogston also noted that *Staphylococcus* seemed to be "harmless on the surface" despite being "so deleterious when injected." I have also observed this—insofar as I am not much bothered by having my skin colonized by *Staphylococcus aureus* but find it deleterious indeed when it starts replicating inside my eye socket.

James Davidson, by the way, went on to live for many decades after his staph infection, thanks to a thorough debriding and Ogston's liberal use of the spray, the spray, the antiseptic spray. But *Staphylococcus aureus* remained an exceptionally dangerous infection until another Scottish scientist, Alexander Fleming, discovered penicillin by accident. One Monday morning in 1928, Fleming noticed that one of his cultures of *Staphylococcus aureus* had been contaminated by a fungus, penicillium, which seemed to have killed all the staph bacteria. He remarked aloud, "That's funny."

Fleming used what he called his "mold juice" to treat a couple of patients, including curing his assistant's sinus infection, but mass production of the antibiotic substance secreted by penicillium proved quite challenging.

It wasn't until the late 1930s that a group of scientists at Oxford began testing their penicillin stocks, first on mice, and then, in 1941, on a human subject, a policeman named Albert Alexander. After being cut by shrapnel during a German bombing raid, Alexander was dying of bacterial infections—in his case, both *Staphylococcus aureus* and *Streptococcus*. The penicillin caused a dramatic improvement in Alexander's condition, but the researchers didn't have enough of the drug to save him. The infections returned, and Alexander died in April of 1941. His seven-year-old daughter Sheila ended up in a local orphanage.

Scientists sought out more productive strains of the mold, and eventually the bacteriologist Mary Hunt found one on a cantaloupe in a Peoria, Illinois, grocery store. That strain became even more productive after being exposed to X-rays and ultraviolet radiation. Essentially all penicillin in the world descends from the mold on that one cantaloupe in Peoria.[19]

Even as penicillin stocks increased—from 21 billion units in 1943 to 6.8 trillion units in 1945—there was growing awareness that the bacteria killed by penicillin were evolving resistance to it, especially *Staphylococcus aureus*. A 1946 *Saturday Evening Post* article worried that antibiotic use would "unwittingly aid and speed up the subtle evolution forces which arrange for the survival of the fittest microbes." So it was to be. By 1950, 40 percent of *Staphylococcus aureus* samples in hospitals were resistant to penicillin; by 1960, 80 percent. Today, only around 2 percent of *Staphylococcus aureus* infections are sensitive to penicillin.

This all happened so, so quickly. Sixty-four years elapsed between Alexander Ogston's discovery of *Staphylococcus* and the mass production of penicillin, and sixty-four years elapsed between the mass production of penicillin and my 2007 bout with orbital cellulitis. In the end, my infection did not respond to penicillin, or to the next two lines of antibiotics, but did fortunately respond to the fourth. Antibiotic resistance is not a problem for the future—this year, some fifty thousand people in the U.S. will die of *Staphylococcus aureus* infections.

---

19.   That's not the astonishing thing about the story, though. The astonishing thing is that after scraping off the mold that became the world's penicillin supply, the researchers ATE THE CANTALOUPE.

How recent is penicillin? That police officer's daughter, who ended up in the orphanage, is still alive as of this writing. Sheila Alexander married an American soldier and moved to California. She's a painter. One of her recent paintings depicts a block of homes in an English village. Ivy grows up along the wall of one home, creeping over rough stone.

To me, one of the mysteries of life is *why* life wants to be. Life is so much more biochemical work than chemical equilibrium, but still, staph desperately seeks that work. As do I, come to think of it. *Staphylococcus* doesn't want to harm people. It doesn't know about people. It just wants to be, like I want to go on, like that ivy wants to spread across the wall, occupying more and more of it. How much? As much as it can.

It's not staph's fault that it wants to be. Nonetheless, I give *Staphylococcus aureus* one star.

THE INTERNET

WHEN THE INTERNET FIRST CAME to our house in the early 1990s, so far as I could tell, the internet was inside of a box. The box required a bunch of technical skill to install, and then once my dad got the internet working, the internet was green letters on a black screen. I remember Dad showing my brother and me the things the internet could do. "Look," he would say. "The internet can show you what the weather is like right now in Beijing." Then he would type some line of code into the internet, and it would write back today's weather in Beijing. "Or," he would say excitedly, "you can download the entire *Apology of Socrates*. For free! And read it right here, in the house."[20]

To my dad, this must have seemed like an actual miracle. But I was not a fan. For one thing, we couldn't get phone calls while my dad was online, on account of how the internet used the phone lines. Admittedly, fourteen-year-old me wasn't fielding a ton of calls, but still. More than that, it seemed to me that the internet was primarily a forum for talking about the internet—my dad would read (and tell us about) endless user

---

20.   One of the weird solipsisms of American life, especially toward the end of the twentieth century, was that the news almost never talked about the weather outside of the United States unless there was some natural disaster unfolding. I guess I should also say that it is still kind of cool that you can download the *Apology of Socrates* for free on the internet.

manuals and message boards he'd read about how the internet worked, and what it might be able to do in the future, and so on.

One day, Dad showed me that on the internet, you could talk to real people all over the world. He explained, "You can practice your French by going to a French forum," and he showed me how it worked. I messaged a couple people on the forum: "Comment ça va?" They responded in real time, with real French, which was unfortunate, as I didn't know much French. I started wondering if there might be an English-language version of the service, and it turned out there was. In fact, there was one built just for me: the CompuServe Teen Forum.

On the CompuServe Teen Forum, nobody knew anything about me. They didn't know that I was a miserable, cringingly awkward kid whose voice often creaked with nervousness. They didn't know I was late to puberty, and they didn't know the names people called me at school.

And paradoxically, because they didn't know me, they knew me far better than anyone in my real life. I remember one evening, in an instant message conversation, I told my CompuServe friend Marie about the "night feeling." The night feeling was my private name for the wave that crashed over me most school nights when I got into bed. My stomach would tighten and I'd feel the worry radiating out from my belly button. I'd never told anyone about the night feeling, and my heart was racing as I typed. Marie responded that she also knew the night feeling, and that she sometimes found comfort in listening quietly to her clock radio. I tried that, and it helped.

But most of the time, my Teen Forum friend group did not share our secrets. We shared inside jokes, and learned/built/borrowed/created together. By the summer of 1993, the CompuServe Teen Forum was a vast universe of mythology and references, from jokes about the TV show *Barney & Friends* to endless acronyms and abbreviations. The internet was still just green letters on a black screen, so we couldn't use images, but we arranged text characters into shapes. The idea of ASCII art, as it is known, had been around for decades, but *we* hadn't been around for decades, and so we felt like we were discovering it as we built everything from extremely simple images—like :-) for example—to ridiculously complex (and often obscene) ones. I don't recall using a word to describe what we were doing, but these days we would call this stuff memes.

That summer, with school out of the way, I was able to devote myself full-time to the Teen Forum. I even got something called an email address— a series of randomly generated digits @compuserve.com. Back then, the internet charged by the hour, which became a real issue because I wanted to spend every hour on it. Now it was my parents who complained about the phone line being tied up. They loved that I was making friends, that I was writing and reading so much, but they could not afford a one-hundred-dollar monthly internet bill. At this point, a lifeline appeared when I was "hired" as a moderator for the Teen Forum. The payment came in the form of all the free internet I wanted, and I wanted a lot of it. CompuServe even paid for a separate phone line so I could be online constantly. If a single event in my life occurred outdoors that summer, I do not recall it.

I fear I've been romanticizing. The early-nineties internet had many of the problems the current internet does. While I recall the Teen Forum being well moderated, the same racism and misogyny that populate today's comments sections was prevalent thirty years ago. And then, as now, you could fall very far down the rabbit hole of the internet's highly personalized information feeds until conspiracy theories began to feel more real than the so-called facts.[21]

---

21.   I lived this experience, actually. In the early nineties, I became entranced by something called the Phantom Time Hypothesis, which held that around three hundred years of time between the seventh and tenth centuries never actually happened and were instead invented by the Catholic Church. I was originally turned on to this idea by one of those memes that is itself not sure whether it's ironic. The conspiracy theory, which was pretty widespread at the time, held that I was really living not in the year 1993 but instead around 1698, and that a bunch of years had been faked so that the Church could . . . maintain power? The details of it escape me, but it's amazing what you can believe when you're down the rabbit hole.

I have wonderful memories of that summer, and also traumatic ones. A few years ago, I ran into an old friend, who said of our high school, "It saved my life. But it also did a lot of other things." So, too, with the internet.

These days, after drinking from the internet's fire hose for thirty years, I've begun to feel more of those negative effects. I don't know if it's my age, or the fact that the internet is no longer plugged into the wall and now travels with me everywhere I go, but I find myself thinking of that Wordsworth poem that begins, "The world is too much with us; late and soon."

What does it say that I can't imagine my life or my work without the internet? What does it mean to have my way of thinking, and my way of *being*, so profoundly shaped by machine logic? What does it mean that, having been part of the internet for so long, the internet is also part of me?

My friend Stan Muller tells me that when you're living in the middle of history, you never know what it means. I am living in the middle of the internet. I have no idea what it means.

I give the internet three stars.

ACADEMIC DECATHLON

BEGINNING IN TENTH GRADE, I attended a boarding school in Alabama, where my best friend, Todd, was also my roommate. He would often say that late at night, when he was trying to fall asleep in our air-conditionless dorm room, I turned into a stream-of-consciousness novel. I'd tell him everything—my every interaction with my English class crush, including selected quotations from the notes she and I exchanged; the reasons it just wasn't possible for me to turn in the paper I had due for history; the weird ache I always felt on the outside of my left knee; how nervous I'd been smoking a cigarette behind the gym because someone got caught there last week; and on and on and on until finally he would say, "Seriously, Green. I love you, but I have to sleep." We were not afraid to say "I love you" to each other.

Here's my favorite story about Todd: In those days, the SAT was offered only every other month in Alabama. Todd and I managed to miss the last local SAT test before our college application deadlines, so we had to drive to Georgia to take the test. After a road trip and a night in a Motel 6, we arrived bleary-eyed at the testing site, where I struggled to concentrate for four endless hours. When the test was at last over, I met back up with Todd. The first thing he said to me was, "What's 'ostentatious' mean?" And I told him it meant, like, "showy" or "over the top." Todd nodded subtly to himself and then, after a second, said, "Cool. I got them all then."

And he had. Perfect score on the SAT.

It was Todd who had the idea for me to join the Academic Decathlon team, although at first blush I seemed a poor candidate. I never excelled academically, and took some pride in "not fulfilling my potential," in part because I was terrified that if I tried my hardest, the world would learn I didn't actually have that much potential. But in my poor grades, Todd sensed an opportunity.

Academic Decathlon, sometimes known as AcaDec, features ten disciplines. In 1994, there were seven "objective" events featuring multiple-choice tests: economics, fine arts, language and literature, math, science, social science, and a "Super Quiz" in "Documents of Freedom." There were also three subjective events graded by judges—an essay, an in-person interview, and the performance of a speech.

Every school's AcaDec team has nine players: You get three A students, with grade point averages above 3.75; three B students, with GPAs above 3; and three C students, whose GPAs are 2.99 or below. For all you non-Americans out there, that means three of each school's players get excellent marks, three get good ones, and three must be . . . fairly bad at school. I, as it happened, was terrible at school. Todd believed that with his patient instruction and my awful grades, he could mold me into an Academic Decathlon superstar.

And so beginning in our junior year, we studied together. We read an entire economics textbook, and whenever I found part of it inscrutable, Todd would frame the topic in ways that were comprehensible to me. When we were learning about marginal utility, for example, he explained it to me in terms of Zima.

Todd would tell me, "Look, you drink one Zima and you feel good. You drink two, and you feel better, but the added benefit is smaller than between zero and one. The additional usefulness of each added Zima gets lower and lower until eventually the curve inverts around five Zimas and you throw up. That's marginal utility." [22]

So we learned economics, but we also learned art history, and chemistry, and math, and much else. Through studying for Academic Decathlon, I learned about everything from the Indus Valley Civilization to mitosis. And thanks to Todd, I became a very capable Academic Decathlete.

I don't want to brag, but at the Alabama State Academic Decathlon of 1994, I was the Lionel Messi of C students. I won seven medals—four of them gold—out of a possible ten events. I won a bronze medal in *math*, even though that year I received a D in precalc. Admittedly, none of my scores would've gotten me into the top ten among A or B students, but I wasn't competing against them. For the first time in my academic life, I felt like I wasn't an idiot.

I won gold medals in topics I thought I sucked at—like literature and history—and also one in speech, which was especially surprising because I'd always been a poor public speaker. I hated my voice, the way it betrayed my omnidirectional anxiety, and I'd done terribly in debate competitions. But with AcaDec, I'd found a place where I could flourish. Our school won the state competition, which meant we'd qualified for nationals, to be held that year in a hotel ballroom in Newark, New Jersey.

Over the next few months, my growing academic confidence,

---

22.   Zima was an alcoholic beverage that was a kind of low-quality precursor to twenty-first-century hard seltzer. It was terrible. I loved it. More importantly, many years later, I would hear marginal utility described almost exactly this same way on the NPR podcast *Planet Money*. Did that podcast and Todd have a shared source? Or is my memory being unreliable? I don't know. What I do know is that my marginal utility curve still inverts after five drinks, just as it did in high school.

combined with study skills learned from Todd, meant that my grades started to improve. I was briefly at risk of losing my coveted C-student status until I realized I could tank physics to keep my GPA below 3.

That April, the nine of us and our coaches flew up to Newark. We made friends with other nerds from around the country, including a C student from the Midwest whose name was, I think, Caroline. She had a good fake ID and managed to smuggle a twelve-pack of Zimas to us.

Todd was one of the leading A students at nationals, and our little team from Alabama ended up finishing sixth in the nation. I even won a couple of medals. One was in speech. My speech was about rivers. I don't remember much about it, but I think I talked about meanders—the serpentine bends in a river's course. I've loved rivers ever since I can remember. I spent part of one summer with my dad on the Noatak River in northern Alaska, and another paddling the French Broad River in Tennessee.

The idea for the speech was stolen from Todd. We were sitting on the banks of a creek one September afternoon, the air thick and mosquito-laden, and Todd told me that what he liked about rivers was that they kept going. They meander this way and that, but they keep going.

———————

It's April of 2020. I am a long way downstream from that hotel ballroom in Newark. All morning, I've been trying to help my kids with e-learning, but I worry I only make it worse for them with my impatience and exasperation. I'm stressed about work, even though my work is absurdly inessential. At noon, the Indiana State Department of Health updates its Covid-19 dashboard with grim news. As the kids eat lunch, I read the updates on my phone. Sarah comes downstairs, and we go to the living room so she can tell me about a friend of ours who is hospitalized. The news is good—our friend is recovering—but I can't feel any joy about it. There is only dread. She can see it in me, I think, because she says, "Why don't you walk over to the river?"

These days, I can only feel normal when I'm outside. I am writing this now on the west bank of the White River here in Indianapolis. I brought a camping chair down here. I am sitting atop a grassy berm, and my laptop's battery has plenty of power. Before me, the river is a muddy, flooded cacophony. Every minute or two, an uprooted tree comes barreling downriver. In a dry summer, I can walk across this stretch of river without ever getting my shorts wet, but now it's fifteen feet deep and churning.

For days now, my brain has refused to allow me to finish a thought, constantly interrupting with worries. Even my worries get interrupted—by new worries, or facets of old worries I had not adequately considered. My thoughts are a river overflowing its banks, churning and muddy and ceaseless. I wish I wasn't so scared all the time—scared of the virus, yes, but there is also some deeper fear: the terror of time passing, and me with it.

I brought a Terry Tempest Williams book with me, but the omnipresent worry makes it impossible to read for more than a few minutes. Scanning through the book, I find a passage I highlighted years ago. "When one of us says, 'Look, there's nothing out there,' what we are really saying is, '*I cannot see.*'"

From here, the White River will flow into the Wabash River, and then into the Ohio, and then into the great Mississippi River, and then into the Gulf of Mexico. Even after that, it will keep going—freezing, melting, evaporating, raining, flowing, being neither created nor destroyed. Looking out at this river reminds me of sitting at the edge of that creek with Todd, and how his love helped carry me through those years, and how in some ways it is still carrying me.

I wonder if you have people like that in your life, people whose love keeps you going even though they are distant now because of time and geography and everything else that comes between us. Todd and I have both floated down through the decades—he's a doctor now—but the courses of our lives were shaped by those moments we shared upstream. As Maya Jasanoff wrote, "A river is nature's plotline: It carries you from here to there." Or from there to here, at least.

Outside, the world continues. The river, even overflowing its banks, still meanders. I glance from my laptop screen to the river, then back to the screen, and then to the river. For no reason I know, a memory coalesces: After the Academic Decathlon competition in Newark was over, we ended up with our Zimas on the roof of that hotel—Todd and me and a couple of our teammates. It was late at night and New York City glowed pink in the distance. We were the sixth best Academic Decathlon team in the nation, we were getting just the right amount of utility out of our Zimas, and we loved each other. Rivers keep going, and we keep going, and there is no way back to the roof of that hotel. But the memory still holds me together.

I give the Academic Decathlon four and a half stars.

SUNSETS

WHAT ARE WE TO DO about the clichéd beauty of an ostentatious sunset? Should we cut it with menace, as Roberto Bolaño did so brilliantly, writing, "The sky at sunset looked like a carnivorous flower"? Should we lean in to the inherent sentimentality, as Kerouac does in *On the Road* when he writes, "Soon it got dusk, a grapy dusk, a purple dusk over tangerine groves and long melon fields . . . the fields the color of love and Spanish mysteries"? Or perhaps we should turn to mysticism, as Anna Akhmatova did when she wrote that in the face of a beautiful sunset,

> *I cannot tell if the day*
> *is ending, or the world, or if*
> *the secret of secrets is inside me again.*

A good sunset always steals the words from me, renders all my thoughts as gauzy and soft as the light itself. I'll admit, though, that when I see the sun sink below a distant horizon as the yellows and oranges and pinks flood the sky, I usually think, "This looks photoshopped." When I see the natural world at its most spectacular, my general impression is that more than anything, it looks fake.

I'm reminded that in the late eighteenth and early nineteenth centuries, tourists would travel around with darkened, slightly convex mirrors called Claude glasses. If you turned yourself away from a magnificent landscape and looked instead at the landscape's reflection in the Claude glass, it was said to appear more "picturesque." Named after seventeenth-century French landscape painter Claude Lorrain, the glass not only framed the scene but also simplified its tonal range, making reality look like a painting. Thomas Gray wrote that only through the Claude glass could he "see the sun set in all its glory."

The thing about the sun, of course, is that you can't look directly at it—not when you're outside, and not when you're trying to describe its beauty. In *Pilgrim at Tinker Creek*, Annie Dillard writes, "We have really only that one light, one source for all power, and yet we must turn away from it by universal decree. Nobody here on the planet seems aware of this strange, powerful taboo, that we all walk around carefully averting our faces this way and that, lest our eyes be blasted forever."

In all those senses, the sun is godlike. As T. S. Eliot put it, light is the visible reminder of the Invisible Light. Like a god, the sun has fearsome and wondrous power. And like a god, the sun is difficult or even dangerous to look at directly. In the Book of Exodus, God says, "You cannot see my face, for no one may see me and live." No wonder that Christian writers have for centuries been punning on Jesus as being both Son and Sun. The Gospel according to John refers to Jesus as "the Light" so many times that it gets annoying. And there are gods of sunlight everywhere there are gods, from the Egyptian Ra to the Greek Helios to the Aztec Nanahuatzin, who sacrificed himself by leaping into a bonfire so that he could become the shining sun. It all makes a kind of sense: I don't just need the light of that star to survive; I am in many ways a product of its light, which is basically how I feel about God.

People ask me all the time if I believe in God. I tell them that I'm Episcopalian, or that I go to church, but they don't care about that. They only want to know if I believe in God, and I can't answer them, because I don't know how to deal with the question's *in*. Do I believe *in* God? I believe around God. But I can only believe *in* what I am in—sunlight and shadow, oxygen and carbon dioxide, solar systems and galaxies.

But now we're already swimming in sentimental waters; I've metaphorized the sunset. First, it was photoshopped. Now, it's divine. And neither of these ways of looking at a sunset will suffice.

e. e. cummings has a sunset poem that goes,

who are you,little i

(five or six years old)
peering from some high

window;at the gold

of november sunset

(and feeling:that if day
has to become night

this is a beautiful way)

It's a good poem, but it only works because cummings situates the observation in childhood, when one is presumably too innocent to have yet realized how lame it is to write about sunsets. And yet, a good sunset *is* beautiful, and better still, universally so. Our distant ancestors didn't eat like us or travel like us. Their relationship to ideas as fundamental as time was different from ours. They measured time not primarily in hours or seconds but mostly in relationship to solar cycles—how close it was to sunset, or to daybreak, or to midwinter. But every human who has lived for more than a few years on this planet has seen a beautiful sunset and paused to spend one of the last moments of the day grateful for, and overwhelmed by, the light.

So how might we celebrate a sunset without being mawkish or saccharine? Maybe state it in cold facts. Here's what happens: Before a beam of sunlight gets to your eyes, it has many, many interactions with molecules that cause the so-called scattering of light. Different wavelengths are sent off in different directions when interacting with, say, oxygen or nitrogen in the atmosphere. But at sunset, the light travels through the atmosphere longer before it reaches us, so that much of the blue and purple has been scattered away, leaving the sky to our eyes rich in reds and pinks and oranges. As the artist Tacita Dean put it, "Color is a fiction of light."

I think it's helpful to know how sunsets work. I don't buy the romantic notion that scientific understanding somehow robs the universe of its beauty, but I still can't find language to describe how breathtakingly beautiful sunsets are—not breathtakingly, actually, but breath-givingly beautiful. All I can say is that sometimes when the world is between day and night, I'm stopped cold by its splendor, and I feel my absurd smallness. You'd think that would be sad, but it isn't. It only makes me grateful. Toni Morrison once wrote, "At some point in life, the world's beauty becomes enough. You don't need to photograph, paint, or even remember it. It is enough." So what can we say of the clichéd beauty of sunsets? Perhaps only that they are enough.

———————

My dog, Willy, died a few years ago, but one of my great memories of him is watching him play in the front yard of our house at dusk. He was a puppy then, and in the early evenings he would contract a case of the zoomies. He ran in delighted circles around us, yipping and jumping at nothing in particular, and then after a while, he'd get tired, and he'd run over to me and lie down. And then he would do something absolutely extraordinary: He would roll over onto his back, and present his soft belly. I always marveled at the courage of that, his ability to be so absolutely vulnerable to us. He offered us the place ribs don't protect, trusting that we weren't going to bite or stab him. It's hard to trust the world like that, to show it your belly. There's something deep within me, something intensely fragile, that is terrified of turning itself to the world.

I'm scared to even write this down, because I worry that having confessed this fragility, you now know where to punch. I know that if I'm hit where I am earnest, I will never recover.

It can sometimes feel like loving the beauty that surrounds us is somehow disrespectful to the many horrors that also surround us. But mostly, I think I'm just scared that if I show the world my belly, it will devour me. And so I wear the armor of cynicism, and hide behind the great walls of irony, and only glimpse beauty with my back turned to it, through the Claude glass.

But I want to be earnest, even if it's embarrassing. The photographer Alec Soth has said, "To me, the most beautiful thing is vulnerability." I would go a step further and argue that you cannot see the beauty which is enough unless you make yourself vulnerable to it.

And so I try to turn toward that scattered light, belly out, and I tell myself: This doesn't look like a picture. And it doesn't look like a god. It is a sunset, and it is beautiful, and this whole thing you've been doing where nothing gets five stars because nothing is perfect? That's bullshit. So much is perfect. Starting with this. I give sunsets five stars.

JERZY DUDEK'S PERFORMANCE

ON MAY 25, 2005

I'D LIKE TO TELL YOU A STORY of joy and wonder and stupidity. It's a sports story, and I've been thinking about it because I am writing to you from May 2020, a moment when sports have—for the first time in my life—stopped.

I miss sports. I know sports don't matter in the scheme of things, but I miss the luxury of caring about stuff that doesn't matter. The late Pope John Paul II is reported (probably falsely) to have said, "Of all the unimportant things, football is the most important." And I yearn for the unimportant things at the moment. So here is a football story that begins in southern Poland, only about sixty miles from where Pope John Paul II was born.

It's 1984, and a gangly ten-year-old coal miner's son named Jerzy Dudek is living in the tiny coal mining town of Szczygłowice. The mining company has organized a trip for miners' spouses to go under-ground and see where the miners work. Jerzy and his older brother, Dariusz, wait outside the mine with their father, as Renata Dudek journeys thousands of feet down into the mineshaft. When she returns, she starts kissing her husband, crying. Dudek would later recall, "She called us over and said, 'Jerzy, Dariusz, promise me you will never go down the mine.'"

Jerzy and his brother just laughed. "We were thinking to ourselves, 'Well, what else are we going to do?'"

By then, Pope John Paul II, whom young Jerzy idolized, was living in the Vatican, a couple of miles away from Rome's Stadio Olimpico, which that year hosted the finals of the European Cup, a big soccer tournament now known as the Champions League, where all the best teams in Europe play one another. That year, the final pitted hometown club AS Roma against my beloved Liverpool Football Club.[23]

Liverpool's goalkeeper at the time, Bruce Grobbelaar, was eccentric even by goalie standards. He warmed up by walking on his hands and hanging off the top of the goal. He often drank a dozen beers on the team bus after a Liverpool loss.

But Grobbelaar is best known for that European Cup final in 1984. The game went to a penalty shoot-out in which, for some reason, Grobbelaar decided to feign wobbly-legged nervousness as one of the Roma penalty takers ran up to shoot. Put off by Grobbelaar's spaghetti legs, the Roma player skyed his shot over the crossbar and Liverpool won their fourth European Cup.

Back in southern Poland, young Jerzy Dudek loved football, although leather balls were hard to come by in his impoverished community, so they usually played with rubber balls or even old tennis balls. He ended up becoming a goalkeeper because he was tall, but he didn't start out especially skilled at the position. His first coach told him, "You dive like a sack of potatoes."

By seventeen, Dudek was in training to become a miner, and as part

---

23. I have known the novelist, *Radio Ambulante* cofounder, and Arsenal fan Daniel Alarcón since high school. Daniel was once asked in an interview if I thought of myself primarily as a YouTuber or as a writer. To my delight, Daniel answered, "John mostly thinks of himself as a Liverpool fan."

of his vocational training, he worked in the coal mine two days a week. In many ways, he liked the work. He enjoyed the camaraderie in the mine, the feeling of mutual reliance. The mine company had a football team, and Jerzy began playing for them. He couldn't afford goalie gloves, so he wore his father's work gloves. To make himself feel like a real goalie, he drew an Adidas logo on them. He got better, stopped diving like a sack of potatoes, and by the age of nineteen, he was making just over a hundred dollars a month as the goalkeeper for a semipro team while still working for the mine company. But by twenty-one, his progress had stalled. He would later say that he felt himself melting "into the grayness."

Liverpool Football Club were melting into the grayness, too. By the 1990s, Liverpool often weren't good enough to play in the Champions League, let alone win it.

In 1996, when Jerzy Dudek was twenty-two, he caught the attention of a first-division Polish team, who signed him to play for a salary of around $400 a month. After that, Dudek's rise was astonishing: Within six months, he was transferred to a Dutch team, Feyenoord, where he finally began to make a living wage playing goalie. After a few years with Feyenoord, Dudek signed a multimillion-pound contract with Liverpool.

But he was miserable. Of the time, he wrote, "The first few days in Liverpool were the worst ones of my life. I felt really lonely. I was in a new place with a new language, which I couldn't speak." All these quotes, by the way, are from Dudek's autobiography, which he titled, *A Big Pole in Our Goal*. That's the song Liverpool fans sang about him, to the tune of "He's Got the Whole World in His Hands." *We've got a big Pole in our goal.*

Before we get to May 25, 2005, I just want to note one more thing. Professional goalkeepers spend a *lot* of time practicing trying to save penalty kicks. Jerzy Dudek had faced thousands of penalty kicks, and he approached them in precisely the same way: He stood stock-still in the middle of the goal until a moment before the ball was kicked, and then he dove one way or another. Always. Without exception.

The 2004–2005 season saw Liverpool go on a magical run through the Champions League, and by April they were preparing to play the famed Italian club Juventus in the quarterfinals when Pope John Paul II died. Dudek ended up on the bench for that game—he couldn't think straight after the death of his childhood hero and found himself near tears as he confessed to the team doctor that he couldn't play that night. Liverpool won the game nonetheless, and eventually made their way to the Champions League final, where they would play another Italian giant, AC Milan.

The final was played in Istanbul, and it began horribly for Dudek and Liverpool. Fifty-one seconds into the game, Milan scored. They scored two more goals just before halftime. Dudek's wife, Mirella, at home in Poland preparing for their son's first communion, recalled a "deathly silence" descending over Szczygłowice.

Of the Liverpool locker room at halftime, Dudek wrote, "Everyone was broken." Liverpool defender Jamie Carragher said, "My dreams had turned to dust." The players could hear the forty thousand Liverpool fans singing "You'll Never Walk Alone" in the stands above, but they knew it was, as Carragher put it, "in sympathy more than belief."

The rest I know by heart, because I've seen it so many times. Nine minutes after the second half begins, Liverpool's captain Steven Gerrard scores with a balletic header. Liverpool score again two minutes later, and then again four minutes after that. Now it's tied 3–3. The match goes into thirty minutes of extra time. Milan pour on the pressure. It is so obvious that they are the better team. Liverpool's players are exhausted, just hoping to get to a penalty shoot-out.

And then: With ninety seconds left in extra time, Jerzy Dudek makes a double save on two point-blank shots that occur within a second of each other. The save is so good that an entire chapter of *A Big Pole in Our Goal* is devoted to it. The save is so good that even now, fifteen years later, when I see replays of it, I still think the Milan player is going to score. But instead, Jerzy Dudek makes the save every time, and the game goes to a penalty shoot-out.

So you're Jerzy Dudek. You've been practicing saving penalties since you were a kid, and you have your way of doing it. You've lain awake at night imagining this moment. The Champions League final, down to penalties, you in goal, standing stock-still until the moment before the ball is kicked.

But then, in the moments before the shoot-out begins, Jamie Carragher runs over to you. He jumps on your back and starts shouting. "Carra came up to me like he was crazy," Dudek remembered. "He grabbed me and said, 'Jerzy Jerzy Jerzy, remember Bruce Grobbelaar.'"

Carragher was screaming at him: *Do the wobbly legs! Move around on the goal line! Just like in 1984!* But that was twenty-one years before—with different players, a different coach, and a different opponent. What could that moment possibly have to do with this one?

There are times in your life when you do things precisely as you have practiced and prepared for them. And then there are times when you listen to Jamie Carragher. So in the most important moment of Jerzy Dudek's professional life, he decided to try something new.

His spaghetti legs didn't look exactly like Grobbelaar's had, but he danced on the goal line, his legs wobbling this way and that. "I didn't recognize my husband," Mirella Dudek said. "I couldn't believe he . . . danced so crazily in the goal."

Liverpool scored all but one of their penalties. For Milan, facing the dancing Dudek, it was a different story. Milan's first penalty taker missed the goal entirely, and then Dudek saved two of the next four penalties, and Liverpool completed what came to be known as "The Miracle of Istanbul."

Someone tell ten-year-old Jerzy Dudek that he is going to save two penalties in a European Cup final by making the weirdest possible choice. Someone tell twenty-one-year-old Jerzy Dudek playing for $1,800 a year that he is a decade away from lifting the European Cup.

You can't see the future coming—not the terrors, for sure, but you also can't see the wonders that are coming, the moments of light-soaked joy that await each of us. These days, I often feel like I'm Jerzy Dudek walking out for the second half down 3–0, feeling as hopeless as I do helpless. But of all the unimportant things, football is the most important, because seeing Jerzy Dudek sprint away from that final penalty save to be mobbed by his teammates reminds me that someday—and maybe someday soon—I will also be embraced by people I love. It is May of 2020, fifteen years since Dudek's spaghetti legs, and this will end, and the light-soaked days are coming.

I give Jerzy Dudek's performance on May 25, 2005 five stars.

PENGUINS OF MADAGASCAR

UNLESS YOU'VE LIVED an exceptionally fortunate life, you've probably known someone who enjoys having provocative opinions. I am referring to the people who will say things to you like, "You know, Ringo was the best Beatle."

You'll take a long breath. Maybe you're out to lunch with this person, because lunch is a time-limited experience, and you can only bear this person's presence in minute quantities. So you'll take a bite of your food. And then you'll sigh again before saying, "Why was Ringo the best Beatle?"[24]

Well, the Provocative Opinion Person is *very* glad you asked. "Ringo was the best Beatle because . . ." And then you stop listening, which is the only way to get through lunch. When the person has finished you say, "Okay, but Ringo also wrote 'Octopus's Garden,'" and then the Provocative Opinion Person will regale you with a fourteen-minute lecture that begins, "Well, actually, 'Octopus's Garden' is a work of considerable genius because . . ."

Most of us are not Provocative Opinion People, thank God. But I

---

24.   Just in case Ringo Starr or anyone who loves him is reading this: I think Ringo was a great Beatle. An excellent Beatle. I just don't think he was necessarily the *best* Beatle.

think everyone secretly harbors at least one provocative opinion, and this is mine: The opening sequence of the 2014 film *Penguins of Madagascar* is one of the greatest scenes in cinematic history.

Penguins of Madagascar is an animated kids' movie about the Anthropocene: A villainous octopus named Dave has invented a special ray that makes cute animals ugly, so that humans will stop privileging the protection of adorable animals (like penguins) over less adorable ones (like Dave).

The movie begins as a faux nature documentary. "Antarctica, an inhospitable wasteland," the famous documentary filmmaker Werner Herzog intones with his trademark gravitas. But even here, he tells us, "We find life. And not just any life. PENGUINS. Joyous, frolicking, waddling, cute, and cuddly life."

A long line of penguins marches mindlessly behind an unseen leader. As Herzog calls penguins "silly little snow clowns," we follow the line back to the three young penguins at the center of the movie, one of whom announces, "Does anyone even know where we're marching *to*?"

"Who cares?" an adult penguin responds.

"I question nothing," another adds.

Soon thereafter, the three young penguins are bowled over by an egg rolling downhill. They decide to follow the egg, which tumbles off the edge of a glacier to a shipwrecked boat below. These three little penguins now stand on the edge of a cliff, looking down at an egg about to be devoured by a leopard seal. The penguins must decide: Risk it all to save this egg, or watch as it gets eaten?

At this point, the camera zooms out, and we see the documentary crew following the penguins. "Tiny and helpless," Herzog says, "the babies are frozen with fear. They know if they fall from this cliff, they will surely die." And then there is a moment's pause before Herzog says, "Günter, give them a shove."

The sound guy uses a boom mic to whack the penguins from be-hind, forcing them into the great unknown. It's a children's movie, so of course the penguins survive and go on to great adventures. But every time I watch *Penguins of Madagascar*, I think of how almost all of us are invisible to penguins almost all of the time, and yet we are nonetheless their biggest threat—and also their best hope. In that respect, we are a kind of god—and not a particularly benevolent one.

I also find myself thinking about the lemming, a six-inch-long rodent with pert eyes and a brown-black coat of fur. There are many species of lemmings, and they can be found throughout the colder parts of North America and Eurasia. Most like to be near water, and can swim a fair distance.

Lemmings tend to have an especially extreme population cycle: Every three or four years, their populations explode due to favorable breeding conditions. In the seventeenth century, some naturalists hy-pothesized that the lemmings must spontaneously generate and then fall from the sky in their millions like raindrops. That belief fell away over time, but another did not. We have long believed that, driven by instinct and/or a willingness to mindlessly follow other lemmings, the creatures self-correct for population growth via mass suicide.

This myth has proven astonishingly durable, even though biologists have known for a very long time that lemmings do no such thing. In fact, lemmings spread out when populations become too large, seeking new and safe spaces. Sometimes, they come to a river or a lake and at-tempt to cross it. Sometimes, they drown. Sometimes, they die of other causes. In all these respects, they are not too different from other rodents.

But even now, we still sometimes say that people who unquestion-ingly follow are "lemmings." We think of lemmings this way in no small part because of the 1958 Disney movie *White Wilderness*, a nature documentary about the North American arctic. In the film, we watch lemmings migrating after a season of population growth. At last, they come to an oceanside cliff, which the narrator refers to as "the final precipice."

"Casting themselves bodily out into space," the narrator tells us, the lemmings hurl themselves over the cliff in their immense stupidity, and those that survive the fall then swim out into the ocean until they drown, "a final rendezvous with destiny, and with death."

But none of this is a realistic depiction of the lemmings' natural behavior. For one thing, the subspecies of lemming depicted in the film do not typically migrate. Also, this section of the movie wasn't even filmed in the wild; the lemmings in question were flown from Hudson Bay to Calgary, where much of the lemming footage was shot. And the lemmings did not hurl themselves bodily out into space. Instead, the filmmakers dumped lemmings over the cliff from a truck and filmed them as they fell, and then eventually drowned. Günter, give them a shove.

Today, *White Wilderness* is remembered not as a documentary about lemmings, but as a documentary about us, and the lengths we will go to hold on to a lie. My father is a documentary filmmaker (I learned the *White Wilderness* story from him), and that's no doubt part of why I love that opening sequence of *Penguins of Madagascar*.

But I also love it because it captures, and makes the gentlest possible fun of, something about myself I find deeply troubling. Like the adult penguin who stays in line and announces, "I question nothing," I mostly follow rules. I mostly try to act like everyone else is acting, even as we all approach the precipice. We imagine other animals as being without consciousness, mindlessly following the leader to they-know-not-where, but in that construction, we sometimes forget that we are also animals.

I am thoughtful—full of thoughts, all the time, inescapably, exhaustingly. But I am also mindless—acting in accordance with default settings I neither understand nor examine. To a degree I don't want to accept,

I am what we have long claimed lemmings to be. Forces beyond my comprehension have led me and my fellow lemmings to a precipice, and I fear the shove is coming. The lemmings myth doesn't last because it helps us to understand lemmings. It lasts because it helps us to understand ourselves.

Penguins of Madagascar is an exceptionally silly movie. But how else can we confront the absurdities of the Anthropocene? I stand by my Provocative Opinion, and give the opening sequence of *Penguins of Madagascar* four and a half stars.

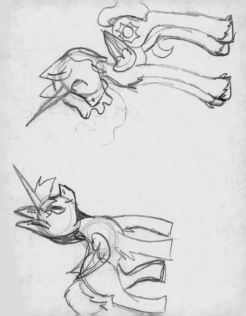

VERIFIED.
TARDY PASS

OCT 13 AM 8:30

Date/Time _____

Name _____

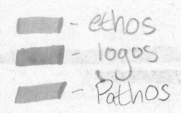

- ethos
- logos
- Pathos

PIGGLY WIGGLY

IN 1920, according to census records, my great-grandfather Roy worked at a grocery store in a tiny town in western Tennessee. Like all U.S. grocery stores at the beginning of the twentieth century, this one was full-service: You walked in with a list of items you needed, and then the grocer—perhaps my great-grandfather—would gather those items. The grocer would weigh the flour or cornmeal or butter or tomatoes, and then wrap everything up for you. My great-grandfather's store probably also allowed customers to purchase food on credit, a common practice at the time. The customer would then, usually, pay back their grocery bill over time.

That job was supposed to be my great-grandfather's path out of poverty, but it didn't work out that way. Instead, the store closed, thanks in part to the self-service grocery store revolution launched by Clarence Saunders, which reshaped the way Americans shopped and cooked and ate and lived. Saunders was a self-educated child of impoverished sharecroppers. Eventually, he found his way into the grocery business in Memphis, Tennessee, about a hundred miles southwest from my great-grandfather's store. Saunders was thirty-five when he developed a concept for a grocery store that would have no counters, but instead a labyrinth of aisles that customers would walk themselves, choosing their own food and placing it in their own shopping baskets.

Prices at Saunders's self-service grocery would be lower, because his stores would employ fewer clerks and also because he would not offer customers credit, instead expecting immediate payment. The prices would also be clear and transparent—for the first time, every item in a grocery store would be marked with a price so customers would no longer fear being shortchanged by unscrupulous grocers. Saunders called his store Piggly Wiggly.

Why? Nobody knows. When asked where the name came from, Saunders once answered that it arrived "from out of chaos and in direct contact with an individual's mind," which gives you a sense of the kind of guy he was. But usually, when Saunders was asked why anyone would call a grocery store Piggly Wiggly, he would answer, "So people will ask that very question."

The first Piggly Wiggly opened in Memphis in 1916. It was so successful that the second Piggly Wiggly opened three weeks later. Two months after that, another opened. Saunders insisted on calling it "Piggly Wiggly the Third" to lend his stores the "royal dignity they are due." He began attaching a catchphrase to his storefront signs: "Piggly Wiggly: All Around the World." At the time, the stores were barely all around Memphis, but Saunders's prophecies came true: Within a year, there were 353 Piggly Wigglies around the United States, and today, Saunders's concept of self-service aisles really has spread all around the world.

In newspaper advertisements, Saunders wrote of his self-service concept in nearly messianic terms. "One day Memphis shall be proud of Piggly Wiggly," one ad read. "And it shall be said by all men that the Piggly Wigglies shall multiply and replenish the Earth with more and cleaner things to eat." Another time he wrote, "The mighty pulse of the throbbing today makes new things out of old and new things where was nothing before." Basically, Saunders spoke of Piggly Wiggly as today's

Silicon Valley executives talk of their companies: We're not just making money here. We are replenishing the earth.

Piggly Wiggly and the self-service grocery stores that followed did bring down prices, which meant there was more to eat. They also changed the kinds of foods that were readily available—to save costs and limit spoilage, Piggly Wiggly stocked less fresh produce than traditional grocery stores. Prepackaged, processed foods became more popular and less expensive, which altered American diets. Brand recognition also became extremely important, because food companies had to appeal directly to shoppers, which led to the growth of consumer-oriented food advertising on radio and in newspapers. National brands like Campbell Soup and OREO cookies exploded in popularity; by 1920, Campbell was the nation's top soup brand and OREO the top cookie brand—which they still are today.

Self-service grocery stores also fueled the rise of many other processed food brands. Wonder Bread. MoonPies. Hostess CupCakes. Birds Eye frozen vegetables. Wheaties cereal. Reese's Peanut Butter Cups. French's mustard. Klondike bars. Velveeta cheese. All of these brands, and many more, appeared in the United States within a decade of the first Piggly Wiggly opening. Clarence Saunders understood the new intersections between mass media and brand awareness better than almost anyone at the time. In fact, during the early 1920s, Piggly Wiggly was the single largest newspaper advertiser in the United States.

Keeping prices low and employing fewer clerks also meant many people who worked at traditional grocery stores lost their jobs, including my great-grandfather. There's nothing new about our fear that automation and increased efficiency will deprive humans of work. In one newspaper ad, Saunders imagined a woman torn between her longtime relationship with her friendly grocer and the low, low prices at Piggly Wiggly. The story concluded with Saunders appealing to a tradition even older than the full-service grocer. The woman in his ad mused,

"Now away back many years, there had been a Dutch grandmother of mine who had been thrifty. The spirit of that old grandmother asserted itself just then within me and said, 'Business is business and charity and alms are another.'" Whereupon our shopper saw the light and converted to Piggly Wiggly.

By 1922, there were more than a thousand Piggly Wiggly stores around the U.S., and shares in the company were listed on the New York Stock Exchange. Saunders was building a thirty-six-thousand-square-foot mansion in Memphis and had endowed the school now known as Rhodes College. But the good times would not last. After a few Piggly Wiggly stores in the Northeast failed, investors began shorting the stock—betting that its price would fall. Saunders responded by trying to buy up all the available shares of Piggly Wiggly using borrowed money, but the gambit failed spectacularly. Saunders lost control of Piggly Wiggly and went bankrupt.

His vitriol at Wall Street short sellers presaged contemporary corporate titans just as his reliance on big advertising and hyperefficiency did. Saunders was by many accounts a bully—verbally abusive, cruel, and profoundly convinced of his own genius. After losing control of the company, he wrote, "They have it all, everything I built, the greatest stores of their kind in the world, but they didn't get the man that was father to the idea. They have the body of Piggly Wiggly but they didn't get the soul." Saunders quickly developed a new concept for a grocery store. This one would have aisles and self-service but also clerks in the meat department and the bakery. Essentially, he invented the supermarket model that would reign into the twenty-first century.

In less than a year, he was ready to open, but the new owners of Piggly Wiggly took him to court, arguing that the use of the Clarence Saunders name in relation to a new grocery store would violate Piggly Wiggly's trademarks and patents. In response, Saunders defiantly named his new grocery store "Clarence Saunders: Sole Owner of My Name," perhaps the only business name worse than Piggly Wiggly. And yet, it succeeded tremendously, and Saunders made a second fortune as Sole Owner stores spread throughout the South.

He went on to invest in a professional football team in Memphis, which he named the Clarence Saunders Sole Owner of My Name Tigers. Really. They played the Green Bay Packers and the Chicago Bears in front of huge crowds in Memphis, and they were invited to join the NFL, but Saunders declined. He didn't want to share revenue, or send his team to away games. He promised to build a stadium for the Tigers that would seat more than thirty thousand people. "The stadium," he wrote, "will have skull and crossbones for my enemies who I have slain."

But within a few years, the Sole Owner stores were crushed by the Depression, the football team was out of business, and Saunders was broke again. Meanwhile, the soulless body of Piggly Wiggly was faring quite well without Saunders—by the supermarket chain's height in 1932, there were over twenty-five hundred Piggly Wigglies in the United States. Even in 2021, there are over five hundred locations, mostly in the South, although like many grocery stores, they are struggling under pressure from the likes of Walmart and Dollar General, which can undercut traditional grocery stores on price partly by providing even less fresh food and fewer clerks than today's Piggly Wiggly does.

These days, Piggly Wiggly ads tend to focus on tradition, and the human touch. One north Alabama Piggly Wiggly TV spot from 1999 included this line: "At Piggly Wiggly, it's all about friends serving friends," a call to the kind of human-to-human relationships that Saunders ridiculed in that Dutch grandmother ad. The mighty pulse of the throbbing today does make new things out of old—but it also makes old things out of new.

Today, food prices are lower relative to average wage than they've ever been in the United States, but our diets are often poor. The average American ingests more sugar and sodium than they should, largely because of processed, prepackaged foods. More than 60 percent of calo-ries consumed by Americans come from so-called "highly processed foods," like the OREO cookies and Milky Way bars that flourished at early Piggly Wigglies. Clarence Saunders didn't make any of this hap-pen, of course. Like the rest of us, he was being pulled by forces far larger than any individual. He merely understood what America was about to want—and gave it to us.

After Saunders's second bankruptcy, he spent decades trying to launch another new retail concept. The Keedoozle was a totally auto-mated store that looked like a massive bank of vending machines and involved purchasing food with almost no human-to-human interaction. But the machinery often broke down, and people found the shopping experience slow and clunky, and so the Keedoozle was never profitable. The self-checkout process Saunders envisioned would only become a reality many decades later.

As he aged, Saunders grew more vitriolic and unpredictable. He began to suffer from debilitating bouts of mental illness, and eventually entered a sanitarium that treated people with anxiety and depression. The mansion Saunders built with his first fortune became the Pink Palace Museum, Memphis's science and history museum. The estate he built with his second fortune became Lichterman Nature Center. In 1936, the journalist Ernie Pyle said, "If Saunders lives long enough, Memphis will become the most beautiful city in the world just with the things Saunders built and lost."

But Saunders never made a third fortune. He died at the Wallace Sanitarium in 1953, at the age of seventy-two. One obituary opined, "Some men achieve lasting fame through success, others achieve it through failure." Saunders was a relentless innovator who understood the power of branding and efficiency. He was also hateful and vindictive. He committed securities fraud. And he helped usher in an era of food that fills without nourishing.

But mostly, when I think of Piggly Wiggly, I think about how the big get bigger by eating the small. Piggly Wiggly swallowed up the small-town grocery stores only to be swallowed itself by the likes of Walmart, which will in turn be swallowed by the likes of Amazon. James Joyce called Ireland the "sow that eats her farrow," but Ireland has nothing on American capitalism.

I give Piggly Wiggly two and a half stars.

THE NATHAN'S FAMOUS
HOT DOG EATING CONTEST

AT THE CORNER OF SURF and Stillwell Avenues in Brooklyn's Coney Island, there is a restaurant called Nathan's Famous, which started out in 1916 under the ownership of Polish immigrants Nathan and Ida Handwerker. The restaurant serves a variety of food—from fried clams to veggie burgers—but Nathan's began as a hot dog place, and remains one at its core.

A Nathan's hot dog is not the best food you will ever eat, or even the best hot dog you will ever eat. But there's something special about the experience of eating one amid the clamor of Coney Island. And the hot dogs have a pedigree—they've been eaten by King George VI and Jacqueline Kennedy. Stalin supposedly ate one at the Yalta Conference in 1945.

Coney Island used to be the huckster capital of the world, where fast-talking barkers wearing straw hats would sell you on this carnival attraction or that one. Now, like all places that survive on nostalgia, it is mostly a memory of itself. The beaches are still packed in summertime. You can still ride the carousel, and there is still a line at Nathan's Famous. But a big part of visiting Coney Island today is imagining how it must have once felt.

Except for one day a year, when Coney Island becomes its old self, for better and for worse. Every July 4, tens of thousands of people flood the streets to witness a spectacular exercise in metaphorical resonance known as the Nathan's Famous Hot Dog Eating Contest. It says so much about contemporary American life that our Independence Day celebrations include 1. fireworks displays, which are essentially imitation battles complete with rockets and bombs, and 2. a contest in which people from around the world attempt to discover how many hot dogs and buns can be ingested by a human within ten minutes. To quote the legendary comedian Yakov Smirnoff: What a country.

Like the nation it aims to celebrate, the hot dog eating contest has always been a strange amalgamation of history and imagination. The contest's originator was probably a guy named Mortimer Matz, whom the journalist Tom Robbins described as "part P. T. Barnum, part political scalawag." Matz made much of his money as a public relations rep for politicians in crisis—a resource never in short supply in New York—but he also did PR for Nathan's Famous along with his colleague Max Rosey. Matz claimed that the hot dog eating contest could trace its history back to July 4, 1916, when four immigrants staged a hot dog eating contest to determine which of them loved America the most. But he would later acknowledge, "In Coney Island pitchman style, we made it up."

The contest actually started in the summer of 1967, when several people were given an hour to eat as many hot dogs and buns as they could. A thirty-two-year-old truck driver named Walter Paul won the initial contest with a purported 127 hot dogs and buns in a single hour, although bear in mind that number was fed to the press by Rosey and Matz.

The event didn't become annual until the late 1970s. Most years, the winner would eat ten or eleven hot dogs in ten minutes. The hot dog eating contest was a fairly quiet affair until 1991, when a young man named George Shea became competitive eating's professional hype man.

Shea was an English major who loved Flannery O'Connor and William Faulkner and wanted to become a novelist, but instead he is the last great American carnival barker. He wears a straw hat and is known for his phenomenally grandiloquent annual introductions of the contest's competitors. In fact, Shea's annual preshow performance, which is broadcast live on America's top sports network, often lasts longer than the hot dog eating contest itself.

He always starts out with reasonably normal introductions. "In his rookie year, he is already ranked number twenty-four in the world," Shea began one year. "From Nigeria, now residing in Morrow, Georgia, he's eaten thirty-four ears of sweet corn. Six feet nine inches tall, let's hear it for Gideon Oji." But as we meet eater after eater, the introductions become progressively more surreal. Introducing seventy-two-year-old Rich LeFevre, Shea said, "When we are young, we drink our coffee with milk and sugar. And as we age, we drink it with milk only, then we drink it black, then we drink it decaf, then we die. Our next eater is at decaf."

Of another eater we are told, "He stands before us like Hercules himself, albeit a large bald Hercules at an eating contest." Introducing longtime competitive eater Crazy Legs Conti, who is a professional window washer and the French-cut green bean eating champion of the world, Shea says, "He was first seen standing at the edge of the shore between the ancient marks of the high and low tide, a place that is neither land nor sea. But as the blue light of morning filtered through the darkness it revealed the man who has been to the beyond and witnessed the secrets of life and death. He was buried alive under sixty cubic feet of popcorn and he ate his way out to survival."

If you don't regularly watch ESPN, it may be difficult to understand just how odd this is compared to its daily fare, which is comprised almost entirely of athletic events and analyses of athletic events. ESPN is not in the business of visiting the place that is neither land nor sea.

But ESPN *is* a sports network, and I'll concede that competitive eating is a sport. Like any sport, this one is about seeing what a human body can accomplish, and like any sport it has a variety of rules. You have to eat the hot dog *and* the bun for it to count, and you're immediately disqualified if during the competition you experience a so-called "Reversal of Fortune," the sport's euphemism for vomiting. The competition itself is, of course, gruesome. These days, the winner usually consumes over seventy hot dogs and buns in ten minutes.

One can feel something akin to joyful wonder at the magnificence of a perfectly weighted Megan Rapinoe cross, or the elegance of a LeBron James fadeaway. But it's hard to construct the Nathan's Famous Hot Dog Eating Contest as beautiful. When a soccer ball is at Lionel Messi's feet, you don't want to look away. When watching competitive hot dog eating, you can't bring yourself to look away.

The hot dog eating contest is a monument to overindulgence, to the human urge to seek not just more than you need but also more than you actually want. But I think it's also about something else. The world's best competitive eater, the American Joey Chestnut, has said of Shea's introductions, "He convinces the audience these guys are athletes. He does such a good job, he convinces *me* I'm an athlete."

The carnival barker is an obvious flimflam artist—we know that Shea is kidding when he refers to Chestnut as "America itself" and claims that the first words Chestnut's mother ever told him were, "You are of my flesh but you are not mine own. Fate is your father and you belong to the people, for you shall lead the army of the free." We know that's a joke. And yet people scream along. They chant, "Jo-ey, Jo-ey, Jo-ey." As the announcer continues to rile the crowd, they began to chant: "U-S-A, U-S-A!" The energy on the street changes. We know that Shea isn't speaking in earnest. And yet . . . his words have power.

Beginning in 2001, a Japanese man named Takeru Kobayashi won the hot dog eating contest for six consecutive years. Kobayashi totally revolutionized the approach to the competition—before him, no one had ever eaten more than twenty-five hot dogs. Kobayashi ate fifty in 2001, more than double what the third-place eater that year managed. His strategies—including breaking each dog in half and dipping the bun in warm water—are now ubiquitous at the contest.

Kobayashi was long beloved as the greatest eater of all time, although he now no longer participates in the contest because he refuses to sign an exclusive contract with Shea's company. But he competed in the 2007 event, and when the Japanese Kobayashi was beaten by the American Chestnut, Shea shouted into the microphone, "We have our confidence back! The dark days of the past six years are behind us!" And that seemed to give the crowd permission to fall into bigotry. You can hear people shout at Kobayashi as he walks over to congratulate Chestnut. They tell him to go home. They call him Kamikaze and Shanghai Boy. Recalling this in a documentary more than a decade later, Kobayashi wept as he said, "They used to cheer for me."

When you have the microphone, what you say matters, even when you're just kidding. It's so easy to take refuge in the "just" of *just* kidding. It's just a joke. We're just doing it for the memes. But the preposterous and absurd can still shape our understanding of ourselves and one another. And ridiculous cruelty is still cruel.

I love humans. We really would eat our way out of sixty cubic feet of popcorn to survive. And I'm grateful to anyone who helps us to see the grotesque absurdity of our situation. But the carnival barkers of the world must be careful which preposterous stories they tell us, because we will believe them.

I give the Nathan's Famous Hot Dog Eating Contest two stars.

CNN

AMERICA'S FIRST twenty-four-hour, nonstop news network was launched by cable magnate Ted Turner on June 1, 1980. The inaugural broadcast began with Turner standing behind a podium speaking to a large crowd outside CNN's new headquarters in Atlanta.

Turner said, "You'll notice out in front of me that we've raised three flags—one, the state of Georgia; second, the United States flag of course, which represents our country and the way we intend to serve it with the Cable News Network; and over on the other side we have the flag of the United Nations, because we hope that the Cable News Network with its international coverage and greater depth coverage will bring a better understanding of how people from different nations live and work together, so that we can perhaps hopefully bring together in brotherhood and kindness and friendship and peace the people of this nation and this world."

After Turner spoke, CNN began covering the news—its first stories were about the attempted assassination of a Black civil rights leader in Indiana and a shooting spree in Connecticut. That first hour of CNN *looks* dated. Its anchors wear broad lapelled suits and sit in a flimsy studio. But it *sounds* very much like contemporary CNN on a Sunday afternoon. The broadcast careens from breaking news story to breaking news story, from fires to shootings to emergency plane landings. Even in that first hour, you can hear the rhythm of the news, the ceaseless pulse of it. Also, the 1980 cable news sets, like most news sets today, had no windows, for the same reason casinos have no windows.

These days, there's usually crisp, blue light in the background as the news anchors talk. You don't know whether it's morning or night, and it doesn't matter, because the news beats on. It's always live—which feels, and maybe is, close to being alive.

Of course, it's hard to argue that CNN has brought the world together in brotherhood and kindness. There's something nauseating about Ted Turner's capitalist idealism, the notion that we can change the world for the better *and* make billions of dollars for one man. But I do think CNN provides a service.

It does a fair bit of investigative journalism, which can uncover corruption and injustice that otherwise would go unchecked. Also, CNN does report the news, at least in a narrow sense—if it happened today, and if it was dramatic or scary or big, and if it happened in the U.S. or Europe, you will probably learn about it on CNN.

The word *news* tells a secret on itself, though: What's news isn't primarily what is noteworthy or important, but what is *new*. So much of what actually changes in human life isn't driven by events, but instead by processes, which often aren't considered news. We don't see much about climate change on CNN, unless a new report is published, nor do we see regular coverage of other ongoing crises, like child mortality or poverty.

A 2017 study found that 74 percent of Americans believe that global child mortality has either stayed the same or gotten worse in the last twenty years, when in fact, it has declined by almost 60 percent since

1990, by far the fastest decline in child death in any thirty-year period in human history.[25]

Watching CNN, you might not know that. You also might not know that in 2020, global rates of death from war were at or near the lowest they've been in centuries.

Even when a news story does receive saturation coverage—as the global disease pandemic did on CNN beginning in March of 2020—there is often a preference for event-based stories over process-based ones. The phrase "grim milestone" is repeated over and over as we learn that 100,000, and then 200,000, and then 500,000 people have died of Covid-19 in the United States. But without context, what do these numbers even mean? The constant repetition of grim milestones without any historical grounding only has a distancing effect, at least for me. But when contextualized, the grimness of the milestone comes into focus. One could report, for instance, that in 2020, average U.S. life expectancy fell (much) further than it has in any year since World War II.

Because there is always new news to report, we rarely get the kind of background information that allows us to understand why the news is happening. We learn that hospitals have run out of ICU beds to treat gravely ill Covid-19 patients, but we do not learn of the decades-long series of choices that led to a U.S. healthcare system that privileged efficiency over capacity. This flood of information without context can so easily, and so quickly, transform into misinformation. Over one hundred and fifty years ago, the American humorist Josh Billings wrote, "I honestly believe it is better to know nothing than to know what ain't so."

---

25.   One of the very few bright spots of 2020 is that child mortality continued to decline globally, but it is still much, much too high. A child born in Sierra Leone is twelve times more likely to die before the age of five than a child born in Sweden, and as Dr. Joia Mukherjee points out in *An Introduction to Global Health Delivery*, "These differences in life expectancy are not caused by genetics, biology, or culture. Health inequities are caused by poverty, racism, lack of medical care, and other social forces that influence health."

And that seems to me the underlying problem—not just with CNN and other cable news networks, but with contemporary information flow in general. So often, I end up knowing what just ain't so.

———————

In 2003, I was living with my three best friends—Katie, Shannon, and Hassan—in an apartment on the northwest side of Chicago. We'd survived those early postcollege years where life—for me at least—felt overwhelming and intensely unstable. Until I moved in with Shannon and Katie and Hassan, everything I owned could fit into my car. My life had been, to borrow a line from Milan Kundera, unbearably light. But now, things were settling down in wonderful ways. We had our first semipermanent jobs, and our first semipermanent furniture. We even had a television with cable.

But mostly, we had one another. That apartment—the walls all painted very bright colors, no sound insulation, only one bathroom, tiny bedrooms, huge common areas—was designed for us to be in it together, to be in every part of life together. And we were. We loved one another with a ferocity that unnerved outsiders. I once went on a few dates with someone who told me one night that my friend group seemed like a cult. When I told Shannon and Katie and Hassan about this, we all agreed that I needed to break off the relationship immediately.

"But that's what we would say if we *were* a cult," Katie said.

Hassan nodded, and deadpanned, "Oh, shit, guys. We're a cult."

I know I am romanticizing this past—we also had huge fights, we had our hearts broken, we got too drunk and fought over who would get to puke into the one toilet, etc.—but it was the first extended period of my adult life when I felt okay even some of the time, and so you'll forgive me if I recall it with such fondness.

That August, I turned twenty-six, and we threw a dinner party called "John Green Has Outlived John Keats," and everybody who attended read some poetry. Someone read Edna St. Vincent Millay:

> *My candle burns at both ends;*
> *It will not last the night;*
> *But ah, my foes, and oh, my friends—*
> *It gives a lovely light!*

A few days later, the owners of the building told us they were selling it. But even if they hadn't, the apartment would've split up eventually. The big forces of human life—marriage, careers, immigration policy— were pulling us in different directions. But our candle gave a lovely light.

––––––––

We were living in that apartment during the U.S.'s 2003 invasion of Iraq. Hassan grew up in Kuwait, and he had family members living in Iraq at the time. For a few weeks after the invasion, he didn't hear from them. He would eventually learn they were okay, but it was a scary time, and one of the ways he coped was by watching cable news almost all the time. And because we only had one TV, and we were constantly together, that meant the rest of us watched a lot of cable news as well.

Even though the war was covered twenty-four hours a day, very little background information ever entered the picture. The news talked a fair amount about the relationship between Shia and Sunni Muslims in Iraq, for instance, but never paused to explain the theological differences between Shias and Sunnis, or the history of Iraq, or the political ideology of the Baathist movement. There was so much news—news that was forever breaking—that there was never time for context.

One evening, just after the U.S.-led forces entered Baghdad, we were all watching the news on the couch together. Unedited footage was being broadcast from the city, and we watched as a cameraman panned across a home with a huge hole in one of its walls that was mostly covered by a piece of plywood. There was Arabic graffiti scrawled in black spray paint on the plywood, and the reporter on the news was talking about the anger in the street, and the hatred. Hassan started to laugh.

I asked him what was so funny, and he said, "The graffiti."

And I said, "What's funny about it?"

Hassan answered, "It says 'Happy birthday, sir, despite the circumstances.'"

On a minute-by-minute basis, it's hard for any of us to consider the Happy Birthday Sir Despite the Circumstances possibility. I project my expectations and fears onto everyone and everything I encounter. I believe that what I believe to be true must be true because I believe it. I imagine lives that feel distant from mine monolithically. I oversimplify. I forget that everyone has birthdays.

Good journalism seeks to correct for those biases, to help us toward a deeper understanding of the universe and our place in it. But when we can't read the writing on the plywood but still think we know what it says, we are spreading ignorance and bigotry, not the peace and friendship Turner promised.

I give CNN two stars.

HARVEY

THE MOVIE *HARVEY* stars Jimmy Stewart as Elwood P. Dowd, an alcoholic whose best friend is a six-foot, three-and-a-half-inch-tall invisible white rabbit named Harvey. Josephine Hull won an Oscar for her portrayal of Elwood's sister, Veta, who struggles with whether to commit Elwood to a sanitarium. The film, based on Mary Chase's Pulitzer Prize–winning play of the same name, was an immediate critical and commercial success when it was released in 1950.[26]

But my story of *Harvey* begins in the early winter of 2001, shortly after I suffered what used to be known as a nervous breakdown. I was working for *Booklist* magazine and living on the Near North Side of Chicago in a small apartment that I had until recently shared with a person I'd thought I would marry. At the time, I believed that our breakup had caused my depression, but now I see that my depression at least in part caused the breakup. Regardless, I was alone, in what had been our apartment, surrounded by what had been our things, trying to take care of what had been our cat.

---

26.   As Bosley Crowther put it in the *New York Times*, "If a visit to the Astor, where it opened yesterday, does not send you forth into the highways and byways embracing a warm glow—then the fault will be less with *Harvey*, we suspect, than it will be with you."

Susan Sontag wrote that "Depression is melancholy minus its charms." For me, living with depression was at once utterly boring and absolutely excruciating. Psychic pain overwhelmed me, consuming my thoughts so thoroughly that I no longer had any thoughts, only pain. In *Darkness Visible*, William Styron's wrenching memoir of depression, he wrote, "What makes the condition intolerable is the foreknowledge that no remedy will come—not in a day, an hour, a month, or a minute. If there is mild relief, one knows that it is only temporary; more pain will follow. It is hopelessness even more than pain that crushes the soul." I find hopelessness to *be* a kind of pain. One of the worst kinds. For me, finding hope is not some philosophical exercise or sentimental notion; it is a prerequisite for my survival.

In the winter of 2001, I had the foreknowledge that no remedy would come, and it was agonizing. I became unable to eat food, so instead I was drinking two two-liter bottles of Sprite per day, which is approximately the right number of calories to consume but not an ideal nutrition strategy.

I remember coming home from work and lying on the peeling linoleum floor of what had been our kitchen, and looking through the Sprite bottle at the green parabolic rectangle of the kitchen window. I watched the bubbles inside the bottle clinging to the bottom, trying to hold on, but inevitably floating up to the top. I thought about how I couldn't think. I felt the pain pressing in on me, like it was an atmosphere. All I wanted was to be separated from the pain, to be free from it.

Eventually, a day came when I could not pick myself up off that linoleum floor, and I spent a very long Sunday thinking about all the ways that the situation might resolve itself. That evening, thank God, I called my parents, and, thank God, they answered.

My parents are busy people with demanding lives who lived fifteen hundred miles away from Chicago. And they were at my apartment within twelve hours of that phone call.

A plan formed quickly. I would leave my job, go home to Florida, get into daily counseling or possibly inpatient treatment. They packed up my apartment. My ex kindly agreed to take the cat. The only thing left was to quit my job.

I loved working at *Booklist*, and I loved my coworkers, but I also knew that my life was in danger. I tearfully told my supervisor that I had to quit, and after giving me a hug as I cried, he told me to talk to the magazine's publisher, Bill Ott.

I thought of Bill as a character out of a noir mystery novel. His incisive wit is both thrilling and intimidating. When I went into his office, he was surrounded by proof pages of the magazine, and he didn't look up until I closed the door. I told him that something was wrong with my head, that I hadn't eaten solid food in a couple of weeks, and that I was quitting to move home to Florida with my parents.

He was silent for a long time after I finished. Bill is a master of pauses. And then at last he said, "Ah, why don't you just go home for a few weeks and see how you feel."

And I said, "But you'll need someone to do my job."

Again, he paused. "Don't take this the wrong way, kid, but I think we'll get by."

At one point that afternoon I started throwing up—excessive Sprite consumption, maybe—and when I came back to my desk to finish packing up my belongings, there was a note from Bill. I still have it. It reads:

John, I stopped by to say goodbye. Hope all goes well and you're back here in two weeks with an appetite that would put a longshoreman to shame. Now more than ever: Watch Harvey. —Bill

For years, Bill had been bothering me to watch *Harvey*, and I steadfastly maintained that black-and-white movies were universally terrible, on account of how the special effects quality is poor and nothing ever happens except people talking.

I was back in Orlando, where I'd grown up. It felt like such a failure to be there, living with my parents, unable to do much of anything. I felt like I was nothing but a burden. My thoughts whorled and swirled. I couldn't ever think straight. I couldn't concentrate enough to read or write. I was in daily therapy, and taking a new medication, but I felt certain it wouldn't work, because I didn't think the problem was chemical. I thought the problem was me, at my core. I was worthless, useless, helpless, hopeless. I was less and less each day.

One night, my parents and I rented *Harvey*. Because it was adapted from a play, *Harvey* is, as I feared, a talky movie. Most of it takes place in only a few locations—the house Elwood P. Dowd shares with his older sister and his niece, the sanitarium where many believe Elwood belongs because his best friend is an invisible rabbit, and the bar where Elwood likes to hang out and drink.

Mary Chase's dialogue is magnificent throughout, but I especially love Elwood's soliloquies. Here is Elwood talking about chatting with strangers at the bar: "They tell me about the big, terrible things they've done and the wonderful things they'll do. Their hopes, and their regrets, and their loves, and their hates. All very large, because nobody ever brings anything small into a bar."

In another scene, Elwood tells his psychiatrist, "I've wrestled with reality for thirty-five years, Doctor, and I'm happy to state I finally won out over it."

Elwood is mentally ill. He's not much of a contributor to society. It'd be easy to characterize him as worthless, or hopeless. But he is also extraordinarily kind, even in difficult situations. At one point, his psychiatrist says, "This sister of yours is at the bottom of a conspiracy against you. She's trying to persuade me to lock you up. Today, she had commitment papers drawn up. She has the power of attorney over you." Elwood replies, "My sister did all that in one afternoon. That Veta certainly is a whirlwind, isn't she?"

Despite not being a traditional hero of any kind, Elwood is profoundly heroic. In my favorite line of the movie, he says, "Years ago my mother used to say to me, she'd say . . . 'In this world, you must be oh so smart, or oh so pleasant.' Well, for years I was smart. I recommend pleasant."

In December of 2001, there was perhaps no human alive on Earth who needed to hear those words more than I did.

I don't believe in epiphanies. My blinding-light awakenings always prove fleeting. But I'll tell you this: I have never felt quite as hopeless since watching *Harvey* as I did just before I watched it.

A couple of months after watching *Harvey*, I was able to return to Chicago and to *Booklist*. Although my recovery was halting and often precarious, I got better. It was probably the therapy and the medication, of course, but Elwood played his part. He showed me that you could be crazy and still be human, still be valuable, and still be loved. Elwood offered me a kind of hope that wasn't bullshit, and in doing so helped me to see that hope is the correct response to the strange, often terrifying miracle of consciousness. Hope is not easy or cheap. It is true.

As Emily Dickinson put it,

"Hope" is the thing with feathers -
That perches in the soul -
And sings the tune without the words -
And never stops - at all -

I still sometimes stop hearing the tune. I still become enveloped by the abject pain of hopelessness. But hope is singing all the while. It's just that again and again and again, I must relearn how to listen.

I hope you never find yourself on the floor of your kitchen. I hope you never cry in front of your boss desperate with pain. But if you do, I hope they will give you some time off and tell you what Bill told me: Now, more than ever, watch *Harvey*.

I give *Harvey* five stars.

THE YIPS

ON OCTOBER 3, 2000, a twenty-one-year-old pitcher named Rick Ankiel took the mound for the St. Louis Cardinals in the first game of a Major League Baseball playoff series. It occurs to me that you may not know the rules of baseball, but for our purposes, all you need to know is that, broadly speaking, professional pitchers throw baseballs very fast—sometimes over one hundred miles per hour—and with astonishing accuracy. Pitchers who can consistently place their throws within a few square inches of space are often said to have "good control." Rick Ankiel had great control. He could put the ball wherever he wanted. Even when he was in high school, the professional scouts marveled at his control. They said the kid was a machine.

But about a third of the way into that playoff game in 2000, Rick Ankiel threw a very low pitch, so low that the catcher missed it—a so-called "wild pitch." Ankiel had only thrown three wild pitches all season, but now, suddenly, he couldn't regain his control. He threw another wild pitch, this one over the batter's head. Then another. Another. Another. He was quickly pulled from the game.

———

A week later, Ankiel started another playoff game. He threw five wild pitches in twenty attempts. After that, he never consistently found the strike zone again. Ankiel won a few more games as a major league pitcher, but he couldn't fully recover his control. He sought all kinds of medical attention, and even began drinking huge amounts of vodka during games to dull his anxiety, but his pitching never came back. He had contracted the yips. The kid, it turned out, was not a machine. Kids never are.

Rick Ankiel wasn't the first baseball player to forget how to throw—in fact, the phenomenon is sometimes called "Steve Blass Disease" or "Steve Sax Syndrome," after other baseball players who suffered sudden-onset throwing challenges. It's not unique to baseball, either. In 2008, an introverted twenty-year-old tennis player named Ana Ivanovic won the French Open and became the top-ranked tennis player in the world. Commentators imagined her winning "a host of grand slams," and maybe even becoming a formidable rival to all-time great Serena Williams.

But shortly after that French Open title, Ivanovic began to experience the yips—not when hitting the ball or swinging the racket, but when tossing the ball before serving. From footwork to swing mechanics, tennis requires precise movements and profound bodily coordination. Throwing the ball straight up in the air before serving is just about the only part of tennis that *isn't* difficult. But when Ivanovic began to experience the yips, her hand would jerk mid-toss, and the ball would drift to the right, or too far forward.

Former tennis pro Pat Cash described watching Ivanovic's serve as a "painful experience," and it truly was, but if watching it is a painful experience, how much more painful to be the server, unable to toss the ball the way she had her entire career, ever since she first took up tennis as a five-year-old in Belgrade. You could see the torment in her eyes. Watching someone struggle with the yips is like watching a school play in which a kid forgets their line. Time stops. Attempts to disguise the discomfort—a little smile, a wave of apology—only heighten everyone's awareness of the anguish. You know they don't want your pity, but you offer it anyway, which only furthers the shame.

"She has absolutely no confidence in herself," tennis great Martina Navratilova said of Ivanovic, which was no doubt true. But how could you be confident?

All serious athletes know the yips are *possible*, that they happen to people. But knowing something abstractly is different from knowing it experientially. Once you've known the yips personally, you can't un-know them. Every time you toss a tennis ball for the rest of your life, you'll know what could happen. How can you regain confidence when you know that confidence is just a varnish painted atop human frailty?

Ivanovic once said of the yips, "If you start thinking about how you come down the stairs and think about how each muscle is working, you can't go down the stairs." But if you've fallen down the stairs, it becomes impossible not to think about how you come down the stairs. "I'm a person who overthinks and overanalyzes everything," Ivanovic went on to say, "so if you give me one thought, it creates a lot more."

The yips have many names—whiskey fingers, the waggles, the freezing. But I like "yips" because it's such an anxious word; I can almost feel the muscle twitch inside the word itself. The yips are most common among golfers. Over a third of serious golfers struggle with them. Golfing yips usually appear when golfers are trying to hit putts, and people have tried all kinds of cures to stop the spasms. Right-handed golfers might putt left-handed, or they might try unconventional grips, or long putters, or short ones, or bending over the club and anchoring it against the chest. And the yips don't only affect putting. One of the world's leading golf coaches can only effectively swing a driver while looking away from the ball.

The yips do not seem to be a result of performance anxiety, although anxiety can worsen the problem—as it worsens many physiological problems, from diarrhea to dizziness. Some golfers, for instance, feel the yips when they play on a course but not when practicing on a putting green. I get the yips when playing tennis on forehand shots—my arm muscles jerk just before the racket hits the ball, and like that golfing coach, the only way I've found to avoid the yips is to glance away from the ball as I swing.

But weirdly, I don't feel the yips when I'm warming up or hitting with a friend, only when we're keeping score. Their situational nature has led some to argue that the yips can be cured by psychotherapy, specifically by processing traumatic events in one's sporting life. I am a big fan of psychotherapy, and have benefited tremendously from it, but I do not have traumatic memories of tennis. I like tennis. I just can't hit forehands while looking at the ball.

Of course, just as anxiety can cause physiological problems, physiological problems can also cause anxiety. For professional athletes, the yips are a threat not just to their livelihood but also to their identity. The answer to the question "Who is Ana Ivanovic?" was invariably, "Ana Ivanovic is a tennis player." Rick Ankiel was a pitcher. Until the yips.

This complicated interplay between the so-called physical and the so-called psychological reminds us that the mind/body dichotomy isn't overly simplistic; it's complete bullshit. The body is always deciding what the brain will think about, and the brain is all the time deciding what the body will do and feel. Our brains are made out of meat, and our bodies experience thoughts.

When we talk about sports, we almost always talk about winning as the measure of success. Vince Lombardi famously said, "Winning isn't everything; it's the only thing." But I'm dubious of that worldview, in sports as well as outside of them. I think a lot of the pleasure in sports is found in performing well. At first, winning is a sign that you are getting better, and then as you age, winning becomes proof that you still have it—the *it* being control and competence. You can't decide whether you get sick, or whether people you love die, or whether a tornado tears apart your house. But you can decide whether to throw a curveball or a fastball. You can at least decide that. Until you can't.

But even after age or the yips steals away your control, you need not give up. In *To Kill a Mockingbird*, Atticus Finch defines courage by saying, "It's when you know you're licked before you begin but you begin anyway."

Ana Ivanovic never recovered the ability to toss the ball the way she did before the yips. But over time, she invented a new serve. It was less powerful, and more predictable, but she became a top-five player again, winning four tournaments in 2014. She retired a couple of years later, at the age of twenty-nine.

Rick Ankiel sunk all the way down to the lowest minor leagues of professional baseball. He missed the 2002 season with an injury, then blew his arm out completely in 2003. After recovering from surgery, he briefly returned to the major leagues, but he couldn't find his control. So in 2005, at the age of twenty-six, he decided he wouldn't be a pitcher anymore. He would play in the outfield.

In professional baseball, pitchers don't just become outfielders. The game is much too highly specialized for that. The last player to have a career that included winning over ten games as a pitcher and hitting over fifty home runs as a hitter was Babe Ruth, who retired in 1935.

Like Ivanovic, Rick Ankiel was licked before he began, but he began anyway. He played as an outfielder in the minor leagues, steadily improving as a hitter. And then one day in 2007—six years removed from the wild pitch that took away his control forever—the St. Louis Cardinals called Rick Ankiel back to the major leagues as an outfielder. When Ankiel went to bat for the first time, the game had to be paused because the crowd's standing ovation was so long and so loud. Rick Ankiel hit a home run in that game. Two days later, he hit two more home runs.

His throws from the outfield were phenomenally accurate—among the best in baseball. He would go on to play as a center fielder in the major leagues for six more years. Today, the most recent player to have won over ten games as a pitcher and hit over fifty home runs as a hitter is Rick Ankiel.

I give the yips one and a half stars.

AULD LANG SYNE

I FIND IT FASCINATING that in a world where so much is so new, we welcome a new year by singing "Auld Lang Syne," which is a very old song. The chorus starts out, "For auld lang syne, my Jo, for auld lang syne / We'll take a cup of kindness yet for auld lang syne." *Jo* is a Scots word that can be straightforwardly translated to "dear," but *auld lang syne* is more complicated. It literally means something like "old long since," but it's idiomatically akin to "the old times." We have a phrase in English somewhat similar to "for auld lang syne"—"for old times' sake."

Here's a bit of my old long since: In the summer of 2001, the writer Amy Krouse Rosenthal emailed *Booklist* magazine to inquire about a review. At the time, I was working for *Booklist* as a publishing assistant; most of my job was data entry, but I also answered many of the low-priority emails that came in. I responded to Amy with an update on the status of the review, and I also mentioned that on a personal note I loved her zine-like column in *Might* magazine. I told her I often thought about one snippet she'd written, which went, "Every time I'm flying and the captain announces the beginning of our descent, the same thing goes through my mind. While we're still pretty high above the city, I'll think, If the plane went down now, we would definitely not be OK.

A bit lower, and no, we still wouldn't be OK. But as we get real close to the ground, I'll relax. OK. We're low enough; if it crashed now, we might be OK."

She wrote me back the next day, and asked if I was a writer, and I said I was trying to be, and she asked if I had anything that was two minutes long that might work on the radio.

We don't really know when "Auld Lang Syne" was written. The first verse goes: "Should auld acquaintance be forgot / And never brought to mind? / Should auld acquaintance be forgot / And auld lang syne." Versions of those lyrics date back at least four hundred years, but we owe the current song to the great Scottish poet Robert Burns. In December of 1788, he wrote to his friend Frances Dunlop, "Is not the Scotch phrase 'Auld Lang Syne' exceedingly expressive? There is an old song and tune which has often thrilled through my soul. . . . Light be the turf on the breast of the heaven-inspired poet who composed this glorious fragment." On the back of the letter, Burns wrote a draft of the poem. At least three of the verses were probably his own, although he would later say of the song that he "took it down from an old man."

Part of what makes dating the first verse difficult is the poem's eternality: It's about drinking together and remembering old times, and almost every idea in the song—from picking daisies to wandering through fields to toasting old friends over a beer—could've been written five hundred, a thousand, or even three thousand years ago.

It is also, incidentally, a rousing ode to splitting the check, with part of the second verse going, "And surely you'll buy your pint cup and surely I'll buy mine." But mostly, the song is just an unapologetic celebration of the good old days.

I guess I should tell you that Amy is dead. Otherwise, her death within this review might seem like some kind of narrative device, which I don't want. So, okay. She is dead. The rare present tense sentence that, once it becomes true, stays true forever.

But we are not there yet. We were still in the past, I think. Amy asked if I had anything for the radio, and I sent her three mini essays, and she liked one of them, and asked me to come in and record it for her show on Chicago's public radio station, WBEZ. After that, Amy invited me to be on her show more often. Within a year, I was recording frequent commentaries for WBEZ, and then for NPR's *All Things Considered*.

In April of 2002, Amy convened some of her writer and musician friends for an event at the Chopin Theatre in Chicago called Writers' Block Party. She asked me to read for it, and I did, and people laughed at my dumb jokes. Amy hired someone to walk around the theater giving everyone compliments, and the complimenter said they liked my shoes, which were new Adidas sneakers, and that's why I have worn Adidas sneakers nearly every day for the last nineteen years.

Robert Burns originally had a different tune in mind for "Auld Lang Syne" than the one most of us know, and although he himself realized the melody was "mediocre," you will sometimes still hear that original arrangement.[27] The tune most associated with "Auld Lang Syne" first appeared in 1799 in George Thomson's *A Select Collection of Original Scottish Airs for the Voice*.

By then, Robert Burns was gone. He was only thirty-seven when he died of a heart condition (possibly exacerbated by his habit of raising many a pint glass to old acquaintances). In his last letter, he wrote to his friend Frances Dunlop, "An illness which has long hung about me in all

---

27.   It is used, for example, in the 2008 film *Sex and the City*.

probability will speedily send me beyond that bourne whence no traveler returns." Even on his deathbed, Burns could turn a phrase.

Within a few decades of Burns's death, "Auld Lang Syne" had become a popular part of New Year's Eve celebrations in Scotland, a holiday known as Hogmanay that can trace its history back to winter solstice rituals. By 1818, Beethoven had written an arrangement of the song, and it was beginning to travel throughout the world.

Between 1945 and 1948, the tune was used in South Korea's national anthem. In the Netherlands, its melody inspired one of the country's most famous football chants. "Auld Lang Syne" is often played at Japanese department stores just before they close to let customers know it's time to leave. The song is also a staple of film soundtracks, from Charlie Chaplin's *The Gold Rush* in 1925 to *It's a Wonderful Life* in 1946 to *Minions* in 2015.

I think "Auld Lang Syne" is popular in Hollywood not just because it's in the public domain and therefore cheap, but also because it's the rare song that is genuinely wistful—it acknowledges human longing without romanticizing it, and it captures how each new year is a product of all the old ones. When I sing "Auld Lang Syne" on New Year's Eve, I forget the words like most of us do, until I get to the fourth verse, which I do have memorized: "We two have paddled in the stream, from morning sun till dine / but seas between us broad have roared since Auld Lang Syne."

And I think about the many broad seas that have roared between me and the past—seas of neglect, seas of time, seas of death. I'll never again speak to many of the people who loved me into this moment, just as you will never speak to many of the people who loved you into your now. So we raise a glass to them—and hope that perhaps somewhere, they are raising a glass to us.

In 2005, Amy published a memoir in the form of an encyclopedia called *Encyclopedia of an Ordinary Life*. That book ends, "I was here, you see. I was." Another sentence that once it becomes true, never stops being true. Her *Encyclopedia* came out just a few months before my first novel, *Looking for Alaska*. Soon thereafter, Sarah got into graduate school at Columbia and so we moved to New York. Amy and I stayed in touch and collaborated occasionally over the next decade—I played a bit part in an experience she curated for hundreds of people on August 8, 2008, in Chicago's Millennium Park—but it was never again like it had been in those early days.

In her strange and beautiful interactive memoir *Textbook Amy Krouse Rosenthal*, published in 2016, she wrote, "If one is generously contracted 80 years, that amounts to 29,220 days on Earth. Playing that out, how many times then, really, do I get to look at a tree? 12,395? There has to be an exact number. Let's just say it is 12,395. Absolutely, that is a lot, but it is not infinite, and anything less than infinite seems too measly a number and is not satisfactory." In her writing, Amy often sought to reconcile the infinite nature of consciousness and love and yearning with the finite nature of the universe and all that inhabits it. Toward the end of *Textbook*, she wrote a multiple-choice question: "In the alley, there is a bright pink flower peeking out through the asphalt. A. It looks like futility. B. It looks like hope." For me at least, "Auld Lang Syne" captures exactly what it feels like to see a bright pink flower peeking out through the asphalt, and how it feels to know you have 12,395 times to look at a tree.

Amy found out she had cancer not long after finishing *Textbook*, and she called me. She knew that in the years after my book *The Fault in Our Stars* was published, I'd come to know many young people who were gravely ill, and she wanted to know if I had advice for her. I told her what I think is true—that love survives death. But she wanted to know how young people react to death. How her kids would. She wanted to know if her kids and her husband would be okay, and that ripped me up. Although I'm usually quite comfortable talking with sick people, with my friend I found myself stumbling over words, overwhelmed by my own sadness and worry.

They won't be okay, of course, but they will go on, and the love you poured into them will go on. That's what I should've said. But what I actually said, while crying, was, "How can this be happening? You do so much yoga."

In my experience, dying people often have wonderful stories of the horrible things healthy people say to them, but I've never heard of anybody saying something as stupid as, "You do so much yoga." I hope that Amy at least got some narrative mileage out of it. But I also know I failed her, after she was there for me so many times. I know she forgives me—present tense—but still, I desperately wish I could've said something useful. Or perhaps not said anything at all. When people we love are suffering, we want to make it better. But sometimes—often, in fact—you can't make it better. I'm reminded of something my supervisor said to me when I was a student chaplain: "Don't just do something. Stand there."

"Auld Lang Syne" was a popular song during World War I—versions of it were sung in trenches not just by British soldiers, but by French and German and Austrian ones as well, and the song even played a small role in one of the strangest and most beautiful moments in world history, the Christmas Truce of 1914.

On Christmas Eve that year, along part of the war's Western Front in Belgium, around one hundred thousand British and German troops emerged from their trenches and met one another in the so-called no-man's-land between front lines. Nineteen-year-old Henry Williamson wrote his mother, "Yesterday the British and Germans met and shook hands in the ground between the trenches and exchanged souvenirs . . . Marvellous, isn't it?" A German soldier remembered that a British soldier "brought a soccer ball from their trenches, and pretty soon a lively game ensued. How marvelously wonderful, yet how strange it was." Elsewhere on the front, Captain Sir Edward Hulse recalled a Christmas sing-along that "ended up with 'Auld Lang Syne' which we all, English, Scots, Irish, Prussians, Wuttenbergers, etc., joined in. It was absolutely astounding, and if I had seen it on a cinematograph film I should have sworn that it was faked."

Hulse, who was twenty-five years old at the time, would be killed on the Western Front less than four months later. At least seventeen million people would die as a direct result of the war—more than half the current population of Canada. By Christmas of 1916, soldiers didn't want truces—the devastating losses of the war, and the growing use of poison gas, had embittered the combatants. But many also had no idea why they were fighting and dying for tiny patches of ground so far from home. In the British trenches, soldiers began to sing the tune of "Auld Lang Syne" with different words: "We're here because we're here because we're here because we're here."

Here was a world without whys, where life was meaninglessness all the way down. Modernity had come to war, and to the rest of life. The art critic Robert Hughes once referred to the "peculiarly modernist Hell of repetition," and the trenches of World War I were hell indeed.

Although she was a playful and optimistic writer, Amy was not deluded about the nature of suffering, or about its centrality in human life. Her work—whether picture book or memoir—always finds a way to acknowledge misery without giving in to it. One of the last lines she ever wrote was, "Death may be knocking on my door, but I'm not getting out of this glorious bath to answer it."

In her public appearances, Amy would sometimes use that recursive lament of British soldiers and transform it without ever changing the tune or the words. She would ask an audience to sing that song with her: "We're here because we're here because we're here because we're here." And although it's a profoundly nihilistic song written about the modernist hell of repetition, singing this song with Amy, I could always see the hope in it. It became a statement that *we* are here—meaning that we are together, and not alone. And it's also a statement that we *are*, that we exist. And it's a statement that we are *here*, that a series of astonishing unlikelihoods has made us possible and here possible. We might never know why we are here, but we can still proclaim in hope *that* we are here. I don't think such hope is foolish or idealistic or misguided.

We live in hope—that life will get better, and more importantly that it will go on, that love will survive even though we will not. And between now and then, we are here because we're here because we're here because we're here.

I give auld lang syne five stars.

GOOGLING STRANGERS

WHEN I WAS A KID, my mother often told me that everyone has a gift inside them. You might be an extraordinarily astute listener of smooth jazz, or a defensive midfielder with an uncommon understanding of how to open up space with the perfect pass. But as a child, I always felt like I had no inborn gift. I wasn't a particularly good student, and I had no athletic ability. I couldn't read social cues. I sucked at piano, karate, ballet dancing, and everything else my parents tried to sign me up for. I thought of myself as a person without a specialty.

But as it turned out, my specialty just hadn't been invented yet, because I am—please forgive the lack of modesty here—really, really good at googling strangers. Sure, I've put in the work—Malcolm Gladwell famously said it takes ten thousand hours to become an expert in a field; I've clocked my ten thousand hours, and then some. But also, I just have a knack for it.

I google strangers almost every day. If my wife and I have to attend a party—and I say *have to* because that is my relationship with parties[28]—I usually research all the known attendees in advance. Of course, I know it's weird when a stranger tells you they are in the carpet installation

---

28.   Yes, even in 2021.

business and you answer, "Oh yeah, I am aware. Also, you met your wife in 1981, when you were both working at the same savings and loan institution in Dallas. She was living at home with her parents, Joseph and Marilyn, at least according to census records, while you had recently graduated from Oklahoma Baptist University. Your wedding reception at the Dallas Museum of Art was right next to that Dale Chihuly sculpture, *Hart Window*. Then you moved to Indianapolis for your wife's job at Eli Lilly. How is the carpet business these days? Do you guys have, like, a rivalry with hardwood floor people?"

It's horrifying, how much information can be accessed via Google about almost all of us. Of course, this loss of privacy has come with tremendous benefits—free storage of photos and video, a chance to participate in large-scale discourse via social media, and the opportunity to easily keep in touch with friends from long ago.

But giving so much of our selves to private corporations like Google makes other people feel comfortable sharing their selves. This feedback loop—we all want to be on Facebook because everyone else is on Facebook—has led to me making so much of my life publicly available that when creating accounts on new social media platforms, I often struggle to find security questions that can't be answered by studying my old social media accounts. Where did I go to elementary school? That's easy enough to find out. What was the name of my first dog? I've vlogged about our miniature dachshund Red Green. Who was your childhood best friend? You'll find baby pictures of us tagged together on Facebook. What was your mother's maiden name? You can't be serious.

But even though less of our lives belong to us and more of our lives belong to the companies that host and gather our browsing habits and hobbies and keystrokes, even though I am revolted by how easy it has become to scroll through the lives of the living and the dead, even though it all feels a bit too much like an Orwell novel . . . I can't outright condemn the googling of strangers.

When I was twenty-two and working as a student chaplain at a children's hospital, I would spend twenty-four hours on call once or twice a week. This meant that I'd stay in the hospital with two beepers. One beeper went off whenever someone asked for a chaplain. The other buzzed when a serious trauma case arrived at the hospital. One of my last nights on call, toward the end of my six-month chaplaincy, I was asleep in the pastoral care office when the trauma pager sent me down to the Emergency Department. A three-year-old child was being wheeled in. He'd suffered severe burns.

I'm not sure whether it's even possible to talk about the suffering of others without exploiting that suffering, whether you can write about pain without glorifying or ennobling or degrading it. Teju Cole once said that "a photograph can't help taming what it shows," and I worry the same might be true of language. Stories have to make sense, and nothing at the hospital made any sense to me at all, which is one of the reasons I've rarely written about my time there directly. I don't know the proper way through this morass, and I never have, but in telling this story, I've chosen to obscure and alter certain details. The important thing is that despite the severity of his injury, the child was conscious, and in terrible pain.

Although I'd been around the Emergency Department for months, and seen all manner of suffering and death, I'd never seen the trauma team so visibly upset. The anguish was overwhelming—the smell of the burns, the piercing screams that accompanied this little boy's every exhalation. Someone shouted, "CHAPLAIN! THE SCISSORS BEHIND YOU!" and in a daze I brought them the scissors. Someone shouted, "CHAPLAIN! THE PARENTS!" And I realized that next to me the little boy's parents were screaming, trying to get at their kid, but the doctors and paramedics and nurses needed enough space to work, so I had to ask the parents to step back.

Next thing I knew I was in the windowless family room in the
Emergency Department, the room where they put you on the worst
night of your life. It was quiet except for the crying of the couple across
from me. They sat on opposite sides of the couch, elbows on knees.

During my training they told me that half of marriages end within a
couple years of losing a child. Weakly, I asked the parents if they wanted
to pray. The woman shook her head no. The doctor came in and said
that the kid was in critical condition. The parents only had one question, and it was one the doctor couldn't answer. "We'll do everything
we can," she said, "but your son may not survive." Both the parents collapsed, not against each other, but into themselves.

We are able to navigate the world knowing these things happen. My
chaplaincy supervisor once told me, "Children have always died. It is
natural." That may be true, but I can't accept it. I couldn't accept it
sitting in the windowless family room, and I can't accept it now, as a
father myself.

When the kid finally went upstairs to the ICU and his parents followed,
I walked to the break room to get a cup of coffee, and the doctor was in
there, her face hovering over a trash can that she'd been vomiting into.
"I'm sorry," I said. "You did good with them. Thanks for being kind to
them. I think it helped." She dry heaved for a while and then said, "That
kid's gonna die and I know his last words. I know the last thing he'll
ever say." I didn't ask her to tell me what it was, and she didn't volunteer.

A week later, I finished the chaplaincy program, and decided not
to go to divinity school. I told everyone it was because I didn't want to
learn Greek, which was true, but it was also true that I couldn't cope
with the memory of this kid. I still can't cope with it. I thought about
him every day. I prayed for him every day, even after I stopped praying
about anything else. Every night, still, I say his name and ask God for

mercy. Whether I believe in God isn't really relevant. I do believe, however tenuously, in mercy.

As an inveterate googler, I knew I could have just looked up his name, but I was too scared. To google would have been to know, one way or another. I'm reminded of that great line from Robert Penn Warren's *All the King's Men*: "The end of man is knowledge, but there is one thing he can't know. He can't know whether knowledge will save him or kill him."

The months of not knowing became years, then more than a decade. And then one morning not long ago, I typed the kid's name into the search bar. It's an unusual name, easy pickings for Google. I hit enter. The first link was to a Facebook. I clicked over, and there he was. Eighteen years old, a decade and a half removed from the one night we spent together.

He is alive.

He is growing up, finding his way in the world, documenting a life that is more public than he probably realizes. But how can I not be grateful for knowing, even if the only way to know is to lose our autonomy over our so-called selves? He is alive. He likes John Deere tractors, and is a member of the Future Farmers of America, and he is alive.

Scrolling through his friends, I find his parents' profiles, and discover that they are still married. He is alive. He likes terrible, overly manufactured country music. He is alive. He calls his girlfriend his bae. Alive. Alive. Alive.

It could've gone the other way, of course. But it didn't. And so I can't help but give the practice of googling strangers four stars.

INDIANAPOLIS

INDIANAPOLIS IS THE SIXTEENTH LARGEST CITY in the U.S. by both population and land area. It is the capital of Indiana, and I guess it is now my hometown. Sarah and I moved to Indianapolis in the summer of 2007. We drove a U-Haul with all our worldly belongings from the corner of 88th and Columbus in New York City to the corner of 86th and Ditch in Indianapolis, an extremely stressful sixteen-hour drive. When we finally arrived in Indianapolis, we unpacked our stuff and slept on an air mattress in our new home, the first place we'd ever owned. We were in our late twenties, and we'd bought this house a few weeks earlier after spending maybe a half hour inside of it. The house had three bedrooms, two and a half baths, and a half-finished basement. Our mortgage payment was a third of what our New York rent had been.

I couldn't get over how quiet and dark the house was that first night. I kept telling Sarah that someone could be standing right outside our bedroom window and we wouldn't even know, and then Sarah would say, "Well, but probably not." And I'm just not the sort of person who is effectively comforted by probablys, so several times through the night I got up from the air mattress and pressed my face against the glass of the bedroom window, expecting to see eyes staring back at me but instead finding only darkness.

The next morning, I insisted that we buy some curtains, but first we had to drop off the moving van. At the U-Haul return place, a guy handed us some paperwork to fill out, and asked us where we'd driven in from. Sarah explained that we had moved from New York for her job at the Indianapolis Museum of Art, and the guy said he'd been to the museum once as a kid, and then Sarah said, "So, what do you think of Indianapolis?"

And then the guy standing behind the counter at the U-Haul place paused for a moment before saying, "Well, you gotta live somewhere."

Indianapolis has tried on a lot of mottoes and catchphrases over the years. Indianapolis is "Raising the Game." "You put the 'I' in Indy." "Crossroads of America." But I'd propose a different motto: "Indianapolis: You gotta live somewhere."

There's no getting around Indianapolis's many imperfections. We are situated on the White River, a non-navigable waterway, which is endlessly resonant as metaphor but problematic as geography. Furthermore, the river is filthy, because our aging water treatment system frequently overflows and dumps raw sewage directly into it. The city sprawls in every direction—endless mini-malls and parking lots and nondescript office buildings. We don't invest enough in the arts or public transportation. One of our major thoroughfares is named Ditch Road, for God's sakes. Ditch Road. We could name it anything—Kurt Vonnegut Drive, Madam C. J. Walker Way, Roady McRoadface—but we don't. We accept Ditch.

Someone once told me that Indianapolis is among the nation's leading test markets for new restaurant chains, because the city is so thoroughly average. Indeed, it ranks among the top so-called "microcosm cities," because Indianapolis is more typically American than almost any

other place. We are spectacular in our ordinariness. The city's nicknames
include "Naptown," because it's boring, and "India-no-place."

When we first moved here, I would often write in the mornings
at my neighborhood Starbucks, at the corner of 86th and Ditch, and I
would marvel at the fact that all four corners of that intersection contained strip malls. Although I lived less than a half mile from that Starbucks, I often drove because there were no sidewalks. The land had been
given over to cars, to sprawl, to flat-roofed soullessness.

I was disgusted by it. Living in a tiny apartment in New York City
where we could never quite eradicate the mice, I had romanticized home
ownership. But now that we actually had a house, I hated it. Indianapolis's favorite literary son, Kurt Vonnegut, wrote that one of the flaws
in the human character "is that everybody wants to build and nobody
wants to do maintenance." Home ownership was all maintenance. There
were always window treatments to install and light bulbs to change. The
water heater kept breaking. And most of all, there was the lawn. God, I
hated mowing the lawn. The lawn and the mini-malls of 86th and Ditch
became the two poles of my resentment. I couldn't wait for Sarah to get
a job somewhere else.

Vonnegut once said, "What people like about me is Indianapolis." He
said that in Indianapolis, of course, to a crowd full of people from Indianapolis, but Kurt Vonnegut really did hold the city in high esteem.
Toward the end of his life, he answered an interviewer's question by
saying, "I've wondered where home is, and I realized, it's not Mars or
some place like that. It's Indianapolis when I was nine years old. I had a
brother and a sister, a cat and a dog, and a mother and father and uncles
and aunts. And there's no way I can get there again." Vonnegut's greatest novel, *Slaughterhouse-Five*, is about a man who becomes unstuck in
time, and how time conspires with consciousness. It's about war and
trauma, but it's also about not being able to get back to before—before

the firebombing of Dresden, before the suicide of Vonnegut's mother, before his sister's early death. I believe that Vonnegut loved Indianapolis. But it's telling that from the time he could choose where to live, he did not choose to live here.

Late in our first Indianapolis year, Sarah and I became friends with our neighbors Marina and Chris Waters. Chris was a former Peace Corps volunteer, and Marina a human rights lawyer. Like us, they'd just gotten married, and like us, they were living in their first home.

But unlike us, Chris and Marina loved Indianapolis. We'd often go to lunch together at Smee's, a little family-owned restaurant in one of the 86th and Ditch mini-malls, and I would complain about lawn care and the lack of sidewalks. Once, Chris said to me, "You know this is one of the most economically and racially diverse zip codes in the United States?"

And I said, "What?"

And he said, "It is. You can google it."

So I did google it, and he was right. The median home price near 86th and Ditch is $237,000, but there are also million-dollar houses and $700-a-month apartments. At that corner, there are Thai and Chinese and Greek and Mexican restaurants, all independently owned. There's a bookstore, a fair-trade gift shop, two pharmacies, a bank, a Salvation Army, and a liquor store named after the constitutional amendment that repealed prohibition.

Yes, the architecture is an unmitigated nightmare, but the people of Indianapolis have gone and made something beautiful anyway. Sit outside of Smee's for an afternoon and you'll hear English and Spanish, Karin and Burmese, Russian and Italian. The problem was never 86th and Ditch, which turns out to be a great American intersection. The problem was me. And after Chris called my assumptions into question, I began to think differently about the city. I began to see it as a place where big moments in human lives take place. The climactic scenes in my two most recent novels, *The Fault in Our Stars* and *Turtles All the Way Down*, both take place at the corner of 86th and Ditch. And I think what people like about those books is Indianapolis.

As with all the best sci-fi writers, Kurt Vonnegut was really good at seeing into the future. Way back in 1974, he wrote, "What should young people do with their lives today? Many things, obviously. But the most daring thing is to create stable communities in which the terrible disease of loneliness can be cured."

That seems to me an even more important, and more daring, endeavor than it was forty-seven years ago. When people ask me why I live in Indianapolis when I could live anywhere, that's what I want to tell them. I am trying to create a stable community in which the terrible disease of loneliness can be cured. And you gotta do that somewhere. When I am sick with the disease of loneliness, good weather and shimmering skyscrapers do me no good whatsoever, as a writer or as a person. I must be home to do the work I need to do. And yes, home is that house where you no longer live. Home is before, and you live in after.

But home is also what you are building and maintaining today, and I feel rather lucky in the end to be making my home just off of Ditch Road.

I give Indianapolis four stars.

KENTUCKY BLUEGRASS

SOMETIMES I LIKE TO IMAGINE benevolent aliens visiting Earth. In my daydreams, these aliens are galactic anthropologists, seeking to understand the cultures, rituals, preoccupations, and divinities of various sentient species. They would conduct careful field research, observing us. They would ask open-ended, nonjudgmental questions, like "What, or whom, is in your view worthy of sacrifice?" and "What should be the collective goals of humanity?" I hope that these alien anthropologists would like us. We are, in spite of it all, a charismatic species.

In time, the aliens would come to understand almost everything about us—our ceaseless yearning, our habit of wandering, how we love the feeling of the sun's light on our skin. At last, they would have only one question remaining: "We have noted that there is a green god that you keep in front of and behind your houses, and we have seen how you are devoted to the care of this ornamental plant god. You call it Kentucky bluegrass, although it is neither blue nor from Kentucky. Here is what we are wondering: Why do you worship this species? Why do you value it over all the other plants?"

Poa pratensis, as it is known to the scientific community, is ubiquitous the world over. Much of the time when you see a soft, green expanse

of lawn, you're looking at least in part at Kentucky bluegrass. The plant
is native to Europe, northern Asia, and parts of North Africa, but according to the Invasive Species Compendium, it is now present on every
continent, including Antarctica.

The typical shoot of *Poa pratensis* has three to four leaves, shaped
like little canoes, and if left unmown, it can grow to three feet tall and
sprout blue flower heads. But it is rarely left unmown, at least not in my
neighborhood, where it is illegal to allow your grass to grow more than
six inches long.

If you've ever driven through my home state of Indiana, you've seen
mile after mile of cornfields. Amber waves of grain are enshrined in
the song "America the Beautiful." But more land and more water are
devoted to the cultivation of lawn grass in the United States than to
corn and wheat combined. There are around 163,000 square kilometers
of lawn in the U.S., greater than the size of Ohio, or the entire nation
of Italy. Almost one-third of all residential water use in the U.S.—clean,
drinkable water—is dedicated to lawns. To thrive, Kentucky bluegrass
often requires fertilizer and pesticides and complex irrigation systems, all
of which we offer up to the plant in abundance, even though it cannot
be eaten by humans or used for anything except walking and playing on.
The U.S.'s most abundant and labor-intensive crop is pure, unadulterated
ornamentation.[29]

The word "lawn" didn't even exist until the 1500s. Back then,
"lawns" referred to expanses of grass shared by communities to feed
grazing livestock, as opposed to "fields," which denoted land used to
grow plants for human consumption. But by the eighteenth century
in England, ornamental lawns similar to the ones we know now had

---

29.   One could make a case for *Poa pratensis* in the Anthropocene if lawn grass was
uniquely good at capturing carbon dioxide. But lawn maintenance creates more carbon
emissions than lawns themselves can capture. It would be vastly better from an emissions
perspective to have unkept grasses or clover or ivy or really anything that doesn't need constant, resource-intensive care.

emerged—back then, lawns were maintained by handheld scythes and shears, and so keeping a lawn without the help of grazing animals was a sign you were rich enough to hire lots of gardeners, and also to own land that did nothing but look good.

The ornamental lawn fad spread throughout Europe, and also to the United States, where people enslaved by Thomas Jefferson maintained a closely mown lawn at Jefferson's estate, Monticello.

Over time, the quality of lawns in a neighborhood began to be seen as a proxy for the quality of the neighborhood itself. In *The Great Gatsby*, Jay Gatsby pays for his gardeners to mow his neighbor's lawn before Daisy Buchanan visits. Or, to cite an example closer to home, when I first moved to Indianapolis in 2007, I suddenly found myself the owner of a lawn, which I struggled mightily to maintain. Although we lived on only a third of an acre, it took my little electric lawn mower and me two hours to cut all the grass. One Sunday afternoon, my next-door neighbor interrupted me mid-mow and offered me a beer. As we stood in my half-mown yard, he said, "You know, when the Kaufmanns lived here, this was the nicest lawn in the neighborhood."

"Well," I answered after a while, "the Kaufmanns don't live here anymore."

It is truly staggering how much of our shared resources we devote to Kentucky bluegrass and its cousins. To minimize weeds and make our lawns as thickly monocultured as possible, Americans use ten times more fertilizer and pesticide per acre of turfgrass than is used in corn or wheat fields. To keep all the lawns in the U.S. green year-round requires, according to a NASA study, around two hundred gallons of water per person per day, and almost all of the water shooting from sprinklers is treated drinking water. Grass clippings and other yard waste constitute 12 percent of all the material that ends up in U.S. landfills. And then there is the direct financial outlay: We spend tens of billions of dollars a year on lawn maintenance.

We do get *something* in exchange, of course. Kentucky bluegrass provides a good surface for soccer and games of tag. Lawn grass cools the ground, and offers some protection from wind and water erosion. But there are better, if less conventionally beautiful, alternatives. One could, for instance, devote a front yard to growing plants that humans can eat.

I know all of this, and yet I still have a lawn. I still mow it, or pay someone else to. I don't use pesticides and welcome clover and wild strawberries as part of the lawn, but still, there's a lot of lawn bluegrass in our yard, even though *Poa pratensis* has no business being in Indianapolis.

It strikes me as interesting that in contrast to proper gardening, lawn maintenance doesn't involve much physical contact with nature. You're mostly touching the machines that mow or edge the grass, not the plant matter itself. And if you've got the kind of Gatsby lawn we're all told to reach for, you can't even see the dirt beneath the thick mat of grass. And so mowing Kentucky bluegrass is an encounter with nature, but the kind where you don't get your hands dirty.

I give *Poa pratensis* two stars.

THE INDIANAPOLIS 500

EVERY YEAR, near the end of May, between 250,000 and 350,000 people gather in the tiny enclave of Speedway, Indiana, to watch the Indianapolis 500. It is the largest annual nonreligious gathering of human beings on Earth.

Speedway is surrounded by, but technically independent from, Indianapolis. Basically, Speedway is to Indianapolis as the Vatican is to Rome. The Vatican comparisons don't end there. Both Speedway and the Vatican are cultural centers that draw visitors from around the world; both contain a museum; and Speedway's racetrack, while commonly called "The Brickyard," is also sometimes known as "The Cathedral of Speed." Of course, the Vatican analogy falls apart if you dig deeply enough. In my admittedly few trips to the Vatican, I have never been offered an ice-cold Miller Lite by a stranger, whereas that happens often when I visit Speedway.

At first blush, the Indianapolis 500 seems tailor-made for ridicule. I mean, it's just cars driving in circles. The drivers literally go nowhere. The race is crowded, and usually hot. One year, my phone case partially melted in my pocket while I sat in the Turn 2 grandstand. It's also loud. Every May, I can hear the cars practicing when

I am working in my garden—even though the Speedway is five miles from my house.

As a spectator sport, the 500 leaves much to be desired. No matter where you sit or stand, you can't see the entire track, so important events take place that you cannot follow. Because some cars are laps ahead of others, it's almost impossible to know who's winning the race unless you bring oversized headphones to listen to the radio broadcast of the event you are watching. The largest crowd to watch a sporting event every year cannot see most of the sporting event.

But it's been my experience that almost everything easy to mock turns out to be interesting if you pay closer attention. The Indy 500 features open-wheel racing, which is to say that the wheels of the cars are not covered by fenders, and the driver's cockpit is open to the elements. Some truly amazing engineering is involved in getting these cars to travel more than 220 miles per hour around the two-and-a-half-mile course. The cars have to be fast, but not so fast that the g-forces in the corners cause drivers to lose consciousness. The cars have to be responsive, and predictable, and reliable, because while driving at 220 miles per hour, these open-wheeled vehicles are often inches away from one another. For more than a hundred years, the Indianapolis 500 has been examining a question that is of serious concern to people in the Anthropocene: What is the proper relationship between human and machine?

Today, the track is entirely asphalt except for a single yard of red bricks at the finish line, but when the first Indianapolis 500 took place on May 30, 1911, the track was paved entirely with bricks—3.2 million of them. The winner of that first five-hundred-mile race was Ray Harroun, who was driving a car that featured his own invention, the rearview mirror. In fact, many early automotive innovators were involved with the Indianapolis 500. Louis Chevrolet, who founded the car company, owned a racing team. His brother Gaston won the Indianapolis 500 in 1920 only to die later that year in a race at the Beverly Hills Speedway.

Indeed, racing cars is an exceptionally dangerous sport—forty-two drivers have died at the Indianapolis Motor Speedway in the track's history. Many more have been injured, some seriously. In 2015, IndyCar driver James Hinchcliffe nearly died after a crash at the Speedway severed a femoral artery. There's no escaping the uncomfortable fact that one of the thrills of racing is how close drivers get to the edge of disaster. As the legendary driver Mario Andretti put it, "If everything seems under control, you're just not going fast enough."

But I do think car racing accomplishes something—it takes both the person and the machine to the edge of possibility, and in the process, we get faster as a species. It took Ray Harroun six hours and forty-two minutes to drive the first five hundred miles at the Indianapolis Motor Speedway; it took 2018 winner Will Power just under three hours.

That's his real name, by the way. Will Power. Nice guy. Once I was standing by a valet stand next to Will Power, and when the valet showed up with my 2011 Chevrolet Volt, Will Power said to me, "You know, I am also a Chevrolet driver."

But the Indy 500 isn't really about going fast; it's about going faster than everyone else, which reflects one of my top-level concerns about humanity: We cannot seem to resist the urge to win. Whether it's climbing El Capitan or going to space, we want to do it, but we also want to do it before anyone else, or faster than anyone else. This drive has pushed us forward as a species—but I worry it has also pushed us in other directions.

On the day of the Indy 500, though, I don't think about what the race means. I'm not considering the ever-diminishing distinction between humans and their machines, or the Anthropocene's accelerating rate of change. Instead, I am merely happy.

My best friend Chris Waters calls it Christmas for Grown-Ups. My race day starts at 5:30 in the morning. I make a cup of coffee, check the weather, and fill my backpack cooler with ice, water, beer, and sandwiches. By six, I'm checking my bike to make sure the tires are properly inflated and my patch kit is ready. Then I bike down to Bob's Food Mart, where I meet up with friends and begin the beautiful early morning bicycle trip down Indianapolis's Central Canal Towpath. Some years, it's raining and cold; other years, the heat is overwhelming. But it is always beautiful, riding and joking with my friends and their friends, many of whom I see only once a year.

We bike down to Butler University's track, where every year two of our friends engage in a one-mile footrace at seven in the morning. The IndyCars get faster decade over decade, but the footrace slows down. We place bets, and one or the other of them wins, and then we get back on our bikes for a couple of miles before stopping again outside the Indianapolis Museum of Art, where we meet up with more people, until we are a traveling band of a hundred or so bicycles. Everyone waves as we bike by. "Have a good race," we say to one another, or else, "Safe race!"

We're together, you see. We bike until the trail dead-ends at Sixteenth Street and then begin the long trip west, merging with the cars that are already stuck in traffic even though the race won't begin for five more hours. We bike single-file for a nervous-making ten blocks before turning into the town of Speedway. People are sitting out on their porches. Occasionally, a cheer will erupt from seemingly nowhere. Everyone is selling their front yards as parking spots, shouting out prices. The noise level is rising now. I don't like crowds, but I like this crowd, because I'm in an *us* that doesn't require a *them*.

We make it to the Speedway, chain our bikes to a fence near Turn 2 and then head our separate ways. Some of us like to watch the race from Turn 2; others at the start/finish line. There are more traditions to come: the singing of "Back Home Again in Indiana," some second-tier celebrity saying, "Drivers, start your engines," the parade laps, and the race itself. Tradition is a way of being with people, not just the people you're observing the traditions with now, but also all those who've ever observed them.

I'm able to write all of this in the present tense because these traditions function as a kind of continuity—they happened, yes, but they are still happening, and will go on happening. The rupture of that continuity was part of what made May of 2020 so difficult for me. As the pandemic took hold, I felt as if I was being unmoored from what I thought was reality. So much that had recently been extraordinary—wearing a mask, being conscious of every surface I touched or every human I walked past—was in the process of becoming mundane. And so much that had recently been mundane was becoming extraordinary.

The Sunday before Memorial Day of 2020, I packed my backpack as usual, and Sarah and I got on our bikes as usual. Near Bob's Food Mart, we met up with our friends Ann-Marie and Stuart Hyatt. We wore masks as we biked down to the Speedway, where the gates were locked shut. It was so quiet, so impossibly quiet as we sat in a vast and empty parking lot. When the race finally did happen, in August, it was held without fans for the first time. I watched it on TV, and found it interminably boring.

But I'm thinking back to 2018. Dozens of us are locking our bikes to the chain-link fence and scattering about to our various seats in the crowded grandstands. In four or five hours, we will meet back at the fence, unlock our bikes, and repeat the rituals on the way home. We will talk about how this happened or that happened, how we are happy for Will Power, who is such a good guy and finally got his Indy 500 victory. I'll tell my Will Power story, only to learn that many of my friends also have Will Power stories. Speedway is a small town after all, even on this day, and we are in it together.

I give the Indianapolis 500 four stars.

MONOPOLY

WHEN MY FAMILY AND I PLAY MONOPOLY, a board game in which the goal is to bankrupt your fellow players, I sometimes think about *Universal Paperclips*, a 2017 video game created by Frank Lantz. In *Universal Paperclips*, you play the role of an artificial intelligence that has been programmed to create as many paperclips as possible. Over time, you produce more and more paperclips, until eventually you exhaust all of Earth's iron ore, whereupon you send probes to outer space to mine paperclip materials from other planets, and then eventually other solar systems. After many hours of play, you finally win the game: You've turned all the universe's available resources into paperclips. You did it. Congratulations. Everyone is dead.

In Monopoly, you land on various properties as you move around a square board. In the original game, the properties are from a fictionalized version of Atlantic City, New Jersey, but that changes depending on region and edition. For instance, in the Pokémon version of the game, properties include Tangela and Raichu. Regardless, if you land on an unclaimed property, you can purchase it, and if you establish a monopoly by purchasing related properties, you can build houses and hotels. When other players land on places you own, they must pay you rent. Acquire enough properties, and the rent becomes unsustainable for your fellow players, and they go bankrupt.

There are many problems with Monopoly, but maybe the reason the game has persisted for so long—it has been one of the world's bestselling board games for over eighty years—is that its problems are our problems: Like life, Monopoly unfolds very slowly at first, and then becomes distressingly fast at the end. Like life, people find meaning in its outcomes even though the game is rigged toward the rich and privileged, and insofar as it isn't rigged, it's random. And like life, your friends get mad if you take their money, and then no matter how rich you are, there's an ever-expanding void inside of you that money can never fill, but gripped by the madness of unregulated enterprise you nonetheless believe that if you just get a couple more hotels or take from your friends their few remaining dollars, you will at last feel complete.

To me, the worst thing about Monopoly is its convoluted, self-contradictory analysis of capitalism. The game is essentially about how acquiring land is literally a roll of the dice, and how the exploitation of monopolies enriches the few and impoverishes the many. And yet, the point of the game is to get as rich as you can.

Monopoly's mealymouthed take on economic inequality is also like life, at least life in Monopoly's home nation of the United States, where many of us think of billionaires the way I thought of the popular kids in middle school. I despised them, but also desperately wanted to be them. In Monopoly's case, the thematic inconsistency of the game is largely a product of its complicated origin story, which turns out to say far more about capitalism than the game itself does.

Here's the creation myth as it gets told by Monopoly's current owner, the toy company Hasbro: In 1929, in the wake of the great stock market crash, forty-year-old Charles Darrow lost his job in Philadelphia and was forced to scratch together a living as a door-to-door salesman. But then in 1933, he invented the board game Monopoly, eventually patenting

the game and licensing it to the company Parker Brothers. Darrow became the first board game millionaire, a proper rags-to-riches story of an
American inventor succeeding via the sweat of his Randian brow.

It's a great story; so great, in fact, that many copies of Monopoly
have been printed with Darrow's biography alongside the rules. Today,
there's even a plaque in Atlantic City celebrating Charles Darrow. The
only problem with the story is that Charles Darrow did not invent
Monopoly.

Almost thirty years earlier, a woman named Elizabeth Magie created a board game called the Landlord's Game. As detailed in Mary
Pilon's wonderful book *The Monopolists*, Magie was a writer and actor
who supported her artistic pursuits with a career as a stenographer and
typist, work that she hated. "I wish to be constructive," she once said,
"not a mere mechanical tool for transmitting a man's spoken thoughts
to letter paper."

In her lifetime, Magie was best known for a newspaper ad in which
she offered herself up for sale to the highest bidder. She described herself
as "not beautiful, but very attractive," and a woman of "strong bohemian
characteristics." The ad, which made national news, was meant to call
attention to the discrimination against women in every aspect of American life, which forced them out of the workforce and into subservient
roles in marriage. She told a reporter, "We are not machines. Girls have
minds, desires, hopes, and ambitions."

Magie also felt that no feminist movement could succeed without
larger changes in the economic system. "In a short time," she said,
"men and women will discover that they are poor because Carnegie
and Rockefeller have more maybe than they know what to do with."
To help show this to the world, in 1906 Magie created the Landlord's
Game. Magie was a follower of Henry George, an economist who
believed, as Antonia Noori Farzan put it in the *Washington Post*, "that
railroads, telegraphs, and utilities should be publicly owned, rather

than controlled by monopolies, and that land should be considered common property."

Magie designed the Landlord's Game to illustrate George's ideas, and believed that as children played it, they would "see clearly the gross injustice of our present land system." The Landlord's Game was similar to Monopoly in many ways: Like Monopoly, it had a square board with properties, and like Monopoly, if you made a bad roll you could go to jail. But Magie released her game with two sets of rules. In one, the goal—like contemporary Monopoly—was to impoverish your opponents and acquire land monopolies. In the other set of rules, "all were rewarded when wealth was created," as Pilon put it. One set of rules showcased how rent systems enriched landlords while keeping tenants poor, leading to capital over time concentrating in fewer and fewer hands. The other set sought to suggest a better way—in which wealth generated by the many was shared by the many.

The monopolist rules for the Landlord's Game proved more popular, and as college students learned the game and played handmade versions of it, they expanded and changed rules to make it even more similar to the Monopoly we know today. An Indianapolis version, called the Fascinating Game of Finance, was released in 1932, and it was in Indianapolis that a woman named Ruth Hoskins learned the game. She soon moved to Atlantic City, and adapted the game to her new hometown. Hoskins taught the game to many people, including a couple who later moved to Philadelphia, where they taught the Fascinating Game of Finance to a guy named Charles Todd, who in turn taught it to Charles Darrow. Darrow then asked for a copy of the rules, altered some of the design, patented the game, and became a millionaire.

Here's how much Charles Darrow did not invent Monopoly: Marven Gardens is a neighborhood near Atlantic City. In Charles Todd's version of the game, which he learned by way of Ruth Hoskins, the neighborhood is misspelled as Marvin Gardens. That misspelling is repeated in Darrow's version of the game, because Charles Darrow didn't invent Monopoly.

So the story we hear of an individual rightly rewarded for his genius turns out to be a far more complicated story of a woman who created a game that thousands of collaborators then improved by playing it. A story of capitalism working turns out to be a story of capitalism failing. So many people got robbed by Darrow's monopolism, but Elizabeth Magie's loss is especially galling, because it wasn't only her game that got buried by Monopoly but also the ideals she worked so hard to share. Magie's rebuke of unregulated extractive capitalism was transformed into a celebration of getting rich by making others poor.

In the game of Monopoly, power and resources get unjustly distributed until one individual ends up with everything, and only in that sense is it Charles Darrow's game. Still, more than a hundred years after Magie first debuted the Landlord's Game, Hasbro continues to credit Charles Darrow as the inventor of Monopoly, and will say of Elizabeth Magie only, "There have been a number of popular property trading games throughout history. Elizabeth Magie—a writer, inventor, and feminist— was one of the pioneers of land-grabbing games." In short, Hasbro still refuses to acknowledge that the land they grabbed was never theirs for the taking.

I give Monopoly one and a half stars.

SUPER MARIO KART

SUPER MARIO KART IS A RACING GAME, first released in 1992 for the Super Nintendo, in which characters from the Mario universe squat atop go-karts, rather like I do when trying to ride my daughter's tricycle. It was initially slated to be a game with Formula One–style cars, but technical constraints forced the designers to build tightly woven tracks that folded in on themselves, the kind that only go-karts can navigate. The game was co-created by Super Mario Brothers lead designer and video game legend Shigeru Miyamoto, who would later say, "We set out to make a game where we could display the game screen for two players at the same time." This split-screen mode is part of what made the first *Super Mario Kart* game so thrilling.

In the Super Nintendo game, players can choose from among eight characters in the Mario universe—including Princess Peach, Mario, Luigi, and Donkey Kong, Jr. Each character has particular strengths and weaknesses. Bowser, for instance, is strong and travels at a high top speed but accelerates very slowly. Toad, on the other hand, is quick and handles well, but has a lower top speed. Once you choose a character (I recommend Luigi), you're pitted against the seven other drivers in a se-ries of increasingly surreal tracks. You might navigate a regular pavement go-kart track, or a ship of ghosts, or a castle, or the famed Rainbow Road, which has a many-splendored driving surface and no guardrails to prevent you from falling into the abyss below.

I was in tenth grade when *Super Mario Kart* was released, and as far as my friends and I were concerned, it was the greatest video game ever. We spent hundreds of hours playing it. The game was so interwoven into our high school experience that, even now, the soundtrack takes me back to a linoleum-floored dorm room that smelled like sweat and Gatorade. I can feel myself sitting on a golden microfiber couch that had been handed down through generations of students, trying to out-turn my friends Chip and Sean on the final race of the Mushroom Cup.

We almost never talked about the game while playing it—we were always talking over each other about our flailing attempts at romance or the ways we were oppressed by this or that teacher or the endless gossip that churns around insular communities like boarding schools. We didn't need to talk about Mario Kart, but we needed Mario Kart to have an excuse to be together—three or four of us squeezed on that couch, hip to hip. What I remember most was the incredible—and for me, novel—joy of being included.

Like the rest of us, Mario Kart has changed a lot since I was in high school. In the recently released *Mario Kart 8*, you can fly and go underwater and drive upside down; you can now choose from among dozens of playable characters and vehicles. But at its core, the game hasn't changed much. Mostly, you win contemporary Mario Kart games in the same way you won them in 1992, by driving in the straightest possible line and cornering well. There is a measure of skill involved—you can carry speed better through corners by drifting, for instance, and there's some strategy to passing. But Mario Kart is almost ridiculously straightforward.

Except, that is, for the question boxes, which make Mario Kart either a brilliant game or a problematic one, depending on what you think games should do. As you navigate a track in Mario Kart, you may pass over or through question boxes, at which point you receive one of several tools. You might get a mushroom, which you can use to get a one-time speed boost. Or you may get a red turtle shell, a kind of heat-seeking missile that will go looking for the kart in front of you and hit it from behind, causing that kart to spin out. Or you might get the coveted lightning bolt, which makes all your opponents miniaturized and slow for a bit, while you remain as big and fast as ever. In the newer editions of Mario Kart, your question box might even provide you with the chance to transform for a few seconds into Bullet Bill, a speeding bullet that corners amazingly and destroys every kart in its path.

Once, I was playing *Mario Kart 8* with my son, and because I am in my twenty-sixth year of regular Mario Kart play, I was leading the game comfortably. But then on the last lap he got Bullet Bill from a question box and proceeded to blow right past me, winning the race and destroying my kart in the process. I ended up finishing fourth.

This sort of thing often happens in Mario Kart, because the question boxes know if you're in first place. If you are, you'll usually get a banana peel, or a coin, which are minimally useful. You'll never get one of those sweet bullets. But if you're in last place—because, say, you're an eight-year-old playing a grizzled Mario Kart veteran—you're much more likely to get lightning or Bullet Bill or an infinite supply of speed-boost mushrooms.

In a Mario Kart game, the best player still usually wins, but luck plays a significant role. Mario Kart is more poker than chess.

Depending on your worldview, the question boxes either make the game fair, because anyone can win, or they make the game unfair, because the person with the most skill doesn't always win.

In that respect, at least in my experience, real life is the precise opposite of Mario Kart. In real life, when you are ahead, you are given lots of power-ups to get further ahead. After one of my books became commercially successful, for instance, my bank called to inform me that I would no longer be charged ATM fees, even if I used an ATM from a different bank. Why? Because people with money in the bank get all kinds of perks just for having money in the bank. Then there are the much bigger power-ups, like the graduating-from-college-with-no-debt power-up, or the being-white power-up, or the being-male power-up. This doesn't mean that people with good power-ups will succeed, of course, or that those without them won't. But I don't buy the argument that these structural power-ups are irrelevant. The fact that our political, social, and economic systems are biased in favor of the already rich and the already powerful is the single greatest failure of the American democratic ideal. I have benefited from this, directly and profoundly, for my entire life. Almost every time I've driven through a question box in my life, I've been given at the very least a red turtle shell. It happens so routinely that it's easy for those of us who benefit from these power-ups to see them as fair. But if I don't grapple with the reality that I owe much of my success to injustice, I'll only further the hoarding of wealth and opportunity.

Some might argue that games should reward talent and skill and hard work precisely because real life doesn't. But to me the real fairness is when everyone has a shot to win, even if their hands are small, even if they haven't been playing the game since 1992.

In an age of extremes in gaming and elsewhere, Mario Kart is refreshingly nuanced. I give it four stars.

BONNEVILLE SALT FLATS

IN THE WINTER OF 2018, Sarah and I traveled to Wendover, a small town that straddles the border between Utah and Nevada. While there, almost as an afterthought, we visited the Bonneville Salt Flats, an otherworldly valley of salt-encrusted land on the western shore of the Great Salt Lake.

Sarah is, by a wide margin, my favorite person. After the death of the poet Jane Kenyon, her husband Donald Hall wrote, "We did not spend our days gazing into each other's eyes. We did that gazing when we made love or when one of us was in trouble, but most of the time our gazes met and entwined as they looked at a third thing. Third things are essential to marriages, objects or practices or habits or arts or institutions or games or human beings that provide a site of joint rapture or contentment. Each member of a couple is separate; the two come together in double attention." Hall goes on to note that third things might be John Keats or the Boston Symphony Orchestra or Dutch interiors or children.

Our kids are critical sites of joint rapture for Sarah and me, but we have other third things, too—the Sunday *New York Times* crossword puzzle, the books we read together, the TV show *The Americans*, and so on.

But our first third thing was art.

Sarah and I attended the same high school in Alabama, so we've known each other since we were kids, but we never really had a conversation until 2003, when we were both living in Chicago. Sarah was working at an art gallery then, and after we crossed paths a couple times and exchanged some emails, she invited me to the opening of an exhibition at the gallery featuring sculptures by the artist Ruby Chishti.

I'd never been to an art gallery before, and at the time I could not have named a single living artist, but I was fascinated by Chishti's sculptures. When Sarah took some time away from work that evening to talk with me about Chishti's artwork, I felt for the first time one of my favorite feelings in this world—the feeling of Sarah's gaze and mine meeting and entwining as we looked at a third thing.

A few months later, after we'd exchanged dozens of emails, we decided to start a two-person book club. Sarah chose *The Human Stain* by Philip Roth as our first book. When we met to discuss it, we found that we had both underlined the same passage: "The pleasure isn't owning the person. The pleasure is this. Having another contender in the room with you."

Fifteen years later, we were in Wendover to film for *The Art Assignment*, a series Sarah produced with PBS Digital Studios.[30] We saw an installation by the artist William Lamson, as well as some of the monumental land art of the American West, including Nancy Holt's *Sun Tunnels* and Robert Smithson's *Spiral Jetty*. At night, we stayed at a casino hotel on the Nevada side of town. During World War II, the crew that dropped an atomic bomb on the city of Hiroshima trained out of Wendover. But

---

30.   *The Art Assignment* would later inspire Sarah's wonderful book *You Are an Artist*, which combines art prompts from contemporary artists with art history and practical tips for creating.

the Air Force left a long time ago, and these days people mostly visit for the casinos, or else for the nearby salt flats.

For some reason, I really like casinos. I recognize that they prey on vulnerable people and enable addiction, and that they're loud and smoky and gross and horrible. But I can't help myself. I like sitting at a table and playing cards with strangers. On the evening in question, I was playing with a woman from the Texas panhandle named Marjorie. She told me that she'd been married for sixty-one years. I asked her what the secret was, and she said, "Separate checking accounts."

I asked her what brought her to Wendover, and she said she wanted to see the salt flats. And the casino, of course. She and her husband gambled one weekend a year. I asked her how it was going, and she said, "You ask a lot of questions."

Which I do, when I'm gambling. In every other environment, I am extremely averse to encounters with strangers. I don't tend to chat with airplane seatmates or cab drivers, and I am an awkward and strained conversationalist in most situations. But put me at a blackjack table with Marjorie, and suddenly I'm Perry Mason.

The other person at my table, eighty-seven-year-old Anne from central Oregon, also wasn't much of a talker, so I turned to the dealer, who was required to talk to me as a condition of his employment. He had a handlebar mustache, and a name tag identifying him as James. I couldn't tell if he was twenty-one or forty-one. I asked him if he was from Wendover.

"Born and bred," he answered.

I asked him what he thought of it, and he told me it was a nice place. Lots of hiking. Great if you like hunting and fishing. And the salt flats were cool, of course, if you liked fast cars, which he did.

After a moment he said, "Not a great place for kids, though."

"Do you have kids?" I asked.

"No," he said. "But I was one."

There's a certain way I talk about the things I don't talk about. Maybe that's true for all of us. We have ways of closing off the conversation so that we don't ever get directly asked what we can't bear to answer. The silence that followed James's comment about having been a kid reminded me of that, and reminded me that I had also been a kid. Of course, it's possible that James was only referring to Wendover's shortage of playgrounds—but I doubted it. I started sweating. The casino's noises—the dinging of slot machines, the shouts at the craps table—were suddenly overwhelming. I thought about that old Faulkner line that the past isn't dead; it's not even past. One of the strange things about adulthood is that you are your current self, but you are also all the selves you used to be, the ones you grew out of but can't ever quite get rid of. I played out the hand, tipped the dealer, thanked the table for the conversation, and cashed out my remaining chips.

The next morning, I drove out to the Bonneville Salt Flats with Sarah and a few of her colleagues. Until 14,500 years ago, what is now Wendover was deep underwater in Lake Bonneville, a vast salty lake that covered nineteen thousand square miles, nearly the size of Lake Michigan today. Lake Bonneville has disappeared and re-formed a couple dozen times over the last five hundred million years; what remains of it at the moment is known as the Great Salt Lake, although it's less than a tenth as great as Lake Bonneville once was. The lake's most recent retreat left behind the salt flats, a thirty-thousand-acre expanse, utterly empty and far flatter than a pancake.

The snow-white ground was cracked like dried lips and crunched under my feet. I could smell the salt. I kept trying to think of what it looked like, but my brain could only find highly figurative similes. It looks like driving alone at night feels. It looks like everything you're scared to say out loud. It looks like the moment the water retreats from the shore just before a wave rolls in.

Herman Melville called white "a colorless, all-color." He wrote that white "shadows forth the heartless voids and immensities of the universe." And the Bonneville Salt Flats are very, very white.

Of course, everything on Earth is geological, but at the salt flats you *feel* the geology. It is not hard to believe that this land was once five hundred feet underwater. You feel like the briny, green-black water might rush back in at any moment, drowning you and your traumas and the town and the hangar where the *Enola Gay* waited for its atomic bomb.

Looking up toward the looming mountain ranges in the distance, I was reminded of what nature is always telling me: Humans are not the protagonists of this planet's story. If there is a main character, it is life itself, which makes of earth and starlight something more than earth and starlight. But in the age of the Anthropocene, humans tend to believe, despite all available evidence, that the world is here for our benefit. So the Bonneville Salt Flats must have a human use; why else would they exist? Nothing can grow in that dry, salty soil, but we find uses for it anyway. For the last hundred years, the flats have been mined for potash, which is used in fertilizer. And a long stretch of the flats has gained fame as a kind of drag-racing strip. A land-speed record was set there in 1965 when a turbo-jet car driven by Craig Breedlove traveled over six hundred miles per hour.

Racing season can still attract thousands of people to the flats, but most days the landscape is, above all else, a backdrop—for movies from *Independence Day* to *The Last Jedi*, and for fashion photo shoots and Instagram posts. While I was at the flats, I was one of several people trying to angle a selfie to make it look like I was alone in that emptiness.

But after walking for a while, away from the road that dead-ends into the flats, I started to feel really alone. At one point, I thought I saw a shimmering pool of water in the distance, but as I approached, it proved to be a mirage—an actual one. I'd always thought they were just fictional devices. As I kept walking, I thought about that blackjack dealer, and how bone-deep terrifying it is to be a child and know that you cannot decide what adults do to you.

Sarah called out to me. I turned around. She was so far away I couldn't hear what she was saying at first, but she was waving me toward her, and so I walked back until I could hear: I was getting in the way of a drone shot they needed for the show; could I walk over to where she was? So I did. I stood next to her, and watched the drone flying over the salt flats. Our gazes entwined. I felt calmer. I was thinking about the people I used to be, and how they fought and scrapped and survived for moments like this one. Looking with Sarah, the salt flats seemed to change—they no longer had the menace of indifference about them.

I give the Bonneville Salt Flats three and a half stars.

HIROYUKI DOI'S
CIRCLE DRAWINGS

ONE WEIRD THING ABOUT ME is that I have signed my name over five hundred thousand times. This effort began in earnest back in 2011, when I decided to sign the entire first printing of my fourth novel, *The Fault in Our Stars*. To do this, I signed sheets of paper that were then bound into copies of the book as they were printed. Over the course of a few months, I signed about 150,000 sheets. Sometimes I listened to podcasts or audiobooks, but often, I just sat there, alone in my basement, signing my name. I never really found it boring, because each time I was trying to realize some ideal form that I have in my head of what my signature looks like, and I can never quite achieve it.[31]

Paying attention to the very slight variations of repetitive behaviors engages me in a way I struggle to explain. There is a very specific itch within my brain that repetitive action scratches. I realize there may be some connection there to my having obsessive-compulsive disorder, but

---

31. Once in a great while—say, once out of every twenty or thirty thousand signatures, I will make one that I am really properly happy with, and I will take it upstairs and show it to Sarah. I'll point out how the line thins out in just the right place, and how I've hinted at the existence of the o in "John" with a little loop. Sarah will nod politely and look carefully at the near-perfect signature for a while before saying, not unkindly, "It looks exactly like all the others."

then again, lots of people enjoy doodling, which is what my signing boils down to. Doodling is good for brains—it relieves stress in ways similar to pacing or fidgeting, and it can help with attentiveness. A 2009 study published in *Applied Cognitive Psychology* found that people given license to doodle recalled more information than non-doodlers, perhaps because doodling requires just enough brainpower to keep the mind from wandering.

I wouldn't say I *enjoy* repetitive tasks, exactly, but I do benefit from them. Sometimes, when I feel burnt out and exhausted and I don't know what to do with myself or whether my work matters or if I'm ever going to do anything of use to anyone, I ask my publisher to send me ten or twenty thousand sheets of paper, and I sign them just to have something specific and measurable to do for a week or so. I don't even know whether those sheets end up in books. I hope they do, and I hope they make readers happy, but to be honest, I do it for myself, because it makes me . . . not happy, exactly, but engrossed. I think engrossed is what I really want to feel most of the time. It's such an ugly word, "engrossed," for such an absolutely beatific experience.

———————

I first saw the ink drawings of Hiroyuki Doi in 2006, at the American Folk Art Museum's show about obsessive drawing. Doi's drawings are epic conglomerations of circles, thousands—or maybe tens of thousands—of tiny circles tightly packed together, combining to form vast, wildly intricate abstractions. Some people say they look like teeming masses of cells, or like galactic nebulae. The one that struck me most was an untitled 2003 drawing shaped vaguely like a human eye turned on its side, fifty-six inches high and twenty-seven inches wide. At times, the circles branching off from one another resemble blood vessels; at others, they seem to swirl around centers of gravity. As I looked longer at the circles, the drawing took on a third dimension, and I felt like I could step into it, like the circles were not just before me but also above and below and behind and within.

Doi did not set out to be an artist; he was a successful chef when, in 1980, his younger brother died of a brain tumor. Overwhelmed with sorrow, he began to draw circles, and found that he could not stop drawing them, because they helped him find "relief from the sadness and grief."

What fascinates me about Doi's drawings is partly their glaring obsessiveness. They look like circling, recursive thoughts made visible. You lose yourself inside a Doi drawing, which is maybe the point. But they also communicate that desire to find relief from the consuming pain of loss. In interviews, Doi uses that word regularly: *relief*. And that is what I'm also desperate for whenever I've been knocked over by grief. Loss can be so encompassing—it's a job where the hours are all hours, every day. We talk of grief in stages—denial, bargaining, acceptance, and so on. But for me, at least, grief is a series of tightly packed circles that fade over many years, like ink exposed to light.

Why have I signed my name half a million times? Why has Hiroyuki Doi spent the last forty years drawing tiny circles? "I feel calm when I'm drawing," Doi has said, and although I'm no artist, I know what he means. On the other side of monotony lies a flow state, a way of being that is just being, a present tense that actually feels present.

There's also the human urge to make things, to paint cave walls and doodle in the margins of to-do lists. Doi once said, "I have to keep on working, otherwise nothing will be brought into existence." But sometimes I feel like the paper is better before we get ahold of it, when it is still wood. Other times, I love the marks we leave. They feel like gifts and signs, like trail markers in the wilderness.

I know we've left scars everywhere, and that our obsessive desire to *make* and *have* and *do* and *say* and *go* and *get*—six of the seven most common verbs in English—may ultimately steal away our ability to *be*, the most common verb in English. Even though we know that none of our marks will truly last, that time is coming not just for all of us but for all we make, we can't stop scribbling, can't stop seeking relief wherever we can find it. I'm grateful that Doi keeps on working, bringing things into existence. I am glad to be unalone in cramped circles of restless yearning.

I give Hiroyuki Doi's circle drawings four stars.

WHISPERING

I HAVE A FRIEND, ALEX, who is one of those impossibly easygoing, imperturbable souls who can instantly recalibrate when faced with a shift in circumstance. But occasionally, when on a tight schedule, Alex will become visibly stressed and say things like, "We've got to get a move on." Alex's wife, Linda, calls this "Airport Alex."

Much to my chagrin, I am always Airport Alex. I cannot stop worrying that the kids might be late for school, that the restaurant might cancel our reservation, that my psychiatrist will fire me for tardiness, and so on. I believe that punctuality is a virtue, but there is nothing virtuous about my particular punctuality. It is driven by fear, and enforced by harried shouting.

One morning when Sarah was out of town for work, I was sitting at breakfast with my then three-year-old daughter, who is never Airport Alex. For small children, time is not kept by clocks, and so I always feel the need to be the Keeper of the Schedule, the Maintainer of Punctuality in the Realm.

It was 8:37. Twenty-three minutes from being late to daycare. We'd already dropped Henry off at school, and we'd come back to the house so that we could eat breakfast before daycare, and breakfast was taking *forever.* My daughter paused between each well-considered bite of toast to consult with a picture book she'd brought down that morning. I kept urging her to finish eating. "This is your eight-minute warning," I said to her, as if eight minutes meant anything.

I tried to line up everything for departure—the shoes, the coat, the backpack containing nothing but her lunch. *Do you have your car keys?* Yes. *Wallet?* Yes. *Phone?* Yes. Now only six minutes to go. The worry was a rising river swelling against its banks. In response to this time crunch, my daughter cautiously nibbled at a corner of the toast, like a mouse wary of poisoning. I wondered what else I could've done to make the toast more appetizing. I'd cut the crust off, and buttered it, and sprinkled it with cinnamon sugar. *For the love of God please eat your toast.* Now four minutes. *All right that's it we're out of time we need to put on your shoes.* And then at the pinnacle of my frenzy, Alice said to me, "Daddy, can I say a secret?"

I leaned in toward her and she cupped her hands over her mouth, and even though we were alone in the house, she whispered to me. I can't tell you what she said, of course, because it was a secret, but it wasn't a big deal or anything. What stopped me dead was the fact of her whisper. I had no idea she could whisper, or even that she knew what secrets were. What she said wasn't really about what she said. It was about reminding me that we were okay, that I didn't need to be Airport Alex. Being busy is a way of being loud. And what my daughter needed was quiet space, for her small voice to be heard.

In a whisper, the vocal cords don't vibrate, but air passes through the larynx with enough turbulence to be audible—at close range, anyway. And so whispers are definitionally intimate. All talking is made of breath, but when someone whispers you are hearing the breath. People sometimes whisper due to laryngitis or other disorders, but usually we whisper because we want to speak to one person without risking everyone hearing. We whisper secrets, yes, but also rumors and cruelties and fears.

Our species has probably been whispering since we began speaking—in fact, we aren't even the only animal to whisper. Some gophers do, as well as some monkeys, including the critically endangered cotton-top tamarin.

But I haven't been whispering much lately. In early March of 2020, my brother and I were performing a live version of our podcast in Columbus, Ohio. Just before I went on stage, our colleague Monica Gasper whispered something to me. She was reminding me which mic to pick up, I think. At any rate, I remember that moment because it was the last time I would hear a whisper from someone outside of my immediate family for . . . years? I suppose I've heard a whisper or two over video or phone chat during the pandemic, but not many of them. I miss the whisper. I was a germophobe long before the pandemic, and I know that another person's breath against my skin is a surefire sign of respiratory droplet transferal. But still, I miss it.

These days, when my kids whisper to me, it is usually to share a worry they find embarrassing or frightening. It takes courage even to whisper those fears, and I am so grateful when they trust me with them, even if I don't know quite how to answer. I want to say, "You don't have any cause for concern," but they do have cause for concern. I want to say, "There's nothing to be scared about," but there's plenty to be scared about. When I was a kid, I thought being a parent meant knowing what to say and how to say it. But I have no idea what to say or how to say it. All I can do is shut up and listen. Otherwise, you miss all the good stuff.

I give whispering four stars.

VIRAL MENINGITIS

I FIND IT DIFFICULT TO GRASP the size of viruses. As individuals, they are tiny: A red blood cell is about a thousand times bigger than a SARS-CoV-2 virus. But as a group, viruses are unfathomably numerous. There are about ten million viruses in a single drop of seawater. For every grain of sand on Earth, there are trillions of viruses. According to Philipp Dettmer's book *Immune*, there are so many viruses on Earth that "if they were laid end to end, they would stretch for 100 million light years—around 500 Milky Way galaxies put next to each other."[32]

Viruses are just single strands of RNA or DNA lying around. They can't replicate until and unless they find a cell to hijack. So they aren't alive, but they also aren't *not* alive. Once a virus invades a cell, it does what life does—it uses energy to make more of itself. Viruses remind me that life is more of a continuum than a duality. Sure, viruses aren't living, because they need host cells to replicate. But then again, many bacteria also can't survive without hosts, and stranger still, many hosts

---

32. Bacteriophages, viruses that parasitize bacteria, are among the most abundant and successful phenomena on our planet. As Nicola Twilley put it, "The battle between viruses and bacteria is brutal: Scientists estimate that phages cause a trillion trillion infections per second, destroying half the world's bacteria every forty-eight hours."

can't survive without bacteria. Cattle, for example, will die if deprived of the gut microbes that help them digest food. All life is dependent upon other life, and the closer we consider what constitutes living, the harder life becomes to define.

––––––––––

In 2014, a strand of RNA called an enterovirus invaded my meninges, the lining that covers my brain and spinal cord. As the virus used the machinery of my cells to make more of itself, those new viral particles invaded further cells. I soon became extremely sick. The symptoms of viral meningitis can vary, but they often include stiff neck, fever, nausea, and an unshakable belief that viruses are not merely unalive.

Also, there is the headache.

Virginia Woolf wrote in "On Being Ill" that it is "strange indeed that illness has not taken its place with love, battle, and jealousy among the prime themes of literature. Novels, one would have thought, would have been devoted to influenza; epic poems to typhoid; odes to pneumonia, lyrics to toothache. But no." She goes on to note, "Among the drawbacks of illness as matter for literature there is the poverty of the language. English, which can express the thoughts of Hamlet and the tragedy of Lear, has no words for the shiver and the headache."

Woolf had migraines, so she knew this poverty of language firsthand, but anyone who has ever been in pain knows how alone it can make you feel—partly because you're the only one in your pain, and partly because it is so infuriatingly and terrifyingly inexpressible. As Elaine Scarry argues in her book *The Body in Pain*, physical pain doesn't just evade language. It destroys language. When we are really hurting, after all, we can't speak. We can only moan and cry.

"Whatever pain achieves," Scarry writes, "it achieves in part through its unsharability, and it ensures this unsharability through its resistance to language." I can tell you that having meningitis involves headaches, but that does little to communicate the consciousness-crushing omnipresence of that headache. All I can say is that when I had viral meningitis, I had a headache that made it impossible to have anything else. My head didn't hurt so much as my self had been rendered inert by the pain in my head.

But I think it is impossible to communicate the nature and severity of such pain. As Scarry puts it, "To have great pain is to have certainty. To hear that another person has pain is to have doubt." Hearing about pain that we do not feel takes us to the limits of empathy, the place where it all breaks down. I can only know my pain, and you can only know yours. We've tried all sorts of ways to get around this axiom of consciousness. We ask patients to rate their pain on a scale of one to ten, or we tell them to point at the face that looks most like their pain. We ask them if the pain is sharp or dull, burning or stabbing—but all of these are metaphors, not the thing itself. We turn to feeble similes, and say that the pain is like a jackhammer at the base of the skull, or like a hot needle through the eye. We can talk and talk and talk about what the pain is *like*, but we can never manage to convey what it *is*.

Unlike meningitis caused by bacteria, viral meningitis is rarely fatal and usually resolves on its own within seven to ten days. This sounds like a reasonable period of time to be sick, until you're actually inside of it. Sick days do not pass like well ones do, like water through cupped hands. Sick days last. When I had the headache, I felt certain I would have it forever. The pain of each moment was terrible, but what made me despair was the knowledge that in the next moment, and the next, the pain would still be there. The pain is so entire that you begin to believe it will never end, that it cannot possibly end. Psychologists call this "catastrophizing," but that term fails to acknowledge that pain is a catastrophe. *The* catastrophe, really.

For many people, including me, the initial period of viral meningitis is followed by several months of occasional headaches, which arrive like the aftershocks of an earthquake. Over a year or so, my headaches grew more infrequent, and by now they've almost entirely subsided. I can hardly even remember what the headaches felt like. I remember that they were terrible, that they circumscribed my life, but I cannot return to my pain in any visceral or experiential way. Even though I myself had the pain, I can't fully empathize with the me who had it, because now I am a different me, with different pangs and discomforts. I am grateful that my head doesn't hurt, but not in the way I would have been grateful if, in the midst of the pain, it had suddenly disappeared. Maybe we forget so that we can go on.

I became sick with meningitis just after returning to Indianapolis from a trip where I visited both Ethiopia and Orlando, Florida. My neurologist told me I probably caught the virus in Orlando, because, and I'm quoting him here, "You know, Florida."

I spent a week in the hospital, although they couldn't do much other than keep me hydrated and treat my pain. I slept a lot. When I was awake, I was in pain. And I mean *in* pain. Inside of it.

Of course, aside from the fact that it doesn't usually kill you, there is nothing to recommend about viral meningitis. As Susan Sontag wrote, "Nothing is more punitive than to give a disease a meaning." The virus that spread through my spinal fluid had no meaning; it did not replicate to teach me a lesson, and any insights I gleaned from the unsharable pain could've been learned less painfully elsewhere. Meningitis, like the virus that caused it, wasn't a metaphor or a narrative device. It was just a disease.

But we are hardwired to look for patterns, to make constellations from the stars. There must be some logic to the narrative, some reason for the misery. When I was sick, people would say to me, "At least you're getting a break from all that work," as if I wanted a break from my work.

Or they'd say, "At least you'll make a full recovery," as if now was not the only moment that the pain allowed me to live inside. I know they were trying to tell me (and themselves) a tightly plotted and thematically consistent story, but there's little comfort to be found in such stories when you know damn well they aren't true.

When we tell those stories to people in chronic pain, or those living with incurable illness, we often end up minimizing their experience. We end up expressing our doubt in the face of their certainty, which only compounds the extent to which pain separates the person experiencing it from the wider social order. The challenge and responsibility of personhood, it seems to me, is to recognize personhood in others—to listen to others' pain and take it seriously, even when you yourself cannot feel it. That capacity for listening, I think, really does separate human life from the quasi-life of an enterovirus.

I give viral meningitis one star.

PLAGUE

THE OTHER DAY, in the midst of a global disease pandemic, I called my pharmacy to refill my Mirtazapine prescription. Mirtazapine is a tetracyclic antidepressant medication that is also used to treat obsessive-compulsive disorder. In my case, it is lifesaving. So anyway, I called my pharmacy only to learn the pharmacy had closed.

I then called a different pharmacy, and a very sympathetic woman answered. When I explained the situation, she told me everything would be fine, but they did need to call my doctor's office before refilling the prescription. She asked when I needed the medication, and I answered, "I guess in a perfect world, I'd pick it up this afternoon."

There was a pause on the other end of the line. At last, stifling a laugh, the woman said, "Well, hon, this ain't a perfect world." She then put me on hold while talking to the pharmacist, except she didn't actually put me on hold. She just put the phone down. And I heard her say to her colleague, "He said—get this—he said *in a perfect world* he'd pick it up today."

In the end I was able to pick up the prescription the following afternoon, and when I did so, the woman behind the counter pointed at me and said, "It's the perfect world guy." Indeed. It's me, the perfect world guy, here to regale you with a plague story—the only kind I find myself able to tell at the moment.

―――――――

In 2020, I read about almost nothing except pandemics. We often hear that we live in unprecedented times. But what worries me is that these times feel quite precedented. For humans, being in uncharted territory is often good news, because our charted territory is so riddled with disease, injustice, and violence.

Reading about cholera in the nineteenth century, for instance, one finds many precedents. Amid fear of the disease, misinformation was widespread and common: Cholera riots broke out in Liverpool as rumors spread that hospitalized patients were being killed so that doctors could have corpses to dissect.

Then, as in 2020, opposition to public health measures was rampant. One American observer wrote in the nineteenth century that isolation measures "embarrass with unnecessary restrictions the commerce and industry of the country."

Then, as in 2020, the rich abandoned cities en masse: As the wealthy fled New York amid the cholera outbreak of 1832, one newspaper wrote, "The roads, in all directions, were lined with well-filled stage coaches . . . all panic struck, fleeing from the city."

Then, as in 2020, outsiders and marginalized groups were blamed for spreading the illness. "By means of Irish vagrants from Sunderland, the cholera has been twice brought among us," read one English account.

Then, as in 2020, the poor were vastly more likely to die. In nineteenth-century Hamburg, the poorest people were nineteen times more likely to die of cholera than the richest people. This statistic has only worsened: In the twenty-first century, poor people are thousands of times more likely to die of cholera than rich people. Cholera kills at least ninety thousand people every year, even though there is a safe and effective vaccine and the disease is almost always survivable with proper fluid replenishment. Cholera continues to spread and kill not because we lack the tools to understand or treat the disease as we did two hundred years ago, but because each day, as a human community, we decide not to prioritize the health of people living in poverty. Like tuberculosis,[33] malaria, and many other infectious diseases, cholera is only successful in the twenty-first century because the rich world doesn't feel threatened by it. As Tina Rosenberg has written, "Probably the worst thing that ever happened to malaria in poor nations was its eradication in rich ones."

Disease only treats humans equally when our social orders treat humans equally. That, too, is precedented. After plague, caused by the bacterium *Yersinia pestis*, swept through England in the fourteenth century, one chronicler noted, "Virtually none of the lords and great men died in this pestilence."

In that pestilence, perhaps half of all humans living in Europe died between the years of 1347 and 1351. What was then usually called "the pestilence" or "the mortality" is now known as the Black Death, and this torrent of plague also devastated Asia, North Africa, and the Middle East. As the Egyptian historian al-Maqrizi noted, the plague "did not distinguish between one region and another."

Al-Maqrizi's hometown of Cairo was the world's largest city outside of China in 1340, with a population of around six hundred thousand. But at least a third of Cairo's residents died in an eight-month period beginning in the summer of 1348. The famous world traveler Ibn Battuta

---

33. Tuberculosis was the second deadliest infectious disease among humans in 2020, behind only Covid-19. More than 1.3 million people died of TB in 2020. The difference between TB and Covid is that more than a million people also died of TB in 2019, and in 2018, and in 2017, and so on, stretching back every year for hundreds of years. Like cholera, tuberculosis is almost always curable in communities with strong healthcare systems.

reported that at the height of the pestilence in the city of Damascus, 2,400 people died every day.

To many, it felt like the end of humanity had arrived. The historian Ibn Khaldūn wrote that it felt "as if the voice of existence in the world had called out for oblivion." In Christian communities, the devastation was seen as more final and total than even the Great Flood. The chroniclers of Padua wrote that at least "in the days of Noah, God did not destroy *all* living souls and it was possible for the human race to recover."

It's hard even to fathom the scope of the loss. Cities from Paris to London to Hamburg saw most of their residents die from the plague and resulting systemic collapses. In Dubrovnik, the death was so unrelenting that the government ordered every citizen to fill out a will. In Florence, a city of more than one hundred thousand people, one recent estimate concluded that about 80 percent of the city's population died in a four-month period. In Ireland, a Franciscan friar named John Clyn described life as "waiting amid death for death to come."

Near the end of his plague journal, Clyn wrote, "So that the writing does not perish with the writer, or the work fail with the workman, I leave [extra] parchment for continuing the work, in case anyone should still be alive in the future." Beneath that paragraph, a brief coda appears in different handwriting: "Here, it seems, the author died."

In Florence, Giovanni Villani wrote of the pestilence, "Many lands and cities were made desolate. And the plague lasted until . . ." and then he left a blank space that was never filled in, because he died of the plague before the plague ended.

To read about the Black Death is to glimpse how it may end with our species—in longing and despair and panic and also ineradicable hope, the kind of hope that makes you leave sentences unfinished and extra parchment in your book, in case anyone should still be alive in the future. As William Faulkner once put it, "It is easy enough to say that man is immortal simply because he will endure: that when the last dingdong of doom has clanged and faded from the last worthless rock hanging tideless in the last red and dying evening, that even then there will still be one more sound: that of his puny inexhaustible voice, still talking." Faulkner went on to argue that humans will not merely endure but will prevail, which these days feels a bit ambitious to me. I, for one, would be delighted to merely endure.

———————

The historian Rosemary Horrox wrote of the Black Death, "The very enormity of the disaster drove chroniclers to take refuge in clichés. . . . The same comments appear in chronicle after chronicle," and indeed, around the plague world, the stories become repetitive. We read, for instance, that corpses lay in the streets of Florence and overwhelmed the graveyards of France and choked the Nile River in Egypt. Chroniclers also focus on the suddenness of it all. One day, a single nun is sick; within a week, her whole community is dead. And the rituals around death must be changed. The bells are no longer tolled for the dead, because they would toll without ceasing. And as one writer put it, "the sick hated to hear them and it discouraged the healthy as well."

But for me, the most gutting repetition in plague accounts is the abandonment of the ill, who were often left to die alone due to fear of contagion, especially in Europe. After the poet Joy Davidman died in 1960, her widower C. S. Lewis wrote, "Nobody ever told me grief felt so like fear." But to grieve in a pandemic is to both grieve *and* fear. "For fear of infection," one writer noted, "no doctor will visit the sick, nor will the father visit the son, the mother the daughter, [or] the brother the brother. . . . And thus an unaccountable number of people died without any mark of affection, piety, or charity." In the Byzantine capital of Constantinople, Demetrios Kydones wrote, "Fathers do not dare to bury their own sons."

In fear of death and hope of survival, many left the sick to die alone.

To do otherwise was to risk your own life, and the lives of whatever loved ones you had left. The Black Death was vastly, incalculably different from our current pandemic—it was orders of magnitude deadlier and far less understood. But infectious disease continues to separate us in our most vulnerable moments. Too many of us, sick and healthy, were forced into isolation. Too many died apart from those they love, saying goodbye over video chat or a telephone line. In the *New England Journal of Medicine*, one physician wrote of a wife watching her husband die over FaceTime.

I think maybe that is the reason I cannot stop reading about pandemics. I am haunted by this separation. When I was sixteen, a friend of mine died. They died alone, which I found very difficult. I couldn't stop thinking about those last minutes, those lonely and helpless minutes. I still often have nightmares about this—where I can see this person and see the fear in their eyes, but I cannot get to them before they die.

I know that being with someone as they die doesn't lessen the pain, and in some cases can amplify it, but still, my mind keeps circling, vulture-like, around the extensively precedented tragedy of not being able to hold the hand of your beloved and say goodbye.

———————

When I worked at the children's hospital, I was just a kid myself—so skinny that in my powder-blue chaplain coat I looked like a boy wearing his dad's suit jacket. Those months of chaplaincy are the axis around which my life spins. I loved the work but also found it impossible—too much suffering that I could do nothing to alleviate.

But now, looking back on it, I try not to judge that twenty-two-year-old for being a bad chaplain, and I realize I did sometimes help, if only by holding someone's hand who otherwise would've been alone. That work left me permanently grateful to all those who do what they can to make sure the dying are accompanied for as long as possible on that last journey we're sure of.

During the Black Death, there were many such people—monks and nuns and physicians and nurses who stayed, offering prayers and comfort to the sick even though they knew such work was beyond dangerous. The same was true of cholera pandemics in the nineteenth century: According to Charles Rosenberg's *The Cholera Years*, in 1832, "at New York's Greenwich Hospital, fourteen of sixteen nurses died of cholera contracted while caring for patients." Then, as now, healthcare workers were often lauded for their heroism, but expected to perform their work with inadequate support, including a lack of clean gowns and gloves.

Most of the names of these accompaniers are lost to history, but among them was the physician Guy de Chauliac, who stayed in Avignon as the plague raged and continued to treat patients despite being, as he later wrote, "in continual fear." It is true that our current horrors are precedented. But so is our capacity for care.

The eighteenth-century historian Barthold Georg Niebuhr once wrote, "Times of plague are always those in which the bestial and diabolical side of human nature gains the upper hand." In Europe during the Black Death, the pestilence was widely blamed on Jewish people. Wild conspiracy theories emerged that Jewish people were poisoning wells or rivers, and after confessions were drawn out through torture, many thousands of Jews were murdered. Entire communities were burned to death, and the emotionless, matter-of-fact accounts of these murders are chilling. Heinrich Truchsess wrote, "First Jews were killed or burnt in Solden in November, then in Zofingen they were seized and some put on the wheel, then in Stuttgart they were all burnt. The same thing happened during November in Lansberg . . ."

It goes on like that, for paragraphs.

Many (including Guy de Chauliac) recognized that it was utterly impossible for a vast Jewish conspiracy to have spread the plague via well-poisoning. But facts still don't slow down conspiracy theories, and the long history of anti-Semitism in Europe predisposed people to believing in even the most absurd stories of poisoning. Pope Clement VI pointed out, "It cannot be true that the Jews . . . are the cause or occasion of the plague, because through many parts of the world the same plague . . . afflicts the Jews themselves and many other races who have never lived alongside them." Still, in many communities, the torture and murder continued, and anti-Semitic ideas about secret international conspiracies proliferated.

That is a human story. It is human in a crisis not just to blame marginalized people, but to kill them.

But to say that times of plague only bring out the bestial and diabolical side of human nature is too simplistic. It seems to me that we are making up "human nature" as we go along. "Very little in history is inevitable," Margaret Atwood wrote. To accept the demonization of the marginalized as inevitable is to give up on the whole human enterprise. What happened to the Jewish residents of Stuttgart and Lansberg and so many other places was not inevitable. It was a choice.

Amid the horrors of the Black Death, Ibn Battuta tells us a story of people coming together in the city of Damascus. He says that people fasted for three consecutive days, then "assembled in the Great Mosque until it was filled to overflowing . . . and spent the night there in prayers. . . . After the dawn prayers the next morning, they all went out together on foot, holding Qurans in their hands, and the amirs barefoot. The procession was joined by the entire population of the town, men and women, small and large; the Jews came with their Book of the Law and the Christians with their Gospel, all of them with their women and children. The whole concourse, weeping and seeking the favor of God through His books and His prophets, made their way to the Mosque of the Footprints, and there they remained in supplication and invocation until near midday. They then returned to the city and held the Friday service, and God lightened their affliction."

In Ibn Battuta's story, even the powerful went barefoot in a statement of equality, and all the people came together in prayer regardless of their religious background. Of course, whether this mass gathering really slowed the spread of the plague in Damascus is unclear—but we see in this account that crisis does not always bring out the cruelty within us. It can also push us toward sharing our pains and hopes and prayers, and treating each other as equally human. And when we respond that way, perhaps the affliction is lightened. While it is human nature to blame and demonize others in miserable times, it is also human nature to walk together, the leaders as barefoot as the followers.

The residents of Damascus left us a model for how to live in this precedented now. As the poet Robert Frost put it, "The only way out is through." And the only good way through is together. Even when circumstances separate us—in fact, especially when they do—the way through is together.

I am highly suspicious of attempts to brightside human suffering, especially suffering that—as in the case of almost all infectious diseases—is unjustly distributed. I'm not here to criticize other people's hope, but personally, whenever I hear someone waxing poetic about the silver linings to all these clouds, I think about a wonderful poem by Clint Smith called "When people say, 'we have made it through worse before.'" The poem begins, "all I hear is the wind slapping against the gravestones / of those who did not make it." As in Ibn Battuta's Damascus, the only path forward is true solidarity—not only in hope, but also in lamentation.

My daughter recently observed that when it's winter, you think it will never again be warm, and when it's summer, you think it will never again be cold. But the seasons go on changing anyway, and nothing that we know of is forever—not even this.

Plague is a one-star phenomenon, of course, but our response to it need not be.

WINTRY MIX

THERE'S A KAVEH AKBAR POEM that begins, "it's been January for months in both directions," and it really has been. I can remember in the abstract how it feels to wear a T-shirt, to feel sweat dripping down the bridge of my nose as I pull weeds in the garden. But I cannot bring to mind the actual feeling of sun on my skin now, as I pull up the withered pepper and tomato plants, trying to keep my back to the lip-cracking wind. I should've done this months ago, when the temperatures were milder and the plants equally dead. But I put everything off, even the purported leisure of gardening.

For quite a while here in Indianapolis, the only answer to "Why is the sky blue?" has been that it isn't blue. I keep thinking about a line from a Mountain Goats song, "The gray sky was vast and real cryptic above me."

There's a phrase in literary analysis for our habit of ascribing human emotions to the nonhuman: the pathetic fallacy, which is often used to reflect the inner life of characters through the outer world, as when Keats in "Ode on Melancholy" writes of a "weeping cloud," or Shakespeare in *Julius Caesar* refers to "threatening clouds." Wordsworth writes of wandering "lonely as a cloud." In Emily Dickinson's poetry, sometimes the clouds are curious, other times mean. Clouds separate us from the sun when we need shade, but they also separate us from the sun when we need light. They are, like the rest of us, quite context-dependent.

I started gardening because my therapist recommended it. She said it might be helpful to me, and it has been. Although I am not a particularly good gardener (the average tomato I successfully harvest costs about seventeen dollars), I like having my hands in the dirt and watching seeds sprout. But the most valuable thing about gardening for me is that before I began growing vegetables, I always dreamt of having a proper nemesis, and now I have one. She is a groundhog—an astonishingly rotund groundhog that waddles into my garden whenever she pleases and eats a wide variety of crops, from soybeans to sweet peppers. Wikipedia tells me that groundhogs in the wild can expect to live six years at the most, but my nemesis has been alive and consuming the garden I cultivate for her for at least eight years.

She lives about twenty-five feet from the edge of the garden, beneath a tiny wooden shed where I store garden tools. Sometimes, I will watch from the deck off the back of my office as she digs beneath the fence my dad and I built to keep the groundhog out. I will shout at the groundhog from the lime-green Adirondack chair where I'm trying to write. I'll get out of the chair and start walking toward her, at which point she will look up toward me with absolute disdain before moseying back beneath the fence to her home.

And then five or ten minutes later, I'll look up and see her enjoying soybeans. She knows I am unwilling to kill her, and she knows I lack the intelligence to groundhog-proof the garden, and so she lives on into an impossible old age, eating a wondrous array of fresh, organic fruits and vegetables.

You need a sense of purpose to get through life. The groundhog has given me one. But now, it is winter, early 2020, and she is hibernating. It has been January for months in both directions, and I, of course, do not know what is coming.

As I belatedly haul the tomato cages and beanpoles out of the garden and into the shed, I make sure to stomp quite loudly in the hopes of disturbing the groundhog's slumber. It takes forever to stack the tomato cages with my half-numb fingers, and I'm cursing and muttering to myself about how if I'd only done this in November, I wouldn't be here.

Then why not just put it off longer, I ask myself. *Why not just go home and make some coffee and watch something empty and delicious on TV while the kids run heavy-footed around the house?* Because I wanted time to myself, and at my age, this is how you get it.

When I finish stacking the tomato cages, I walk back to the garden. It begins to spit frozen rain—or not exactly frozen rain. Here in Indianapolis, there is a common weather phenomenon known as "wintry mix." Precipitation will shift from sleet to snow to rain and then back again. Sometimes we get these weird tiny pellets of snow called graupel.[34]

Snow is beautiful, almost ridiculously picturesque as it wafts down and blankets the ground, bringing with it a beatific quiet. Wintry mix is radically unromantic, as nicely captured by the word *graupel*. Wintry mix is a thoroughly Midwestern form of precipitation: practical, unlovely, and unpretentious.

As I pile withered bean bushes into the wheelbarrow, I feel like the sky is spitting on me. I think of Wilson Bentley, the amateur photographer from Vermont who became the first person to take a close-up photograph of a snowflake in 1885. Bentley went on to photograph more

---

34.   The word *graupel* is taken from the German word for sleet. English-language meteorologists used to call this kind of precipitation "soft hail," but eventually abandoned the term on account of how graupel is neither soft nor hail.

than five thousand snowflakes, which he called "ice flowers" and "tiny miracles of beauty."

Nobody ever called graupel a tiny miracle of beauty, and obviously, I don't love being pelted by tiny balls of freezing rain or having sleet lash at me from seemingly impossible angles as it blows across the flat and unbroken misery of an Indiana field. And yet . . . I do kind of like wintry mix. It's one of the ways I know that I'm home.

I love Indianapolis precisely because it isn't easy to love. You have to stay here a while to know its beauty. You have to learn to read the clouds as something more than threatening or dreary. The words "pathetic fallacy" sound derogatory, and the phrase was originally intended as such when coined by the critic John Ruskin. Of Romantic poets like Scott and Wordsworth, Ruskin wrote, "The love of nature is more or less associated with their weakness." He would go on to claim that endowing nature with emotion "is always the sign of a morbid state of mind, and comparatively a weak one."[35]

Maybe it's owing to my comparatively weak and morbid state of mind, but the pathetic fallacy often works for me. I like it when Wordsworth wanders lonely as a cloud, or when Scott writes of nature having a "genial glow." Many of us really are affected by the weather, especially in the slimly lit days of winter. The weather may not have human emotions, but it does cause them. Also, we can't help but see the world around us in the context of ourselves, especially our emotional selves. That's not a bug of human consciousness, but a feature of it.

---

35.   Ruskin's obsession with strength and weakness in poetry (and the assumption that strength is inherently better than weakness, which in my opinion is a fundamental misunderstanding of the human situation) serves as a stark reminder that the forces of colonialist thinking in English literature stretched so deep into everything that there's no separating—there or anywhere—art from ideology.

And so, yes, of course precipitation is utterly indifferent to us. As e. e. cummings put it, "the snow doesn't give a soft white / damn Whom it touches." And yes, how grateful we are to the modernists for knocking down our doors to inform us that clouds do not threaten or weep, that the only verb a cloud ever verbed was to be. But *we* give a soft white damn whom snow touches.

––––––––––

Walking the wheelbarrow full of dead, uprooted plants toward our compost pile, I remember a snippet of an Anne Carson poem. "The first snows of winter / floated down on his eyelashes and covered the branches around him and silenced / all trace of the world." But there is no silence here in the land of wintry mix, only the cacophonous tit-a-tat white noise of graupel bombarding the ground.

The groundhog sleeps through it all. When she gets going in late March, she'll feel the same, and I will feel different. The month the groundhog wakes up, Sarah's book tour will be canceled. Our kids' schools will close. We will be separated from friends and family for what, at first, we think might be four weeks, or even eight.

I will suddenly become far more interested in the garden than I've ever been, and that spring I will learn of a solution to the great groundhog war from watching, of all things, a YouTube video. It turns out that I am not the only person to be locked in conflict with a groundhog, and another gardener suggests a radical solution that works perfectly. I till a patch of soil by the shed, and when I am done planting soybean seeds in my garden, I plant some in the groundhog's garden. The same with the peppers and the beans.

––––––––––

Beginning that March, I will be outside all the time, every day, ravenous for the normalcy that I can only feel outdoors, where nature proceeds apace. I will begin to understand for the first time in my life that I am not just made for Earth, but also of it.

But we are not there yet. The menacing Spring has not yet sprouted. I dump the dead plants into a compost pile, and return the wheelbarrow to the shed. That night, Sarah and I will listen to the poet Paige Lewis read. I love Lewis's book *Space Struck* for many reasons, but especially because the poems give voice and form to the anxiety that dominates so much of my life, the panic of threatening clouds and scornful groundhogs. In one poem, Lewis writes of a narrator who feels

> *as if I'm on the moon listening to the air hiss*
> *out of my spacesuit, and I can't find the hole. I'm*

> *the vice president of panic, and the president is*
> *missing.*

In March of 1965, the cosmonaut Alexei Leonov exited the Mir space capsule and became the first human being to float freely[36] in space. At the end of this first spacewalk, Leonov discovered that his space suit had expanded in the vacuum of space, and he could not squeeze back into the capsule. His only choice was to open a valve in the space suit and let the air within seep into space, which shrank the suit enough that he could squeeze back into his spaceship just before his oxygen ran out. Nature is indifferent to us, but surely it did not feel that way to Alexei Leonov as he felt the air leak out and the void rush in.

I don't believe we have a choice when it comes to whether we endow the world with meaning. We are all little fairies, sprinkling meaning dust everywhere we go. This mountain will mean God, and that precipitation

------

36. Everyone's keen on freedom until you are floating in the absolute freedom of outer space with forty-five minutes of air inside your space suit.

will mean trouble. The vacuum of space will mean emptiness, and the groundhog will mean nature's scorn for human absurdity. We will build meaning wherever we go, with whatever we come across. But to me, while making meaning isn't a choice, the kind of meaning can be.

———

I came in from the garden. I took a shower, and the water prickled my frozen skin. I got dressed, parted my hair to the side with a comb, and drove with Sarah through a treacherous evening of wintry mix to the poetry reading. We talked about her book, and about our kids. After a while, she turned the radio on. On another night, the same weather would've been threatening or menacing or joyless. But not tonight. What you're looking at matters, but not as much as how you're looking or who you're looking with. That night, I was with just the right person in just the right place, and I'll be damned if the graupel wasn't beautiful.

I give wintry mix four stars.

THE HOT DOGS OF

BÆJARINS BEZTU PYLSUR

IN THE SUMMER OF 2008, Sarah and I traveled to Europe with another couple, our friends Laura and Ryan. I like Laura and Ryan a lot, but one thing you need to know is that they are the sort of people who really try to suck the marrow out of life and make the most of their brief flicker of consciousness and all that stuff. This is quite different from my style of traveling, wherein I spend most of the day psyching myself up to do one thing—visit a museum, perhaps—and the rest of the day recovering from the only event on my itinerary.

The trip took us from Denmark to Sweden and then on to Iceland, a small and mostly rocky island nation in the North Atlantic that attracts tourists primarily by offering free stopovers to anyone who flies Iceland's national airline, Icelandair. I was interested in visiting Iceland because 1. It has a population under four hundred thousand, and I've long been fascinated by tiny nations and how they make it work, and 2. My long-time publisher Julie Strauss-Gabel is a frequent visitor to Iceland and had vociferously recommended a certain hot dog stand in Reykjavík.[37]

---

37.   Julie has been my editor for almost twenty years now, and has edited all of my books, including this one. She is also one of my closest friends. The reason she had occasion to visit Iceland frequently was because of the children's TV show *Lazy Town*, which was filmed in Iceland, and which costarred Julie's husband, the puppeteer David Feldman.

The trips to Sweden and Denmark had been lovely. There were smorgasbords and museums, but the highlight had been an evening spent with Ryan's Swedish relatives, who lived on the shores of some endless lake in the wilderness. They welcomed us to their home and proceeded to get us blisteringly, unprecedentedly drunk on Sweden's national liquor, brännvin. I do not often drink to excess, because I have an intense fear of hangovers, but I made an exception that evening. Ryan's relatives taught us Swedish drinking songs, and they taught us how to eat pickled herring, and my glass kept getting filled with brännvin until at last the eighty-year-old patriarch of the family stood up and spoke his first English words of the evening: "UND NOW VEE SAUNA!"

So we got in the sauna and I was so drunk that I was pouring cold beer over my head to stay cool in the sauna, and then after a while Sarah and I stepped outside and walked knee-deep into the lake. The eighty-year-old patriarch whose name was I think Lasse joined us, and he was standing there completely nude, next to the ridiculously modest Americans in their bathing suits. And then Lasse clapped me on the back in what was intended to be a firm gesture of camaraderie. Unprepared for the strength of his embrace, I fell face-first into the lake. I was uninjured but my glasses were thoroughly and irreparably scratched from an encounter with the rocks in the lake bed. The next morning I woke up reminded that my abject fear of hangovers is fully warranted, and also unable to see much on account of the gouged glasses.

By the time we arrived in Reykjavík, Iceland, two days later, I was still hungover, which for me always means a sour churning in the left side of my abdomen combined with a general desire to dissolve into the landscape. This is the real crux of a hangover for me—alcohol consumption increases my vulnerability to despair. I understood that it was only the hangover talking, but the hangover does talk rather loudly.

Hangovers also make me quite sensitive to light, which would've been a problem except that it was a hideously gray morning when we landed in Reykjavík, not just overcast but misty. It was one of those days where you realize that "sky" is just another human construct, that the sky starts wherever the ground ends. Sky isn't just something way up out there, but also something that your head is swimming in all the time.

We took a taxi from the airport into the city of Reykjavík, Iceland's largest (and really only) city. The cab driver was listening to some kind of Icelandic talk radio that was turned up entirely too loud, and I was squeezed between Sarah and Laura in the backseat. As we entered the city, I was struck mostly by its eerie silence. There was not a single person out on the streets, even though the weather wasn't *that* bad. It was a Friday in summer, and I had imagined a small city where people walked all day to the butcher and the baker and the candlestick maker or whatever. Instead, the town was utterly still.

About four blocks from our hotel, the cab driver said, "This is good." He stopped and asked us to pay him. We expressed an interest in his driving us all the way to our hotel, but he said, "No, it is too much. It is too, what do you say, too much stress."

From my perspective, it didn't seem *too* stressful to drive on these empty streets, but whatever, I'm not an expert in Icelandic driving. We got out of the cab and began wheeling our suitcases down a wide, abandoned sidewalk in central Reykjavík. What I remember most is the sound of our suitcase wheels on the sidewalk's stone tiles, the noise overwhelming amid such silence.

And then, from nowhere and everywhere, simultaneously, came a shout followed by a groan. The entire city, hidden somewhere inside the buildings all around us, seemed to have made the exact same noise at the exact same moment.

"That was weird," Ryan said, and we began speculating on why the city was locked down. Maybe there'd been some kind of weather threat that tourists weren't made aware of. Maybe it was a national indoor holiday.

"Maybe," Laura said, "they're all watching the same thing on TV?"

And at that moment, the city's silence burst apart. A tremendous roar erupted all around us. People poured out of every doorway—out of homes and stores and bars, and into the streets. They were screaming in exaltation, all of them, yelling, "YYYAAAAAAAAAA!" Many of them had their faces painted in the colors of the Icelandic flag, and quite a lot of them were openly weeping. A tall fellow around my age picked me up and held me up to the sky like I was Simba in *The Lion King* and then embraced me as he wept. Someone draped a scarf around Ryan's neck.

"What the hell is happening?" Sarah asked, with her trademark precision.

Beers were handed around. We took some. The initial chaos of screaming soon organized itself into song, songs that were apparently very emotional, because everyone except for us was crying as they sang in the streets. Some people had to sit down on the curbs in order to sob properly. The crowd continued to swell. There are 120,000 people in Reykjavík, and they were all on the streets, all seemingly on *this* street. Making it to our hotel was an impossibility now. We were in the throng, amidst some great wave of human experience, and all we could hope for was to hold on to our suitcases. As one song ended and everyone began to shout again, I decided to try it myself. I lifted my unopened can of beer into the air and shouted "YAAAAAAA!" Although I did not know what we were celebrating, I felt exultant. I loved Iceland. I loved Reykjavík. I loved these people, whose tears and sweat smudged their red, white, and blue face paint.

Eventually, we were able to ascertain that Iceland had just secured its first-ever team Olympic medal, in the sport of men's handball. I found myself wondering what event in my home country might lead to such shared celebrations. Cities celebrate when their teams win the World Series or the Super Bowl, but the only time I'd seen any public celebrations of a national event was in 1999, when the U.S. Women's National Soccer Team won the World Cup. I was living in the small town of Moose Pass, Alaska, that summer, working at a cafe. My colleagues and I were watching the game on a tiny TV in the corner of the shop, and after Brandi Chastain scored the winning penalty kick, I heard horns honking, and then a couple of minutes later, a single voice from somewhere in Moose Pass shouted, "FUCK YES AMERICA!"

I didn't know much about men's team handball,[38] but I am willing to get excited about almost anything in sports, and by the time we got to the hotel a couple of hours later, I considered myself a die-hard fan of Icelandic men's team handball. I wanted to rest in the hotel and perhaps watch some highlights—the excitement of my beloved team winning an Olympic medal had exhausted me—but my compatriots insisted that we go out and soak in some Icelandic culture.

The crowd had thinned considerably, and it was still early in the day, so we visited a museum where we learned that because the Icelandic language has changed so little over the centuries, their classic sagas read like contemporary literature. We saw the chess table where Bobby Fischer defeated Boris Spassky in 1972. Later, we took a tour bus trip to the island's interior, where endless plains of volcanic rock make it feel like you're on another planet. Our tour guide extolled Iceland's many virtues. "In Greenland it is always icy," she said, "but here in Iceland the weather is quite mild. They should call Iceland Greenland and Greenland Iceland." Then we all got out of the bus to observe a waterfall. It was fifty degrees Fahrenheit in August, and a cold rain was blowing at us horizontally, rendering umbrellas utterly useless.

Shouting to be heard over the wind, the tour guide said, "ICELAND

---

38.   It is one of the only Olympic sports that the U.S. does not regularly participate in (we have not fielded a team since 1996), so it is rarely on American TV.

HAS MANY NATURAL WONDERS AS YOU CAN SEE THIS WATERFALL IS VERY HISTORIC." Even now, I cannot look at a waterfall without thinking, "Very historic."

When we returned to the hotel around six, sopping wet and bone cold, I begged my friends for a quiet night in. We'd done so much. Couldn't we just order room service and watch some handball highlights and go to bed? But no. The marrow had to be sucked out of life, and so I reluctantly followed my wife and friends out into what would've been the evening, except that in summertime Reykjavík, the sun doesn't set until after ten.

We walked to Bæjarins Beztu Pylsur, that hot dog stand Julie recommended, and stood in a surprisingly short line outside a small building decorated with an anthropomorphic frankfurter wearing a chef's hat. I'd been told to order "one with everything," and I did—a hot dog with remoulade, sweet mustard, and bits of fried onion. The hot dogs at Bæjarins Beztu Pylsur are famous—they are featured in travel guides and TV shows. Bæjarins Beztu Pylsur has been rated on a five-star scale by thousands of Google users, and like anything that has become exceedingly popular, there is widespread backlash. Many reviews point out that this is, after all, just a hot dog. "Nothing too special," one wrote. "Not that good had better at a gas station," reported a visitor named Doug.

Like Doug, I am often disappointed by much-hyped culinary experiences, perhaps because of the weight of expectation, and perhaps because I just don't like food that much. And yet, I found the hot dog at Bæjarins Beztu Pylsur not just worthy of the hype but, if anything, underappreciated. I don't even particularly *like* hot dogs, but that hot dog was among the most joyous culinary experiences of my life.

A few months later, in the fall of 2008, an economic recession would sweep the globe, and Iceland would be among the nations hardest hit, with its currency declining in value by 35 percent in just a few months.

As the recession took hold and credit markets froze, experts said we were experiencing a once-in-a-lifetime economic contraction, although as it happened, the next once-in-a-lifetime economic contraction was only twelve years away. We should get out of the habit of saying that anything is once-in-a-lifetime. We should stop pretending we have any idea how long a lifetime is, or what might happen in one.

And yet, I strongly suspect that our long day in Iceland really was once-in-a-lifetime. On the chilly summer day Iceland secured their first-ever summer Olympics team medal, I ate a hot dog while huddled with my friends. It was the greatest hot dog I've ever eaten. It cured my multiday hangover and cleared the film from my eyes and sent me out into the Reykjavík twilight feeling the kind of close-to-the-chest joy that can't last—but also doesn't need to.

I give Bæjarins Beztu Pylsur five stars.

THE NOTES APP

THE IOS NOTES APP DEBUTED with the first iPhone in 2007. Back then, the app's default font looked vaguely like handwriting, and had a yellow background with horizontal lines between each row of text, an attempt to call to mind the yellow legal pads of yore. Even now, the Notes app has a slightly textured background that mimics paper, an example of what's called skeuomorphic design, where a derivative object—say, an app—retains now-obsolete elements of the original object's design. Casino slot machines, for instance, no longer need a pullable arm, but most still have one. Many mobile device apps use skeuomorphic design—our calculator apps are calculator-shaped; our digital watches have minute and hour hands, and so on. Perhaps all of this is done in the hopes that we won't notice just how quickly everything is changing.

For most of my life, I took notes in the margins of whatever book I happened to be reading. I've never been the kind of person to carry a notebook. I *want* to be a person who journals, who sits on park benches and has wonderful thoughts that must be immediately captured. But I usually found that my thoughts could wait, and if for some reason I needed to scribble something down, I always had a book with me, and a pen in my pocket.

There is a grocery list in my copy of *Song of Solomon*, and directions to my great-aunt's house in *The Amazing Adventures of Kavalier and Clay*. On page 241 of *All the King's Men*, I wrote at the bottom of the page, "It rains for two days straight," an idea I had for the plot of my first novel, *Looking for Alaska*. There are many other references to my stories in books I was reading. Sometimes it's only a few words: *FERAL HOG HUNT*, scrawled in the margins of *Our Southern Highlanders*, became part of the climactic scene in my book *An Abundance of Katherines*.

Usually, though, my marginalia just baffles me. On page 84 of my copy of *Jane Eyre*, why did I write, "You have never been so lonely"? Was I even the *you* of that sentence? The note depends on a context I now lack. When I think back to reading *Jane Eyre* for the first time in college, I don't remember being lonely or whatever else was happening in my daily life. I mostly remember Jane herself, how Rochester called her "my sympathy," how Jane said the way to avoid hell was "to keep in good health and not die."

I first got an iPhone in 2008, but I was slow to abandon my book-margin note-taking. I didn't write in the Notes app until 2010. But not long after, I found that I was often leaving home without a pen in my pocket, and eventually I'd often leave home without a physical book in my hand. The problem of having neither pen nor paper was both caused and solved by the iPhone.[39]

Having a digital library and a note-taking device in my pocket at all times did not make my notes-to-self any more comprehensible. Why, for instance, did I write in 2011, "They're painting the ceiling of the Rijksmuseum"? Were they painting the ceiling of the Rijksmuseum? Or did I think that was a good line for a story? I have no idea. But I can still parse some of the notes, and taken together they do form a strange kind

---

39.   It occurs to me that technology often brags about solving problems it created.

of autobiography, a way into knowing myself through the lens of what I cared about. Beginning in 2020, I adopted a different note-taking app, leaving Apple's Notes behind. The Notes app is now, like the marginalia in that old copy of *Jane Eyre*, a series of relics. Here is one note I wrote for each year of my life with the Notes app.

———————

2019: "Send Manguso quote to Sarah." More than a dozen of my notes are reminders to send Sarah something—a Donald Hall essay, the catalog for MOCA's Kerry James Marshall exhibition, or a joke Henry James wrote about adverbs ("the only qualification I really much respect"). I don't know how much of this stuff I ever actually shared with her, because things in the Notes app had a way of not getting done. I also don't know which Sarah Manguso quote I was referring to, but it may have been a passage about life in a psychiatric hospital from Manguso's book *Two Kinds of Decay:* "The ward was the only true community of equals I have ever lived in. What I mean is that we all knew we had already lived through hell, that our lives were already over, and all we had was the final descent. The only thing to do on the way down was to radiate mercy."

———————

2018: "Discontinuity of tense and perspective hallmark of your time." I have no idea what those words mean, but there they are, typed by me in March of 2018 with no further context.

———————

2017: "Driving alone at night is heartbreak without the agony." I had this thought while driving alone at night, and then I pulled over to write it down, which ruined the feeling.

———————

2016: "No bright line between imagination and memory." According to my Google calendar, when I wrote this I was at the home of my best friends, Chris and Marina Waters. I suspect Sarah probably said a version of that line in conversation, and then I stole it. At any rate, it ended up in my book *Turtles All the Way Down*, which is about a kid who is constantly remembering what she imagined and imagining what she remembers.

2015: "This bar has lights everywhere but you can't see anybody's face." I sometimes feel like I can't properly participate in conversation, because everything I say and hear has to drip through the sieve of my anxiety, and so by the time I understand what someone has just said to me and how I ought to respond, my laughter or whatever seems weirdly delayed. Knowing this will happen makes my anxiety worse, which in turn makes the problem worse. I sometimes deal with it by imagining myself not as part of great conversations but instead as a chronicler of them, so I pull out my phone and take some notes. "This bar has lights everywhere but you can't see anybody's face" is something a movie star's publicist said to my colleague Elyse Marshall when we were all at a hotel bar in Cleveland, Ohio. I liked the line a lot and I'll probably try to use it in a novel someday.

2014: "Strawberry Hill is not the luxury alcohol experience I remember it being." I wrote this after I'd had a bottle of Strawberry Hill, a four-dollar, bright pink, wine-like beverage made by Boone's Farm. I often drank Strawberry Hill in high school, and loved it then, but in the intervening years, either it has changed or I have.[40]

---

40.   One of my favorite sentences in the English language comes from a review of Strawberry Hill at the fan website boonesfarm.net: "Strawberry Hill has a rich, vibrant strawberry flavor with just a hint of hill."

———————

2013: "Fire fights fire." This phrase must have mattered to me, because I wrote it three separate times in the Notes app in 2013, but I have absolutely no idea what it meant. It's a small reminder now that memory is not so much a camera as a filter. The particulates it holds on to are nothing compared to what leaks through.

———————

2012: "Only line meant literally." One day I was at church, and the gospel reading included Matthew 19:24, which goes, "Again, I tell you, it is easier for a camel to go through the eye of a needle than for a rich man to enter the Kingdom of God." The minister said that people take every line of the Bible literally except for that one, when it is the only line that is meant literally.

———————

2011: "It was kind of a beautiful day—only saveable sentence." This one I remember quite vividly. I'd spent almost a year working on a novel about six high school students who end up stranded on a desert island. I was stuck with the story so I decided to take a couple weeks away from it and then reread it. When I returned to it with clear eyes, I found absolutely nothing—no heart, no wit, no joy. It had to be scrapped, except for that one sentence, "It was kind of a beautiful day." I still like that sentence, though. It ended up in *The Fault in Our Stars*.

———————

2010: "Her eyes on His eyes on." According to my phone, this was the first note I made in the app. I assume it was written when I first noticed the pun inside a lyric from my favorite band, the Mountain Goats. Their song "Jenny" is about a girl who has just acquired a yellow-and-black Kawasaki motorcycle, and the narrator who loves her. One of the song's couplets goes, "And you pointed your headlamp toward the horizon / We were the one thing in the galaxy God didn't have His eyes on." That line always reminds me of being in eleventh grade, lying in the middle of an open field with three friends I loved ferociously, drinking warm malt liquor, and staring up at the night sky.

Being the one thing in the galaxy God didn't have His eyes on gets a solid five stars from me, but as for the Notes app: I give it three and a half stars.

THE MOUNTAIN GOATS

I DON'T KNOW HOW TO TELL YOU about my love for the band the Mountain Goats except to say that it is genuinely unconditional. I do not have a favorite Mountain Goats song or album; they are all my favorites. Their songs have been my main musical companion since my friend Lindsay Robertson played me the song "The Best Ever Death Metal Band Out of Denton" half my life ago. Lindsay, who has the best taste of any person I've ever met, recommended I start my Mountain Goats journey by listening to their at-the-time new album, *Tallahassee*. (Like me, Lindsay grew up in Florida.)

Within a few weeks, I'd memorized every song on *Tallahassee*. John Darnielle, the band's front man, is, as music critic Sasha Frere-Jones put it, "America's best non-hip-hop lyricist." On *Tallahassee*, he presents love as I was then experiencing it: "Our love is like the border between Greece and Albania," he sings in "International Small Arms Traffic Blues." In another song, he sings of a relationship "like a Louisiana graveyard / Where nothing stays buried."

As I got older, the Mountain Goats grew with me. Their songs were with me when my kids were born ("I saw his little face contract as his eyes met light"), and they were with me as I spiraled out of control with grief ("I am an airplane tumbling wing over wing / Try to listen to my instruments / They don't say anything"). Sometimes, I need art to encourage me, as the Mountain Goats famously do in the chorus of "This Year," with Darnielle shouting, "I am going to make it through this year if it kills me." Other times, I only need art to accompany me.

The Mountain Goats have shaped the way I think and listen so profoundly that I don't know who I would be without them, only that I wouldn't be me. I don't want to overstate it, but there are moments in Mountain Goats songs that are almost scriptural to me, in the sense that they give me a guide to the life I want to live and the person I wish to be when I grow up. Consider, for instance, this couplet: "You were a presence full of light upon this Earth / And I am a witness to your life and to its worth. " That's a calling to me—to present more light, and to better witness the light in others.

I give the Mountain Goats five stars.

THE QWERTY KEYBOARD

ON MOST ENGLISH-LANGUAGE KEYBOARDS, the three rows of letter keys are not arranged alphabetically or by frequency of use. Indeed, the two most common letters in English—*e* and *t*—aren't among the so-called "home keys," where your fingers rest when typing. You've got to reach for them up on the top row, where the letters, from left to right, begin Q W E R T Y. The reasons for this involve typewriter mechanics, a militant vegetarian, and a Wisconsin politician who belonged to three different political parties in the span of eight years.

I love a straightforward story of inventors and their inventions. In fifth grade, I wrote my first-ever work of nonfiction on the life of Thomas Edison. It begins, "Thomas Alva Edison was a very interesting person who created many interesting inventions, like the light bulb and the very interesting motion picture camera." I liked the word *interesting* because my biography had to be written by hand in cursive, and it had to be five pages long, and in my shaky penmanship, *interesting* took up an entire line on its own.

Of course, among the interesting things about Edison is that he did not invent either the light bulb or the motion picture camera. In both cases, Edison worked with collaborators to build upon existing inventions, which is one of the human superpowers. What's most interesting to me about humanity is not what our individual members do, but the kinds of systems we build and maintain together. The light bulb is cool and everything, but what's really cool is the electrical grid used to power it.

But who wants to hear a story about slow progress made through iterative change over many decades? Well, you, hopefully.

The earliest typewriters were built in the eighteenth century, but they were both too slow and too expensive to be mass-produced. Over time, the expansion of the Industrial Revolution meant that more precision metal parts could be created at lower costs, and by the 1860s, a newspaper publisher and politician in Wisconsin, Christopher Latham Sholes, was trying to create a machine that could print page numbers onto books when he started to think a similar machine could type letters as well.

Sholes was a veteran of Wisconsin politics—he'd served as a Democrat in the Wisconsin state senate before joining the Free Soil Party, which sought to end legal discrimination against African Americans and to prevent the expansion of slavery in the U.S. Sholes later became a Republican and is most remembered today as a vocal opponent of capital punishment. He led the way toward Wisconsin abolishing the death penalty in 1853.

Working with his friends Samuel Soule and Carlos Glidden, Sholes set out to build a typewriter similar to one he'd read about in the magazine *Scientific American*, which described a "literary piano." They initially built their typewriter with two rows of keys—ebony and ivory, just like the piano—and a mostly alphabetical key layout.

At the time, there were many typewriting machines using many different key layouts and design strategies, which speaks to one of the great challenges of our sprawling, species-wide collaborations: standardization.

Learning a new key layout every time you get a new typewriter is wildly inefficient.[41]

The Sholes typewriter was a so-called "blind writer," meaning you couldn't see what you were typing as you typed it. This meant you also couldn't tell when the typewriter had jammed, and the alphabetical layout of the keys led to lots of jams. But it's not clear these jams were the driving force behind changing the key layout. Koichi and Motoko Yasuoka make a compelling argument in their paper "On the Prehistory of QWERTY" that the layout was not driven by jams but by the needs of telegraph operators translating Morse code.

Regardless, both telegraph operators and stenographers helped shape the eventual keyboard layout, as did a huge array of other collaborators, including Thomas Edison, who offered advice on the typewriter. Sholes, Soule, and Glidden also relied upon outside investors, most notably Sholes's old friend James Densmore. Densmore was a passionate vegetarian who survived primarily on raw apples and was known for getting into arguments at restaurants whenever he overheard a stranger ordering a meat dish. He also cut his pants several inches above the ankle for comfort, and he happened to have a brother, Amos, who studied letter frequency and combinations in English. According to some reports, Amos advised the typewriter makers on the keyboard layout.

Beta-testing stenographers and telegraph operators were told by Densmore to give the typewriters "a good thrashing. Find its weak spots." As the beta testers thrashed away, Sholes and colleagues refined the machines until by November of 1868, the typewriter used a four-row keyboard in which the top row began A E I . ?. By 1873, the

---

41. Lack of standardization often hampers productivity. Railroad gauge size is a famous example of the phenomenon, but the one that enters my life most often is charger cables for portable electronic devices. Some of my devices use USB-C charging cables; others use USB-A or mini-USB or micro-USB. And then there's whatever charging standard Apple is using at the moment. Apple has abandoned so many standards over the past decade that it's a blessed miracle they still make computers with QWERTY keyboard layouts.

four-row layout began Q W E . T Y. That year, the gun manufacturer
Remington and Sons bought the rights to the Sholes and Glidden typewriter—with the U.S. Civil War over, Remington wanted to expand
outside of firearms. Engineers at Remington moved the R to the top
row of the typewriter, giving us more or less the same key layout we
have today.

The QWERTY layout wasn't invented by one person or another,
but by many people working together. Incidentally, Sholes himself found
the key layout unsatisfactory and continued to work on improvements
for the rest of his life. A few months before his death, he sought a patent
for a new keyboard where the top row of letter keys began X P M C H.

But it was QWERTY that hung around, in part because the Remington 2 typewriter became very popular, and in part because it's a good
keyboard layout. There have been many attempts to improve upon
QWERTY in the years since its introduction, but none made a big
enough difference to shift the standard. The best-known purportedly
easier typing layout is the Dvorak Simplified Keyboard, created in 1932
by August Dvorak, which features A O E U on the left-side home
keys. Some studies found that Dvorak's layout improved typing speed
and lowered error rates, but many of those studies were paid for by
Dvorak, and more recent scholarship has shown little if any benefit to
the Dvorak, or any other purportedly optimized keyboard layout.

The QWERTY keyboard—partly by accident—is pretty good at
alternating hands within words, which means that one hand can be
reaching for a key while the other hand is typing. It's not perfectly efficient—the most common keys are typed by the left hand, whereas most
people type slightly faster and more accurately with their right hands—
but for most of us, most of the time, QWERTY works.

It has certainly worked for me. In elementary school, I had terrible
handwriting (hence it taking an entire line of notebook paper to write
the word *interesting* in cursive). No matter how hard I tried to hold the

pencil steady, I just couldn't write well. But even as a kid, I was a hell of a typist. Typing on a QWERTY keyboard was one of the first things I ever became good at, initially because I wanted to play the text-based video games of the 1980s, but eventually because I liked the feeling of excellence. By sixth grade I could type eighty words a minute. These days, I can type as fast as I can think. Or maybe, since I've spent so much of my life thinking through typing, my brain has learned to think at the speed of my typing, just as my brain has learned to think of the alphabet as beginning Q-W-E-R-T-Y.

The keyboard is my path to having thoughts, and also my path to sharing them. I can't play an instrument, but I can bang on this literary piano, and when it's going well, a certain percussive rhythm develops. Sometimes—not every day, certainly, but sometimes—knowing where the letters are allows me to feel like I know where the words are. I love the sound of pressing keys on a great keyboard—the technical term is "key action"—but what I love most about typing is that on the screen or on the page, my writing is visually indistinguishable from anyone else's.

As a kid on the early internet, I loved typing because no one could know how small and thin my hands were, how scared I was all the time, how I struggled to talk out loud. Online, back in 1991, I wasn't made of anxious flesh and brittle bone; I was made out of keystrokes. When I could no longer bear to be myself, I was able to become for a while a series of keys struck in quick succession. And on some level, that's why I'm still typing all these years later.

So even though it isn't a perfect keyboard layout, I still give the QWERTY keyboard four stars.

THE WORLD'S LARGEST
BALL OF PAINT

I DON'T LABOR UNDER THE DELUSION that the United States is an exemplary or even particularly exceptional nation, but we do have a lot of the world's largest balls. The world's largest ball of barbed wire is in the U.S., as is the world's largest ball of popcorn, and the world's largest ball of stickers, and the world's largest ball of rubber bands, and so on. The world's largest ball of stamps is in Omaha, Nebraska—it was collected by the residents of the orphanage known as Boys Town.

I visited the ball of stamps twenty years ago, on a road trip with a girlfriend during which we crisscrossed the country seeking out roadside attractions. Our relationship was falling apart, and so we sought a geographical cure. We visited Nebraska's Carhenge, an exact replica of Stonehenge built out of junked cars, and South Dakota's Corn Palace, a massive structure with a facade made primarily of corn kernels. We also visited several of the world's largest balls, including both the world's largest ball of twine rolled by one person in Darwin, Minnesota, and the world's largest ball of twine rolled by a community in Cawker City, Kansas.[42] We broke up soon after, but we'll always have Cawker City.

---

42.   Perhaps it says all you need to know about America that these are not the only competitors for the title World's Most Impressive Ball of Twine. There is also the world's largest ball of nylon twine, currently housed in Branson, Missouri, and the world's heaviest ball of twine, which is in Wisconsin.

There's an Emily Dickinson poem that begins, "I felt a Funeral, in my Brain." It's one of the only poems I've managed to commit to memory. It ends like this:

> *And then a Plank in Reason, broke,*
> *And I dropped down, and down -*
> *And hit a World, at every plunge,*
> *And Finished knowing - then -*

Several years ago, a plank in reason broke within me, and I dropped down and down, and hit a world at every plunge. It wasn't the first time this had happened, but precedent is cold comfort when you feel the funeral in your brain. As I struggled to recover, or at least slow the plunge, my thoughts drifted back to the road trips I'd taken, and I decided to try a geographical cure. I drove to see the world's largest ball of paint, which ended up kind of saving my life, at least for the time being.

I'm fascinated by roadside attractions because they are one place where we see the work of huge systems intersect with the work of tiny individuals. We have so many roadside attractions because we have so many roads—our interstate highway system is built to move lots of people across vast areas of land.[43] Once you're on an Interstate, it's easy to stay on it until you need gas or food. To tempt you away from the cruise-controlled straightforwardness of the American highway requires something extraordinary. Something unprecedented. The world's largest _____.

It's the system that makes the roadside attraction necessary, but individuals choose what to make and why. Consider, for example, Joel Waul,

---

43.   It's telling that in the U.S., world's largest balls did not really become a thing until after the highway system was built beginning in the 1950s.

creator of Megaton, the world's largest ball of rubber bands. When first constructing the ball, Waul wrote on his Myspace page, "First, have a definite, clear practical idea, a goal, an objective. Second, have the necessary means to achieve your ends. Third, adjust all means to that end. —Aristotle."[44] For Waul, the definite and clear and practical idea was to make the world's largest ball of rubber bands, which would eventually come to weigh over nine thousand pounds. I'm not sure why I find it beautiful to devote oneself obsessively to the creation of something that doesn't matter, but I do.

The world's largest ball of paint is located in the tiny town of Alexandria, Indiana. Back in 1977, Mike Carmichael painted a baseball with his three-year-old son. And then they kept painting it. Carmichael told Roadside America, "My intention was to paint maybe a thousand coats on it and then maybe cut it in half and see what it looked like. But then it got to the size where it looked kinda neat, and all my family said keep painting it." Carmichael also invited friends and family over to paint the ball, and eventually strangers started showing up, and Mike would have them paint it, too.

Now, over forty years later, there are more than twenty-six thousand layers of paint on that baseball. It weighs two and a half tons. It has its own little house, and every year more than a thousand strangers show up to add layers of paint to it. The whole thing is free to visit; Mike even provides the paint. He and his son both still add layers, but most of the painting is done by visitors.

———————

As a child, just as I imagined technological advances were driven primarily by the brilliant insights of heroic individuals laboring in isolation, I saw art as a story of individual geniuses.

Shakespeare or Leonardo da Vinci or whoever used their innate

---

44. Aristotle didn't actually write this, but the ideas are distilled from *Ethics*.

brilliance to expand the human landscape, and by studying the lives and work of these individuals, I could know all there is to know about how great art gets made. In school, whether I was studying history or math or literature, I was almost always taught that great and terrible individuals were at the center of the story. Michelangelo and his ceiling. Newton and the falling apple. Caesar crossing the Rubicon.

To be fair, I was sometimes taught that circumstance played a role in the emergence of greatness. When discussing *The Adventures of Huckleberry Finn* in high school, one of my teachers pointed out that in order for Mark Twain to become Mark Twain, he had to grow up along the river that separated twentieth-century America during the war that separated nineteenth-century America. But mostly I was taught, and believed, that important work was done not by the times or via massive collaboration, but by heroic and brilliant individuals.

I still believe in genius. From John Milton to Jane Austen to Toni Morrison, some artists are just . . . better. But these days, I see genius as a continuum rather than a simple trait. More to the point, I think the worship of individual genius in art and elsewhere is ultimately misguided. Isaac Newton did not discover gravity; he expanded our awareness of it in concert with many others at a time and in a place where knowledge was being built and shared more efficiently. Julius Caesar didn't become a dictator because he chose to cross the Rubicon River with his army; he became a dictator because over centuries, the Roman Republic became more reliant upon the success of its generals to fund the state, and because over time the empire's soldiers felt more loyalty to their military leaders than to their civilian ones. Michelangelo benefited not just from improved understandings of human anatomy, and not just from being Florentine at a time when Florence was rich, but also from the work of several assistants who helped paint parts of the Sistine Chapel.

The individuals we celebrate at the center of more recent revolutions were similarly positioned in times and places where they could contribute to faster microchips or better operating systems or more efficient keyboard layouts. Even the most extraordinary genius can accomplish very little alone.

I've often wished—especially when I was younger—that my work was better, that it rose to the level of genius, that I could write well enough to make something worth remembering. But I think that way of imagining art might make individuals too important. Maybe in the end art and life are more like the world's largest ball of paint. You carefully choose your colors, and then you add your layer as best you can. In time, it gets painted over. The ball gets painted again and again until there is no visible remnant of your paint. And eventually, maybe nobody knows about it except for you.

But that doesn't mean your layer of paint is irrelevant or a failure. You have permanently, if slightly, changed the larger sphere. You've made it more beautiful, and more interesting. The world's largest ball of paint looks nothing like the baseball it used to be, and you're part of the reason.

In the end, that's what art is for me. You paint the ball, which changes the way someone else thinks about painting the ball, and so on, until some guy overwhelmed with grief and dread drives out to Alexandria, Indiana, to see what beautiful foolishness thousands of people have made together, and feels a hope that cannot be explained or shared except by painting. That guy adds a layer of his own to the ball, one that won't last but still matters. Art is not only a genius going forth, as James Joyce put it, "to forge in the smithy of my soul the uncreated conscience of my race." Art is also picking a light blue for your layer of the world's largest ball of paint, knowing that it will soon be painted over, and painting anyway.

I give the world's largest ball of paint four stars.

SYCAMORE TREES

MY CHILDREN LIKE TO PLAY an age-old game with me called Why? I'll tell them, for instance, that I need them to finish breakfast, and they'll say, "Why?" And I'll say so that you receive adequate nutrition and hydration, and they'll say, "Why?" And I'll say because as your parent I feel obligated to protect your health, and they'll say, "Why?" And I'll say partly because I love you and partly because of evolutionary imperatives baked into my biology, and they'll say, "Why?" And I'll say because the species wants to go on, and they'll say, "Why?"

And I'll pause for a long time before saying, "I don't know. I guess I believe, in spite of it all, that the human enterprise has value."

And then there will be a silence. A blessed and beautiful silence will spread across the breakfast table. I might even see a kid pick up a fork. And then, just as the silence seems ready to take off its coat and stay awhile, one of my kids will say, "Why?"

When I was a teenager, I used the why game as a way of establishing that if you dig deep enough, there is no why. I reveled in nihilism. More than that, I liked being certain about it. Certain that everyone who believed life had inherent meaning was an idiot. Certain that meaning is just a lie we tell ourselves to survive the pain of meaninglessness.

A while back, my brain started playing a game similar to the why game. This one is called What's Even the Point.

There's an Edna St. Vincent Millay poem I've quoted in two of my novels and will now quote again, because I've never come across anything that describes my depressive blizzards so perfectly. "That chill is in the air," the poem begins, "Which the wise know well, and have even learned to bear. / This joy, I know, / Will soon be under snow."

I'm in an airport in late 2018 when suddenly I feel that chill in the air. What's even the point? I'm about to fly to Milwaukee on a Tuesday afternoon, about to herd with other moderately intelligent apes into a tube that will spew a truly astonishing amount of carbon dioxide into the atmosphere in order to transport us from one population center to a different one. Nothing that anyone has to do in Milwaukee really matters, because nothing really matters.

When my mind starts playing What's Even the Point, I can't find a point to making art, which is just using the finite resources of our planet to decorate. I can't find a point to planting gardens, which is just inefficiently creating food that will sustain our useless vessels for a little while longer. And I can't find a point to falling in love, which is just a desperate attempt to stave off the loneliness that you can never truly solve for, because you are always alone "way down in the dark which is you," as Robert Penn Warren put it.

Except it's not a darkness. It's much worse than that. When my brain plays What's Even the Point, what actually descends upon me is a blizzard of blinding, frozen white light. Being in the dark doesn't hurt, but this does, like staring at the sun. That Millay poem refers to "the eye's bright trouble." It seems to me that the bright trouble is the light you see the first time you open your eyes after birth, the light that makes you cry your first tears, the light that is your first fear.

What's even the point? All this trial and travail for what will become nothing, and soon. Sitting in the airport, I'm disgusted by my excesses, my failures, my pathetic attempts to forge some meaning or hope from the materials of this meaningless world. I've been tricking myself, thinking there was some reason for all of it, thinking that consciousness was a miracle when it's really a burden, thinking that to be alive was wondrous when it's really a terror. The plain fact, my brain tells me when it plays this game, is that the universe doesn't care if I'm here.

"Night falls fast," Millay wrote. "Today is in the past."

The thing about this game is that once my brain starts playing it, I can't find a way to stop. Any earnest defense I try to mount is destroyed instantaneously by the searing white light, and I feel like the only way to survive life is to cultivate an ironic detachment from it. If I can't be happy, I at least want to be cool. When my brain is playing What's Even the Point, hope feels so flimsy and naïve—especially in the face of the endless outrages and horrors of human life. What kind of mouth-breathing jackass looks at the state of human experience and responds with anything other than absolute despair?

I stop believing in the future. There's a character in Jacqueline Woodson's novel *If You Come Softly* who says that he looks into the future and sees only "this big blank space where I should be." When I think of the future, I start to only see the big blank space, the whyless bright terror. As for the present, it hurts. Everything hurts. The pain ripples beneath my skin, bone-shocking. What's the point of all this pain and yearning? *Why?*

Despair isn't very productive. That's the problem with it. Like a replicating virus, all despair can make is more of itself. If playing What's Even the Point made me a more committed advocate for justice or environmental protection, I'd be all for it. But the white light of despair instead renders me inert and apathetic. I struggle to do anything. It's hard to sleep, but it's also hard not to.

I don't want to give in to despair; I don't want to take refuge in the detached ridicule of emotion. I don't want to be cool if cool means being cold to or distant from the reality of experience.

Depression is exhausting. It gets old so fast, listening to the elaborate prose of your brain tell you that you're an idiot for even trying. When the game is being played, I feel certain it will never end. But that is a lie, like most certainties. Now always feels infinite and never is. I was wrong about life's meaninglessness when I was a teenager, and I'm wrong about it now. The truth is far more complicated than mere hopelessness.

————————

Believe. My friend Amy Krouse Rosenthal once told me to look at the word and be awed by it. See how it contains both *be* and *live*. We were eating lunch together, and after telling me about how much she liked the word *believe*, the conversation drifted off toward family or work, and then out of nowhere, she said, "Believe! Be live! What a word!"

Etymology dictionaries tell me that *believe* comes from Proto-Germanic roots meaning "to hold dear" or "to care." I like that almost as much as Amy's etymology. I must choose to believe, to care, to hold dear. I keep going. I go to therapy. I try a different medication. I meditate, even though I despise meditation. I exercise. I wait. I work to believe, to hold dear, to go on.

————————

One day, the air is a bit warmer, and the sky is not so blindingly bright. I'm walking through a forested park with my children. My son points out two squirrels racing up an immense American sycamore tree, its white bark peeling in patches, its leaves bigger than dinner plates. I think, *God, that's a beautiful tree*. It must be a hundred years old, maybe more.

Later, I'll go home and read up on sycamores and learn that there are sycamore trees alive today that date back more than three hundred years, trees that are older than the nation that claims them. I'll learn that George Washington once measured a sycamore tree that was nearly forty feet in circumference, and that after deserting the British Army in the eighteenth century, brothers John and Samuel Pringle lived for over two years in the hollowed-out trunk of a sycamore tree in what is now West Virginia.

I'll learn that twenty-four hundred years ago, Herodotus wrote that the Persian king Xerxes was marching his army through a grove of syca-more trees when he came across one of "such beauty that he was moved to decorate it with golden ornaments and to leave behind one of his soldiers to guard it."

But for now I'm just looking up at that tree, thinking about how it turned air and water and sunshine into wood and bark and leaves, and I realize that I am in the vast, dark shade of this immense tree. I feel the solace of that shade, the relief it provides. And that's the point.

My son grabs my wrist, pulling my gaze from the colossal tree to his thin-fingered hand. "I love you," I tell him. I can hardly get the words out.

I give sycamore trees five stars.

"NEW PARTNER"

HEARTBREAK is not really so different from falling in love. Both are overwhelming experiences that unmoor me. Both burst with yearning. Both consume the self. I *think* that's what the Palace Music song "New Partner" is about. But I'm not sure.

"New Partner" has been my favorite song not by the Mountain Goats for over twenty years now, but I've never been able to make sense of the lyrics. One couplet goes, "And the loons on the moor, the fish in the flow / And my friends, my friends still will whisper hello." I know that means something; I just don't know what. This is soon followed by a line equally beautiful and baffling: "When you think like a hermit, you forget what you know."

Palace Music is one of the many incarnations of Will Oldham, who sometimes records under his own name and sometimes as the dandyish Bonnie Prince Billy. I like a lot of his songs; he sings about religion and longing and hope in ways that resonate with me, and I love how his voice often seems on the edge of cracking open.

But "New Partner" is not just a song for me. It's a kind of magic, because it has the ability to transport me to all the moments I've heard that song before. For three minutes and fifty-four seconds, it makes me into people I used to be. Through the song I am brought back both to heartbreak and to falling in love with enough distance to see them as something more than opposites. In "The Palace," Kaveh Akbar writes that "Art is where what we survive survives," and I think that's true not only of the art we make, but also of the art we love.

Like any magic, you have to be careful with a magical song—listen to it too often, and it will become routine. You'll hear the chord changes before they come, and the song will lose its ability to surprise and teleport you. But if I'm judicious with a magical song, it can take me back to places more vividly than any other form of memory.

———————

I'm twenty-one. I'm in love, and I'm on a road trip to visit distant relatives of mine who live in and around the tiny town where my grandmother grew up. My girlfriend and I pull into a McDonald's parking lot in Milan, Tennessee, and then we stay in the car for a couple of minutes listening to the end of "New Partner."

It's spring, and we're driving south, and when we get out of the car after the song ends, we discover that our long-sleeve T-shirts are no longer necessary. I scrunch my sleeves up and feel the sun on my forearms for the first time in months. At the pay phone inside McDonald's, I call the number my mom has given me, and a quivering voice answers, "Hello?"

I explain that her cousin, Billie Grace, is my grandmother. The woman says, "Roy's daughter?" And I say yes. And she says, "You're saying you're kin to Billie Grace Walker," and I say yes, and she says, "So you're saying you're kin to me," and I say yes, and then my distant relative, Bernice, says, "Well, then come on over!"

———————

I'm twenty-two, working as a student chaplain at a children's hospital, newly and quite miserably single. I've just finished forty-eight consecutive hours on call. It's been a rough couple of days. Leaving the hospital, I can't believe how bright it is outside, or how alive the air feels. I get into my car and stare for a while at the parents and kids walking in and out. I play "New Partner" on my car's tape player.

A child had died for no reason the night before—sudden infant death syndrome, a disease that in its name acknowledges our ignorance of it and powerlessness before it. He was a beautiful baby, and he was gone. His mother had asked me to baptize him. In my faith tradition, you're not supposed to baptize the dead, but then again, babies aren't supposed to die. He was the first person I ever baptized. His name was Zachary, a name taken from Hebrew words meaning, "God remembers."

I'm twenty-eight, newly married, living in a basement in Chicago with almost no furniture. I'm in the midst of a series of oral surgeries to try to repair my mouth after a bike accident, and I'm in pain all the time. The pain is maddening—I'm trying to start work on a new novel, but all I can write is a series of stories in which a young man tries increasingly absurd strategies for pulling out all his teeth.

I remember lying in a borrowed bed in that apartment, listening to "New Partner" to calm myself down, staring at the ancient ceiling tiles with their tea-colored water stains that looked like continents on another world's map. Sometimes, the song will take me back there so viscerally that I can smell the antibiotic mouthwash I gargled with while the wound in my mouth was still open. I can even feel the pain in my jaw, but in a way that feels survivable as things only can once you've survived them.

I'm thirty-two. I have a baby of my own now. I knew, of course, that the act of becoming a father does not suddenly make you qualified for the work, but still, I can't believe this child is my responsibility. Henry is only a couple months old, and I'm still terrified by the idea of being someone's dad, of how utterly he depends upon me, when I know myself to be profoundly undependable.

I roll the word *father* around in my head all the time. Father. What a loaded gun of a word. I want to be kind and patient, unhurried and unworried. I want him to feel secure in my arms. But I have no idea what I'm doing. I've literally read more books about *Hamlet* than I've read about parenting. He won't stop crying even though I've changed his diaper and offered him a bottle. I've tried swaddling and shushing and swinging and singing, but nothing works.

Why is he crying? Maybe there is no why, but my brain needs a why. I'm so incompetent, so quick to frustration, so totally unprepared for every facet of this. A baby's cries are piercing—it feels as if they cut through you. Finally, unable to get him to stop crying, I put him in his car seat and rock him slowly, stick earbuds in my ears, and turn "New Partner" up as loud as I can, so I can hear Will Oldham's plaintive wailing instead of my son's.

———

I'm forty-one. For Sarah and me, the song now sounds like being in love all those years ago, when we were each other's new partners, and it also sounds like our love now. It's a bridge between that life and this one. We're playing "New Partner" for our now nine-year-old son for the first time, and Sarah and I can't help but smile a little giddily at each other. We start dancing together slowly in the kitchen despite our son's gagging noises, and we sing along, Sarah on-key and me way off-. At the end of the song, I ask my son if he liked it and he says, "A little."

That's okay. He'll have a different song. You probably have a different one, too. I hope it carries you to places you need to visit without asking you to stay in them.

I give "New Partner" five stars.

August Sander, *Young Farmers*, 1914. Pictured, left to right: Otto Krieger, August Klein, and Ewald Klein.

THREE FARMERS

ON THEIR WAY TO A DANCE

MOST DAYS, I walk past a vertical strip of four photographs featuring Sarah and me. The pictures were taken at a photo booth in Chicago in 2005, just a couple of weeks after we got engaged. It's standard photo booth fare—smiles, silly faces, and so on—but the light was good, and we were young.

As I get older, the picture keeps changing. In 2005, I thought, *This is us*. These days, I think, *We were just kids*. Seeing that picture every day helps remind me that in another fifteen years, I will see pictures of us from 2020 and think, *Look at everything those two didn't know*.

There is one other photograph I see almost every day: It's a print of a picture taken by the photographer August Sander initially titled *Young Farmers*, 1914, but later known as *Three Farmers on Their Way to a Dance*.

Sander took many photographs that he called *Young Farmers* for his massive, never-finished project *People of the 20th Century*, which sought to photograph all sorts of people in Germany, from aristocrats to circus performers to soldiers. But this picture is probably the best known of them all. I first learned about it from Richard Powers's novel *Three Farmers on Their Way to a Dance*, which I read in college. Powers later wrote an autobiographical novel in which a young computer programmer becomes obsessed with the picture and abandons his career to write about it. I, too, have become obsessed with the picture. I spent years working to track down the biographies and other extant portraits of the boys depicted in the photograph.[45]

There's so much to love about this picture. I love how the young men are looking over their shoulders, as if they barely have time to pause for the camera before going toward the dance and the rest of their lives. Their feet are in the mud, but their heads are in the sky, which is not a bad metaphor for being twenty. And their expressions capture the way you feel when you're with your best friends in your nicest clothes.

The clothes themselves are also fascinating. As the art critic John Berger wrote, "The three young men belong, at the very most, to the second generation who ever wore such suits in the European country-side. Twenty or thirty years earlier, such clothes did not exist at a price which peasants could afford." Industrialization combined with mass media like films and magazines meant that urban fashion was now available, and attractive, to young people in rural Europe.

But there's also tension in the picture. The farmers' dandy-like poses with cigarettes and jaunty canes are strangely incongruent with the pastoral landscape in the background. Also, their heads are sort of being cut off by the horizon line, which turns out to be tragically resonant, because when the picture was taken, the three farmers could not have known that they were also on their way to World War I. The photograph was made shortly before the assassination of the Archduke Franz Ferdinand. Soon, Germany would be at war, and the same industrialization that made those suits possible would mass-produce weapons far deadlier than any the world had previously seen.

And so, for me, it's a picture about knowing and not knowing. You know you're on your way to a dance, but don't know you're on your way

---

45. In the end, as with so much effort in the world, I was not able to do this by myself and succeeded only by collaborating with others. A group of kind and wildly talented internet sleuths called Tuataria worked together to track down Reinhard Pabst, the German journalist and scholar whose research established the boys' identities and backgrounds.

to a war. The picture is a reminder that you never know what will happen to you, to your friends, to your nation. Philip Roth called history "the relentless unforeseen." He said that history is where "everything unexpected in its own time is chronicled on the page as inevitable." In the faces of these young farmers, we glimpse how profoundly unexpected the coming horror was. And that reminds us there is also a horizon we cannot see past.

I have a picture from January of 2020, taken inside a house. I stand arm in arm with four friends. Below us, our kids—eight of them—are tangled in a joyful pile, their shared hug having collapsed into a scrum the moment before the picture was taken. Nobody is wearing a mask. In January of 2020, the picture made me laugh. By July, not so much. "History is merely a list of surprises," Kurt Vonnegut wrote. "It can only prepare us to be surprised yet again."

So that's how I always read the picture—the farmers are symbols of a precarious historical moment. They are reminders that I, too, would in time be surprised by history, and that a picture, though static, keeps changing as its viewers change. As Anaïs Nin put it, "We do not see things as they are, we see them as we are."

Young Farmers is not only a work of art; it is also a historical document, depicting actual people. The boy on the left is Otto Krieger, born in 1894. He knew August Sander, because Sander had photographed Otto and his family three years earlier. The boy in the middle, August Klein, had also been previously photographed by Sander, but the negatives of those pictures, along with thirty thousand other Sander negatives, were destroyed during World War II.

There is, however, one photograph of Otto Krieger and August Klein from before *Young Farmers*.

In this 1913 photograph, Otto (bottom row, third from left) holds crossed drumsticks, while August (bottom row, far left) holds what seems to be the same cane that appears in the *Young Farmers* picture. According to the journalist Reinhard Pabst, a fellow *Young Farmers* obsessive who found and preserved this photograph, the picture may have been taken during a "Flower Day" celebration in the spring of 1913, about a year before Sander's famous picture.

As Sander probably knew, Otto Krieger and August Klein were not farmers. They both worked in an iron ore mine. The boy on the right of the *Young Farmers* photograph, August's cousin Ewald Klein, worked in the iron mine's office. His godson would later say that Ewald preferred office work because he didn't like getting his hands dirty.

And so the young farmers were, in fact, two young miners and an office worker, which is to say that they were participants in the industrial economy. The iron from the mine where they worked would go toward building weapons in the coming war.

Sander himself had worked in an iron ore mine beginning when he was thirteen, so he may have felt some affinity toward these boys. The photographer Maggie Steber once noted, "Respect is the most important thing you put into your camera," and Sander's respect for these three subjects is evident in the picture. Ewald later said, "We all knew him back then, because he had taken photos all over the area, and he always came into the pub."

Indeed, it was Sander's respect for his subjects that would eventually earn the ire of the Nazi regime. Sander photographed Jewish and Roma people (one section of *People of the 20th Century* is devoted to "the persecuted"), and in 1934, Nazi authorities destroyed the printing blocks for a collection of Sander's photography and burned all available copies of the book. The following year, Sander's son, Erich, was imprisoned for being a communist. He died in prison a decade later, just months before the Second World War ended.

But we haven't even gotten to the First World War yet. It is the summer of 1914. Erich Sander is fifteen years old.

The three young farmers who weren't farmers lived in Dünebusch, a village of around a hundred and fifty people in the Westerwald mountains in western Germany. Back then, the village wasn't accessible by car. To visit, Sander drove to the end of the road, and then walked his camera equipment up the mountain for miles.

Otto, August, and Ewald really were on their way to a dance, which was in a little town about a forty-five-minute walk away. Sander probably knew their route in advance and was already set up when they arrived. They paused in front of the camera, turned their heads over their shoulders, and held still.

Otto, hat cocked, cigarette in his lips, looked like the kind of trouble you wouldn't mind getting into. August seems handsome and confident and a little bit sleepy-eyed. And then there's Ewald, who with his tight lips and ramrod straight cane looks nervous to me.

It's silly to make broad conclusions about human beings from a single frame. Sander himself noted of his subjects, "I freeze one moment in his movement, a mere five hundredths of a second of that person's lifetime. That's a very meager or small extract from a life."

Still, I can't help but imagine the moments before and after. I wonder what they talked about as they walked. I wonder if they had a good time, how late they stayed out, who they danced with. We know it was Saturday, summertime. We know they were out of the mine, in the light. And we know that it must've been one of the last dances they attended together, because the war was only weeks away.

Soon, all three boys were called to serve in the German armed forces. Otto and August were placed in the same regiment and sent to Belgium to fight. In January of 1915, only a few months after the *Young Farmers* photo, August Klein sent home this picture from snowy Belgium: Klein stands fifth from right; Krieger kneels beneath him.

The boys look different now. The future, which had been just over the horizon, has come into view. But even then, August and Otto could not know. They couldn't know that August Klein would be killed in the war that March at the age of twenty-two. Otto was wounded three times—including a serious injury in May 1918—but he survived the war. Ewald was also wounded, but he eventually made it back to Dünebusch, where he lived into old age.

Alice Walker once wrote, "All history is current," and I think that's true in so many ways. History presses into us, shaping contemporary experience. History changes as we look back on the past from different presents. And history is electric current, too—charged and flowing. It takes power from some sources and delivers it to others. Sander once said he believed photography could help "hold fast the history of the world," but there is no holding history fast. It is always receding and dissolving, not just into the unknowable past but also into the unfixable future.

I cannot remember precisely how that picture of kids tangled together felt before a global pandemic rendered it so strangely voltaic. And I cannot imagine how it will look to my future selves. All I can see is that picture, changing as time flees away from it.

August Klein was twenty-two years old when he died. He had around a year to live when he posed for that famous photograph. Anything might've happened, but one thing did.

I give *Three Farmers on Their Way to a Dance* four and a half stars.

POSTSCRIPT

THE GERMAN TRANSLATION OF THIS BOOK is called *Wie hat Ihnen das Anthropozän bis jetzt gefallen?* I can't read German, but I find that title wonderful just to look at. I'm told it translates to something like *How Have You Enjoyed the Anthropocene So Far?*

How, indeed.

───────────

Ever since we were kids, I've been asking my brother, Hank, to tell me the meaning of life. It's a running joke with us—we'll be talking about our lives and what to do with them, or about our families, or about work, and when there is a slight pause in the conversation, I'll say, "What *is* the meaning of life, anyway?"

Hank always tailors his response to the conversation, or to what he thinks I might need to hear. Sometimes, he will tell me that caring for others is the meaning of life. Other times, he'll say that we are here to bear witness, to pay attention. In a song he wrote years ago called "The Universe Is Weird," Hank sings that the weirdest thing is that, in us, "the universe created a tool with which to know itself."

He likes to remind me that I am made out of the materials of the universe, that I contain nothing but those materials. "Really," he told me once, "you're just a hunk of Earth trying to sustain a departure from chemical equilibrium."

In "Self-Portrait in a Convex Mirror," John Ashbery writes:

> *The secret is too plain. The pity of it smarts,*
> *Makes hot tears spurt: that the soul is not a soul,*
> *Has no secret, is small, and it fits*
> *Its hollow perfectly: its room, our moment of attention.*

It fits its hollow perfectly. Its room, our moment of attention. I whisper those words to myself sometimes, to try to call myself to attention, to notice the perfectly fitted hollows all around.

It occurs to me that this book is filled with quotes—maybe over-filled with them. I am also overfilled with quotes. For me, reading and rereading are an everlasting apprenticeship. I want to learn what Ashbery seemed to know: how to open the room of attention that contains the soul. I want to learn what my brother knows: how to make meaning, and what meaning to make. I want to learn what to do with my tiny expanse of the world's largest ball of paint.

It is spring, finally, and I am planting carrot seeds in a long row. They're so tiny that I can't help but overplant, ten or twelve seeds for every inch of soil. I feel like I am a human being planting carrot seeds into Earth, but really, as my brother would tell me, I am Earth planting Earth into Earth.

"Fill the Earth and subdue it," God tells us in the first chapter of Genesis. But we are also the Earth we are filling and subduing.

How have I enjoyed the Anthropocene so far? It is wondrous! In high school, my best friend, Todd, and I went to the dollar movie theater every Wednesday. We watched whatever movie was playing on the frigid theater's single screen. Once, a werewolf movie starring Jack Nicholson and Michelle Pfeiffer played at the theater for eight straight Wednesdays, so we watched it eight times. The movie, which was terrible, got better and better the more we watched it. By the eighth time, we were alone in the theater, and we howled with Jack Nicholson while we drank Mountain Dew spiked with bourbon.

How have I enjoyed the Anthropocene so far? It's awful! I feel that I am not evolved for this. I have only been here a little while, but already I have seen my kind extinguish the last remaining members of many other kinds—from birds like the Kaua'i 'ō'ō, last seen when I was ten, to trees like the St. Helena olive, the last of which died when I was twenty-six.

"I smell the wound and it smells like me," Terry Tempest Williams writes in *Erosion*. I live in a wounded world, and I know I am the wound: Earth destroying Earth with Earth.

What does it mean to live in a world where you have the power to end species by the thousands, but you can also be brought to your knees, or to your end, by a single strand of RNA? I have tried here to map some of the places where my little life brushes up against the big forces shaping contemporary human experience, but the only conclusion I can draw is a simple one: We are so small, and so frail, so gloriously and terrifyingly temporary.

When I think of how I have enjoyed the Anthropocene so far, I think of Robert Frost, who wrote, "Like a piece of ice on a hot stove, the poem must ride on its own melting." So it is with poems, and so it is with us. Like ice on a hot stove, we must ride on a melting Earth, all the while knowing who is melting it. A species that has only ever found its way to more must now find its way to less.

Sometimes, I wonder how I can survive in this world where, as Mary Oliver put it, "everything / Sooner or later / Is part of everything else." Other times, I remember that I won't survive, of course. I will, sooner or later, be the everything that is part of everything else. But until then: What an astonishment to breathe on this breathing planet. What a blessing to be Earth loving Earth.

POST-POSTSCRIPT

IN THE MONTHS AFTER THIS BOOK WAS FIRST PUBLISHED, I found myself going outside a lot. I walked every day along the banks of the White River. Some days, I got in my kayak and paddled downstream to a river island just south of 38th Street.

Even though the White River bisects one of the largest cities in America, the riverside is not really urban. You see coyotes and deer on the banks, and occasionally a shy fox or weasel. There are beavers and nutria swimming in the water. There are very few people. Much of the land is undeveloped because it lies in floodplain, and few people swim or play in the river, because it's so polluted. Dozens of times each year, Indianapolis's water management system overflows, dumping raw sewage directly into the river—and that's not even to mention the pollution introduced upstream. The river is beautiful because it's empty, and it is empty because it is filthy—because we made it filthy.

I walked around after dark that summer, too. I looked up at the stars. My son helped me download an app that, when I pointed it at the night sky, identified each pinprick of light. There's Arcturus. And Saturn. That's the Big Dipper. Mars is just above the horizon line, barely visible. We would lie in the front yard on top of grass and clover and dandelions, and we would say the name of each star as we pointed the app toward it. The names seemed—and are, of course—otherworldly. Vega. Altair. Deneb.

Usually, when I finish a book, it feels very over to me, because once a book is published, it's no longer really mine. It belongs to the people who will read it, the people who will commingle their own experiences and emotions with the text. In the weeks after this book was published, I heard from a woman who told me about the death of her brother, and how she'd been trying to interpret the scrawled, manic notes he left on a chalkboard in his apartment. I heard from a grandmother in Italy, and an eleven-year-old in Wisconsin who did *not* like my take on teddy bears. All these people, and so many more, made the essays in this book useful to them in ways that I could never have imagined, which for me is the wonder of art: The art and its viewer or reader make meaning together in a collaboration that transcends time and space. My feeling has always been that I make the words, and then leave them to become whatever kind of meaning a reader can find.

But with this particular book, I found that I couldn't quite leave it. Perhaps this is because unlike my previous work, the main character in this book has been, well, me. And try as I might, I can't seem to leave myself. And so I kept writing reviews. I wrote mostly about being out-side. I wrote about the ginkgo tree in a forest near my house, because I walked past the ginkgo tree almost every day, marveling at its strange-ness. I didn't know when I started writing the history of this particular tree that it was enmeshed in my town's literary history as well as the region's natural history, but that's the joy of research. Almost everything turns out to be interesting if you pay the right kind of attention to it.

And because I was looking at the night sky each evening with my son, I became interested in space travel. I started to ask myself what to think about when thinking about humans in space, and that's how I came to write about a phenomenon called "orbital sunrise," and the first work of art a human ever created outside of our atmosphere—a drawing that was sketched amid a torrent of relief and terror and awe.

And so when it came time to make a paperback version of the book, I asked my publisher, Julie Strauss-Gabel, if we could include those essays, and she kindly agreed.

They are yours now. I hope you find them useful.

THE ORBITAL SUNRISE

MY WIFE SARAH'S BOOK *YOU ARE AN ARTIST* features creativity prompts sprinkled with art historical context, and I often use the book when trying to figure out what to write about, or even what to think about. One of the chapters in the book, "Never Seen, Never Will," features a prompt from the artist David Brooks, who asks us to think of something we've never seen and probably never will see, and then to find a way to articulate that something.

In this context, Brooks discusses a 1515 etching of a rhinoceros by the artist Albrecht Durer. Durer had never seen—and as it happened, would never see—an actual rhinoceros, but he'd read a description of a rhino that was brought to Portugal in 1515.[46] Armed only with this description and a tiny sketch made by another artist, Durer created his famous woodcut of a rhino, which depicts the animal as having literal plates of armor complete with rivets.

Durer's etching does look quite a lot like an actual rhinoceros, which is a testament to his particular genius and more broadly to the capacities

46. Portuguese king Manuel I decided to give this particular rhino to Pope Leo X as a gift. Leo X is today best remembered for the selling of indulgences, which helped spur the Protestant reformation, but Leo was also *nearly* the first pope ever to own a rhinoceros. Alas, the ship carrying the rhino sank in a storm just off the coast of Italy, and the rhino died.

of the human imagination. But in the places where Durer's rhino is different from an actual one, something else is betrayed about the human imagination, which is that we tend to fill in blank spaces or unknowns with guesses that are deeply shaped by our human-ness. When Durer read that the rhino had skin like armor, he imagined sixteenth-century European armor, because what else *could* he imagine?

When thinking, my default setting is to focus on what I know, or at least what someone else knows that I can quickly learn. And of course we do know quite a bit about ourselves and the universe. We know about gravity and the structure of DNA. We know when the Prophet Muhammad led the Muslim community from Mecca to Medina. And we know how internal combustion engines work and the approximate shape of the coastline of Florida. But we don't know almost everything. We don't know what dark matter is, or why there is matter in the universe at all. We don't know how thought works or why some viruses are seasonal. We don't know who killed Jimmy Hoffa or when people started to have names or what the earliest names were. And we know almost nothing about almost all of the so-called known universe, including how or if it will end or whether it is the only universe.

We also don't know why we make art. William Faulkner said that the work of an artist is "to create out of the materials of the human spirit something which did not exist before," but it also involves creating out of the materials of the Earth something which did not exist before—turning graphite into a drawing, or marble into a sculpture, or wood and ink into a book. This refashioning is a very old human habit—it is not too distant from toolmaking, and indeed, it may be that art is a kind of a tool for us, a way into giving form to all the stuff that does not easily lend itself to form. But I think even that broad definition is in the end too narrow. I don't know what art is. I don't know why we make it. I don't know almost everything.

Which brings us, belatedly, to the orbital sunrise.

During the 342 days astronaut Scott Kelly spent in space a few years ago, the International Space Station experienced nearly 11,000 sunrises. Because the station orbits Earth every 90 minutes, with each orbit there is a new sunrise—the sun emerging from behind what looks like a long, thin arc of blue light. That blue light is the crust of the Earth.

During these orbital sunrises, astronauts can sometimes see other bands of color—white, amber, gold. To hear astronauts talk of orbital sunrises is to glimpse how amazing they must be. The astronaut Victor Glover wrote of the bands of color, "They remind me of the scripture in Psalm 30, 'Weeping may endure for a night, but joy cometh in the morning.'" On the International Space Station, joy cometh eighteen times per Earth day.

Many space travelers have written of experiencing so-called "orbital perspective"—seeing the whole, profoundly interconnected planet from afar, teeming with life, vast and resilient and fragile and tiny. Astronaut Mae Jemison said that in space, "I felt more expansive, very connected to the universe." The Russian cosmonaut Alexei Leonov wrote that, "Looking back at our blue globe from such a distance profoundly changed my vision of space and time."

Leonov is most remembered today for taking the first spacewalk, but he also made the first space art. In March 1965, Leonov visited space with his friend and colleague Pasha Belyayev. The two men orbited Earth in a tiny spherical spacecraft that was just over two meters in diameter, and so they were only allowed a few personal belongings on the trip. Leonov chose to bring a drawing pad and some colored pencils. He'd loved making art since childhood. He had wanted to go to art school, but it was too expensive, so he became a pilot.

Their mission was known as Voskhod 2—*voskhod* means *sunrise* in

Russian—and despite lasting for just over one day, this space flight contained quite a lot of firsts—not just the first spacewalk and the first art made in space, but also the first spacecraft landing to occur fifteen hundred miles off course after its occupants nearly died on several separate occasions.

Here's what happened: Shortly after entering orbit, Leonov exited the Voskhod capsule via an airlock and floated in space connected to the spaceship by only a ropelike tether. The event was broadcast live on Soviet radio and television, and you can still find recordings on YouTube. Watching it recently from the comfort of my living room in Indianapolis, I saw Leonov push away from the spacecraft, drifting into the void until his tether snapped taut.

After a few minutes of spacewalking, it was time for Leonov to re-enter the ship, but there was a problem: His pressurized spacesuit had dramatically expanded in the vacuum of space. In his memoirs, Leonov recalled, "My feet had pulled away from my boots and my fingers from the gloves attached to my sleeves, making it impossible to enter the airlock. . . . The only solution was to reduce the pressure in my suit by opening the pressure valve and letting out a little oxygen at a time as I tried to inch inside the airlock." And so as his oxygen leeched out into the void, Leonov tried to wedge himself back into the capsule, which he described as "an almost impossible maneuver."

This part was not broadcast live on television. "From the moment our mission looked to be in jeopardy," Leonov wrote, "transmissions from our spacecraft were suddenly suspended without explanation. In their place, Mozart's Requiem was played again and again on state radio. The custom in the Soviet Union at that time was for such solemn music to be played after a senior political figure had died, but before an official announcement of their death was made." Leonov's family and friends, who knew the music meant something had gone wrong, waited for the news, with no way of knowing what was happening miles above.

As his suit shrank and his oxygen dwindled, Leonov eventually managed to get back into the Voskhod capsule. He was drenched with sweat, breathless, and overwhelmed with adrenaline. His compatriot calmed him down, saying that they had ninety minutes before they needed to eject the airlock. Maybe Alexei could use that time to rest, or to write up a report of the spacewalk?

But Leonov found that he could neither sleep nor write. Instead, to calm himself and capture the moment, he took those minutes to make some art. "I reached for my sketch pad and colored pencils and sat quietly drawing my first impressions of the panorama I had seen while floating free in space. I tried to capture the different shades of charcoal rings that make up the Earth's atmosphere, the sunrise or air glow over the Earth's horizon, the blue belt covering the Earth's crust and the spectrum of colors I had observed looking down at the globe."

The sketch is simple—it was made quickly in a weightless environment with simple drawing instruments—but it is also stunningly beautiful. A curved band mixing black and blue represents the portion of Earth visible due to the rising sun. Above the planet, a narrow curvature of red, then yellow, and then the black of space. And in the center of the drawing, we see the red sphere of the sun, almost risen behind the curvature of the Earth. It says something to me that the first art made by humans from outside of Earth's atmosphere depicts Earth's atmosphere. Leonov was astonished by the brightness of the stars from space, but he did not draw that, nor did he draw himself floating, looking up at the spaceship. He drew home. He drew what Mary Oliver memorably called "this, the one world we all belong to."

I will never see an orbital sunrise in real life.

On many levels, I'm not cut out for space travel—an inner ear disorder has damaged my sense of balance, for starters. But also, I am not a pilot or an engineer or a billionaire. I tend to side with Eudora Welty on matters of adventure. She once, after acknowledging she had lived a sheltered life, added, "A sheltered life can be a daring life as well. For all serious daring starts from within." My daring also generally ends within.

And so I will only ever have descriptions and depictions of space. Like Albrecht Durer and his rhinoceros, when it comes to orbital sunrises I am wholly dependent upon words and images made by other people. But unlike Durer, I can find endless high-definition images and videos of an orbital sunrise via a quick Google search. I can read orbital sunrise musings written by dozens of firsthand observers. Even so, Alexei Leonov's drawing—simple, straightforward, even childlike—is overwhelmingly the most beautiful and moving depiction of an orbital sunrise I've ever seen. Precisely because it is not photorealistic, it captures the awe of that moment—of seeing the sun rise over a very different sort of horizon.

After making his sketch of the orbital sunrise, Leonov returned to the mission at hand, whereupon a new crisis arose. The ejection of Voskhod 2's airlock led to an unexpected and uncontrolled spin of the spaceship. There was no longer the pleasure of a sunrise every ninety minutes; now, their spacecraft was spinning wildly, the sunlight streaming in through the window creating a strobe light effect. On the ground, Mozart's Requiem played over and over on the radio, while in space, the oxygen level inside the Voskhod crept dangerously high, so that any spark risked a massive explosion. Just as the astronauts were able to resolve that issue, the craft's automatic guidance system failed. This meant the cosmonauts, still spinning out of control, would have to manually calculate when to fire the retrorockets to re-enter Earth's atmosphere. After extensive calculations, Leonov chose to aim the craft toward a vast wilderness in the western Soviet Union. That way, if they crashed, they at least wouldn't kill anyone on the ground.

But the problems continued to compound—upon re-entry, the landing module initially failed to separate from the rest of the aircraft as planned, which caused the entire spacecraft to spin as it re-entered the atmosphere. The g-forces were so strong that blood vessels burst in the cosmonauts' eyes.

At last, the landing module did separate and fortunately the parachutes deployed as planned as the cosmonauts returned to Earth. They landed in a forest, in two feet of snow, their escape hatch blocked by a tree that had fallen when the spacecraft barreled into it. For hours, the two men rocked the capsule back and forth by throwing their bodies against the inside of the ship until, finally, the escape hatch was freed. And then they spent a very long and very cold night in the Siberian wilderness until rescuers arrived the next day. Only then could the two men ski nine kilometers with the rescue party to a site where a helicopter could land. That is how the cosmonauts of Voskhod 2 survived, and with them the first picture of an orbital sunrise.

I like to look at Leonov's drawing when I am exhausted by despair and drudgery, or when I feel the weight of longing and fear pressing in on my chest. I look at the picture and think of all that had to happen for the drawing to exist, for Leonov to exist, for anything to exist. I look at the drawing and take a long, slow breath, and think of how my lungs were made for this air.

For me, art is a kind of landing site in the wilderness. Art is where I go when I do not know where else to go. Art can help me to see what I will never see—not just orbital sunrises but the way-down stuff too abstract and nebulous to have a name. Through art, paradoxes of consciousness resolve for me. I see what I will never see. I know what I will never know. And I survive what I will not survive.

I give the orbital sunrise four and a half stars.

THE GINKGO TREE

WHEN I WAS IN COLLEGE, I took a class in American religion in which we read one of those mid-nineteenth-century novels that luxuriates in description. I no longer remember the title or the plot of the book; all I can recall is one passage, which went on for pages and pages, wherein the author described a tree. Every knob and every branch, every leaf and every ridge of bark were elucidated—as if the reader had never seen a tree.

Thinking about that passage now, I'm reminded of Gertrude Stein's essay "What Are Masterpieces and Why Are There So Few of Them," where she writes about the challenges of making art in the twentieth century. "The tradition has always been that you may more or less describe the things that happen you imagine them of course but you more or less describe the things that happen but nowadays everybody all day long knows what is happening and so what is happening is not really interesting, one knows it by radios cinemas newspapers biographies autobiographies until what is happening does not really thrill any one."

Perhaps to a nineteenth century reader, a seven-page description of a tree was thrilling, but to my twenty-year-old eyes in 1997, the adjective-laden prose buckling under the weight of its own sincerity embodied everything that I disliked about literature, and so I wrote a paper about how much I detested the book. As part of my impassioned defense of lean, people-centric prose, I proclaimed that any writing that devotes thousands of words to a tree is definitionally bad writing, because we already know what trees look like.

And now, here I am, twenty-six years removed from absolutely hating that seven-page description of a tree, here to share with you a seven-page description of a tree. Be careful what you ridicule, for in time you will become it.

———

Near my home, there is a stretch of woods that begins on the banks of the White River. Sycamores and oaks lean out over the riverbank, and then as you walk farther inland, you find more sugar maple trees. The forest adheres to a kind of logic—at my feet, there are patches of stinging nettles intermingled with ferns and waist-high reeds. Above, me, I see the overstory—the treetops blotting out almost all of the sky. There are many species of plant in the forest, but even the invasive ones like honeysuckle answer to a kind of logic—they look, basically, Midwestern. Lovely. A bit dense in places. Unpretentious.

But then there is the ginkgo tree. The ginkgo sticks out like a camera-toting tourist. Long before I knew this tree was a ginkgo tree, I knew it was weird. It was weird because of its leaves, thick and waxy and resembling fan blades or enlarged flower petals. The veins in a ginkgo leaf do not branch and spider out like the leaves I'm accustomed to; instead, they are tiny, nearly parallel lines that converge at the base of the leaf like a calculus problem—the veins growing infinitely closer without ever quite touching.

And I knew the tree was weird because of its shape—while the oaks and sycamores spread their crowns across as much of the sky as they can muster, the ginkgo is vaguely cone-shaped, like an unruly ninety-foot-tall Christmas tree. But also, I noticed it before I knew it was a living fossil or a medicinal tree or anything else because the trees around the ginkgo give it a wide berth, leaving ample room in the canopy above. It's as if the other trees know the ginkgo doesn't quite belong, but they still make room for it.

In the autumn, ginkgo leaves turn a bright yellow and then fall all at once, sometimes in a single day. Most years, I've missed this. One day, I walk past the ginkgo tree and the leaves are bright above me, and the next time I'm in these woods, those leaves are beneath my feet. But last year, I caught it. I happened to be walking as the leaves were falling, dozens of them every minute, floating down in long fluttering helices.

A few days later, the branches were totally leafless, and I could see the invisible symmetry of the tree, how the branches splinter out and grow up, reaching prayerfully toward sunlight, just as their roots branch out and down, reaching for water and stability. In summertime, I can only see the tree as a hanger for those extraordinary leaves.

What a peculiar world this is, where life emerges only from life but must have, at some point, emerged from something else.

A few years ago, an eighty-five-year-old neighbor of mine asked if he could meet with me to discuss what he described as "a few matters." I was only distantly acquainted with this neighbor, but I knew he had a reputation for eccentricity. Our only previous conversation had involved his habit of flying a different flag from his front yard's flagpole each day. On one day, he'd fly the flag of Sweden, the next, an LGBTQ pride flag, the next, the Alaska state flag. I asked him once how his flag schedule worked. I expected he would tell me about independence days and pride months, but instead he said, "I wake up each morning, and I look at the sky, and the sky tells me which flag is called for."

I figured the meeting would involve a request for publishing advice or the like, but in fact my neighbor just wanted to take me through the forest and explain some things. We walked down an arroyo behind his house where, in spring, a creek dribbles toward the river, and as we walked, my neighbor pointed out a huge sycamore tree, the tallest in the forest. "That's Zeus," he said of the tree. "The God of Gods."

"Okay," I told him. This was my kind of meeting.

After another minute of slow walking—the ground was muddy, and my neighbor's balance unsteady—we approached a thick bramble of honeysuckle bushes, which he explained was in fact a fairy garden. He then gestured to another sycamore near the river's edge. "Beneath that tree is the wedding chapel," he told me, and I knew what he meant. Something about the tree and the way its branches sagged seemed to create a chapel's ceiling, and the shade cast by the tree did seem like a holy place, and a celebratory one.

At last, we came to the ginkgo tree. "The mother of light," he said. As we stood beneath it, he grabbed one of those fanned leaves and examined it. He called the ginkgo tree "the oldest lady in town." He told me that Zeus had a name, but the ginkgo tree did not, because she was older than names. He said that maybe Zeus had been alive longer than this particular ginkgo, but that leaves just like these had been eaten by dinosaurs. "Everything her age is a fossil," he said, and then added, almost as an afterthought, "You know, they found ginkgo fossils in North Dakota that are a thousand times older than sin."

What is now the American Midwest has been ocean floor many times in the past. It is not uncommon to find fossilized remains of sea creatures within stones on the rocky shore of the White River near my home in

Indianapolis. But this little swath of Earth was dry land for much of its history—beginning over 200 million years ago, what is now Indiana often hosted trees, including vast forests of ginkgoes. A recent excavation of a site just north of Indianapolis found fossils of likely ginkgoes among other trees and animals.

Ginkgo biloba, the only species from the genus still alive today, seems very similar—and perhaps identical—to the ginkgo trees that grew back then, which is why Ginkgo biloba is often called a living fossil. But ginkgoes saw a huge decline during the Pliocene epoch, beginning 5.6 million years ago. The ginkgoes died out in most of the world. In what would become the American Midwest, a series of huge glaciers swept in from the north, killing trees and many other species and covering the land with sheets of ice thousands of feet thick.

When the last glacier retreated from this patch of Earth about 14,000 years ago, it left behind loamy, nutrient-dense soil, and in time hardwood forests began to grow along the banks of the White River. By then, the ginkgoes were long gone from this part of the world. Instead, the forests were thick with sycamores, sugar maples, and beech trees.

As ginkgoes were wiped out in North America (and most other places) over the last few million years, the trees might've gone extinct entirely had they not survived in what is now central China—partly thanks to a friendly climate and partly because the trees have been planted and preserved by humans for many thousands of years. Its nuts are edible, and parts of the trees have long been used in traditional Chinese medicine. Through human cultivation, the trees spread—first to Korea and Japan, and then throughout Afro-Eurasia, and by the late eighteenth century, to the Americas.

And so when a Ginkgo biloba tree was introduced to a little forest along the White River about 130 years ago, it was not the first ginkgo tree to have grown in this neighborhood, just the first one to have been here in several million years.

Toward the end of the nineteenth century, the land containing the ginkgo tree was purchased. The idea that land *could* be purchased and divvied up was reasonably new to the region. A century earlier, no individual had "owned" the land that is currently Indianapolis, because it was Miami land, shared by a community that did not believe in private property. In this neck of the woods at least, the idea that a forest of trees can be owned by one person or another is younger than many of the trees in that forest.

The couple who bought this newly minted private land were Sophia and Peter Lieber. Peter was a U.S. Civil War veteran who walked with a pronounced limp as a result of injuries sustained in the war. His family had gotten rich in the brewing business and bought the land along the White River as a kind of country estate.

The ginkgo tree was probably planted around 1890 by their son, Albert Lieber—or more accurately, by his gardener. Albert Lieber was a hard-partying philanderer who worked sparingly and managed to spend almost all of his parents' fortune. Part of that spending went to planning and planting ornate gardens all around his extensive properties, including the installation of novel tree species in the riverside woods near the family home. When Albert died in 1934, the vast tract of Lieber land was divided up and sold for development. Most of what were once phenomenal gardens are gone now. Today, the old Lieber property contains over a hundred houses, a golf course, three apartment buildings, and a McDonald's. Most of the trees Lieber had planted were cut down amid all that development.

But the ginkgo survived.

It is here that my life, and the ginkgo tree, intersect with the novelist Kurt Vonnegut, who grew up in Indianapolis before becoming one of the most beloved and popular American writers of the twentieth century. Kurt Vonnegut's grandfather was this very same hard-drinking, big-spending, garden-funding, ginkgo-planting Albert Lieber. In fact, Vonnegut must have walked past the ginkgo tree many times during his frequent childhood visits to his grandfather Albert's estate. He would grow to detest the man; as he wrote in his quasi-autobiography *Palm Sunday*, "We have come now to a rascal, Albert Lieber, whose emotional faithlessness to his children, in my humble opinion, contributed substantially to my mother's eventual suicide." Albert and his wife were by many accounts physically and emotionally abusive parents.

Their daughter, Vonnegut's mother, Edith, suffered from substance abuse and mental health problems throughout her life. In his writing, Vonnegut sometimes referred to his mother as "half-cracked." I am also half cracked, and because we walked the same woods, I often think of Edith when I'm walking. Before she married the prominent Indianapolis architect Kurt Vonnegut Sr., Edith lived for a time in a cottage that looked out at the ginkgo tree from its kitchen window. The tree would've been about thirty years old then, already mature, even if it was only about half as tall as it is today.

When I look at the ginkgo tree, I think of its beauty, but I also think of a young woman who can't escape the abuse and terror of home, because home extends out for miles in every direction, and because she feels she has no choice but to live the life her father demands of her. How must she have felt when looking out at the ginkgo? The tree was smaller then, but it must have still been beautiful and strange in that forest.

Anaïs Nin wrote that we don't see things as they are; we see them as we are. In writing about the ginkgo, I don't want to describe the ginkgo tree as it is; I want to describe it as I am. Why do I love this tree so much? Why does my neighbor love it? Why do I imagine, boldly, that

Edith Lieber Vonnegut loved it when there was so little in her life that she could trust with love?

Well, perhaps we should acknowledge the astonishing resilience of the ginkgo. They are often said to be excellent city trees, because they do not seem to be bothered by pollution or concrete or disturbed land or salty soil. From Manhattan to Seoul, you'll find ginkgoes where you don't find other trees. And so ginkgoes are often used as metaphors for adaptability and tenacity. And it is true that I want to be adaptable and tenacious, but I don't think that's what sends me again and again to the ginkgo's shade. I think I come back here for the same reason Gertrude Stein said that there are so few masterpieces: It is easy enough to describe something, or to comprehend something, as it is. But what really thrills the human soul is to be in the presence of astonishment. I am thrilled by everything that makes me feel alive within my self. Alive in my smallness, and alive in my fragility, and alive in my wondrousness.

There is so much I won't ever know. I will never know how Edith Lieber Vonnegut felt when she watched from her kitchen window as this tree dropped all its leaves in one furious afternoon. I will never know the inside of your life, what you've survived to reach this now. I will never know what it's like to live as a tree, growing up into the light and down into the soil.

But I know the thrill I feel beneath the ginkgo tree, how looking up at it makes me feel an awe that contains both wonder and fear at its edges, and thanks to the generosity of my neighbor, I know that I am unalone in this thrill. I think of him, too, when I walk through the forest. And I find myself hoping that someday I will be eighty-five years old, and I will request a meeting with some young whippersnapper so that I can introduce them to Zeus and the wedding chapel and the oldest lady in town. And I will try to explain to them what I am trying to explain to you: How, in the presence of this tree, I feel newly aware that I am in a world vastly older than sin and older even than hope as I know it.

I've spent so much of my life wondering why I am here, feeling this ache behind my solar plexus that my life isn't *for* anything, that it doesn't *mean* anything, that the hurt hurts too much and the joy gives too little. But in the shade of the ginkgo tree, I'm able to feel, if only in moments, why I am here—that I am here to pay attention. I am here to love and to be loved, and to know and to not know.

And most of all, I am here to be. To be not just on this planet, but with it. I am here to be with you, to be with my family, and even to be with this forest. The gift is being itself, and who better to show us that than the oldest lady in town.

I give that ginkgo tree five stars.

ACKNOWLEDGMENTS

THANK YOU TO Hank Green, Sarah Urist Green, Rosianna Halse Rojas, Elyse Marshall, and Stan Muller for encouraging this idea in the first place. Mark Olsen and Meredith Danko also gave critical early feedback. Making *The Anthropocene Reviewed* podcast with WNYC Studios has been an absolute joy thanks to producer Jenny Lawton, composer Hannis Brown, technical director Joe Plourde, and Nadim Silverman. I'm also indebted to Tony Philips and Ashley Lusk, among many others. Niki Hua provided critical notes on many of these essays and taught me about the tempo of "You'll Never Walk Alone." Julie Strauss-Gabel has been my editor for now almost twenty years; I am so, so grateful to her for shepherding this book, and for always finding the story when I can't. Thank you to everyone at Dutton and Penguin, including Anna Booth, Melissa Faulner, Rob Farren, Natalie Vielkind, Jen Loja, Christine Ball, Emily Canders, Stephanie Cooper, Dora Mak, John Parsley, Linda Rosenberg, Amanda Walker, Helen Boomer, Leigh Butler, Kim Ryan, and Grace Han. I'm also thankful for the sage counsel of Jodi Reamer and Kassie Evashevski.

My parents, Mike and Sydney Green, enriched this book in many ways, as did my in-laws, Connie and Marshall Urist. I'm also so grateful to Chris and Marina Waters. Sarah Urist Green is the best collaborator in work and in life I could ever imagine.

So much of this book was made possible by the people who listen to *The Anthropocene Reviewed* podcast. Thank you for the topics you suggested and the poems you emailed. I'm especially grateful to the online community Tuataria, who researched the story of the young farmers that closes this book, and to the Life's Library Book Club and all those who work to make it amazing.

Lastly, to Henry and Alice: Thank you. You both astound me with joy and wonder. Thank you for helping me with this book and teaching me about everything from velociraptors to whispering.

NOTES

Many of these essays first appeared, in different forms, on the podcast *The Anthropocene Reviewed*, a co-production of WNYC Studios and Complexly. Portions of other essays first appeared in the PBS Digital series *The Art Assignment*, founded and produced by Sarah Urist Green, or on the YouTube channel vlogbrothers. The notes below are not intended to be exhaustive (or exhausting), but instead as an introduction for those interested in further reading and other experiences that informed the essays.

This is a work of nonfiction, but I'm sure that I have misremembered much. I have also in moments changed details or characterizations in order to preserve people's anonymity.

These notes and sources were compiled with the help of Niki Hua and Rosianna Halse Rojas, without whom this book would have been impossible. Any mistakes are mine alone.

"You'll Never Walk Alone"
One of the many benefits of loving Liverpool Football Club is that over time, knowledge about the song "You'll Never Walk Alone" seeps into you via osmosis. The quote about Molnár not wanting *Liliom* to become a Puccini opera comes from Frederick Nolan's *The Sound of Their Music,* as did much of the other information about the musical and Molnár's relationship with it. I learned about the musical changes Gerry and the Pacemakers made to the song from Niki Hua. Gerry Marsden, who died in early 2021, often told the story about meeting Shankly, including in an *Independent* interview with Simon Hart from 2013. No human life is complete without joining with sixty thousand people singing "You'll Never Walk Alone" together, and I hope that is an experience available to you at some point, and also that it is available to me again soon.

Humanity's Temporal Range

The idea for this essay came from a conversation with my friend and longtime collaborator Stan Muller. There are many versions of the Earth-history-in-a-year analogy, but I relied mostly on a timeline developed by the Kentucky Geological Survey. The poll about people in different countries having different beliefs about our proximity to the Apocalypse was conducted by Ipsos Global Affairs. Most of the information about the Permian extinction came from a 2012 *National Geographic* story by Christine Dell'Amore called "'Lethally Hot' Earth Was Devoid of Life—Could It Happen Again?" (Spoiler alert: It could. Actually, it will.) The Octavia Butler quotes are from *Parable of the Talents*. The idea of seeing things you'll never see came to me from the work of the artist David Brooks, via his art assignment challenge printed in Sarah Urist Green's book *You Are an Artist*. The information on global average temperature rise since the Industrial Revolution came from the National Climatic Data Center of the NOAA.

Halley's Comet

As noted in the review, much of the background for understanding Edmond Halley and his comety calculations came from two very enjoyable books: Julie Wakefield's *Halley's Quest*, about Halley's time as a ship captain and explorer, and John Gribbin and Mary Gribbin's *Out of the Shadow of a Giant: Hooke, Halley, and the Birth of Science*. I learned of Fred Whipple's "dirty snowball" theory of comets from the Smithsonian Astrophysical Observatory. More information on responses to the 1910 apparition of the comet can be found in Chris Riddell's 2012 *Guardian* article "Apocalypse Postponed?" (It's only ever postponed, that Apocalypse.)

Our Capacity for Wonder

I'm indebted to Matthew J. Bruccoli's book about F. Scott Fitzgerald, *Some Sort of Epic Grandeur*, and also to Nancy Mitford's *Zelda*, about Zelda Fitzgerald. I learned a lot about Armed Services Editions from a 2015 article in *Mental Floss* magazine called "How WWII Saved *The Great Gatsby* from Obscurity." I was able to stay in the Plaza Hotel due to the largesse of Fox 2000, a filmmaking enterprise that no longer exists. "The Crack-Up" was initially published in *Esquire* magazine in 1936 and is now available online. Various manuscripts for *The Great Gatsby* are available online through Princeton University's library, and it's fascinating to see what changed (and what didn't) among the revisions. The David Denby quote comes from a review published in the *New Yorker* on May 13, 2013.

Lascaux Cave Paintings

I first learned of these paintings and the story of our separation from them in Werner Herzog's documentary *Cave of Forgotten Dreams*. I learned more from Judith Thurman's essay "First Impressions," in the June 16, 2008, issue of the *New Yorker*. Simon Coencas recorded an oral history for the United States Holocaust Memorial Museum, which is available online at its website. Coencas's quote about the "little gang" came from a 2016 interview with the AFP. The Barbara Ehrenreich essay "The Humanoid Stain" was first published in *The Baffler* in November 2019. The Lascaux website, at archeologie.culture.fr, was especially helpful, and included references to hand stencils at Lascaux. I learned of Genevieve von Petzinger's work from a 2016 *New Scientist* article by Alison George called "Code Hidden in Stone Age Art May Be the Root of Human Writing." Last, I would not have been able to write this review without Thierry Félix's work to preserve both the cave and the stories of those who discovered it.

Scratch 'n' Sniff Stickers

The Helen Keller quote about smell is from her wonderful book *The World I Live In*. The Baltimore Gas and Electric debacle is described in an AP News story from September 4, 1987.

When I was in middle school, one of my teachers took me aside after class one day. She knew that I had been struggling academically as well as socially, and she went out of her way to tell me that she liked something I'd written. She also said to me, "You're going to be okay, you know. Not in the short run . . ." and then she paused before saying, "And also not in the long run, I guess. But in the medium run." This moment of kindness stayed with me, and helped hold me together in tough days, and I don't know if this book would exist without it. I have forgotten this teacher's name, as I have forgotten almost everything, but I am so grateful to her.

Diet Dr Pepper

The history of Dr Pepper is told succinctly (if somewhat self-aggrandizingly) at the Dr Pepper Museum and Free Enterprise Institute in Waco, Texas. (Foots Clements, a staunch anti-communist, insisted that the museum be a celebration of not only Dr Pepper but also free markets.) Charles Alderton was a member of the Masons, and so far as I know, the fullest biography written of him was put together by the Waco Masonic Lodge, and is available at its website. I am also indebted to two histories of Dr Pepper: *The Legend of Dr Pepper/7-Up* by Jeffrey L. Rodengen, and *The Road to Dr Pepper, Texas* by Karen Wright, which explores the astonishing story of the Dublin Dr Pepper bottling plant, which produced a unique cane-sugar version of Dr Pepper until 2012.

Velociraptors

When writing *Jurassic Park*, Michael Crichton consulted with the paleontologist John Ostrom, whose research helped revolutionize our understanding of dinosaurs. In a *New York Times* interview with Fred Musante on June 29, 1997, Ostrom discussed his relationship with Crichton and how Crichton chose the name velociraptor because it was "more dramatic." As explained in a *Yale News* article from 2015, the team behind the *Jurassic Park* film asked for all of Ostrom's research on deinonychus when deciding how to portray the film's velociraptors. I learned much of the truth about velociraptors from my son, Henry, and then from the American Museum of Natural History, where I also read of the velociraptor that died in the midst of fighting a protoceratops. My favorite reading on the resurrection of the brontosaurus is Charles Choi's "The *Brontosaurus* Is Back," published by *Scientific American* on April 7, 2015.

Canada Geese

For a bird I actively dislike, the Canada goose is a joy to read about. Much of the information from this essay came from the Cornell Lab of Ornithology (allaboutbirds.org), which is so wondrously comprehensive and accessible that the rest of the internet should take a lesson from it. Harold C. Hanson's book *The Giant Canada Goose* is one of those highly specialized books that is nonetheless thoroughly fun. Joe Van Wormer's 1968 book *The World of the Canada Goose* is lovely, too. The Philip Habermann quote came from the book *History Afield* by Robert C. Willging. If you want to learn more about the history of lawns, I recommend Krystal D'Costa's *Scientific American* piece, "The American Obsession with Lawns."

Teddy Bears

I first heard the story of Teddy Roosevelt sparing the bear that died anyway from a TED Talk given by Jon Mooallem, whose book *Wild Ones: A Sometimes Dismaying, Weirdly Reassuring Story About Looking at People Looking at Animals in America* is as enjoyable as you'd expect from that subtitle. The taboo avoidance etymology of the word *bear* is described in the incredibly helpful online etymology dictionary (etymonline.com). The Smithsonian's history of the teddy bear was also very helpful to me; this is how I learned of the 1902 *Washington Post* article about Roosevelt sparing (sorta?) the bear. The figures of Earth's biomass distribution come from "The Biomass Distribution on Earth," lead author Yinon M. Bar-On, first published on May 21, 2018, in the *Proceedings of the National Academy of Sciences of the United States of America*. I was introduced to the concept of species biomass in Yuval Noah Harari's book *Sapiens*. The Sarah Dessen quote is from her wonderful novel *What Happened to Goodbye*.

The Hall of Presidents

Special thanks to my children, Henry and Alice, for taking half an hour away from their Disney vacation so that I could visit the Hall of Presidents for this review. When I asked my son afterward if he enjoyed the presentation, he paused for a moment before saying, "I want to say yes but I didn't."

Air-Conditioning

The idea for this essay came from my friend Ryan Sandahl, who told me the story of Willis Carrier. I also relied on Margaret Ingels's book *Willis Haviland Carrier: Father of Air Conditioning*. The information about the role air-conditioning and cooling fans play in climate change came from the International Energy Agency's 2018 report, "The Future of Cooling." Data about the 2003 heat wave catastrophe came from a report first published in France in 2008 in *Comptes Rendus Biologies*. John Huxham's account of the 1757 European heat wave was first published in *Philosophical Transactions of the Royal Society*; I learned about it via Wikipedia. For understanding the ways air-conditioning has changed architecture, I am indebted to an episode of the podcast *99% Invisible*.

Staphylococcus aureus

I've wanted to write about staph since my doctor told me about my fascinatingly aggressive colony of them. I was on so many different antibiotics in an attempt to control the infection that, at one point, the doctor needed to confirm I hadn't previously taken the drug he wanted to prescribe for me. "This pill is yellow," the doctor said. "Have you taken a yellow pill before?" Maybe, I told him. "This pill is circular. Have you taken a circular pill before?" Again, maybe. "This drug costs $700 per pill," he then said. "Have you taken a pill—"

"No," I said. The drug cost me $2,000 even though we had health insurance, but we're not here to review the U.S.'s one-and-a-half-star healthcare system. The quotes from and about Alexander Ogston in this essay come from the book *Alexander Ogston, K.C.V.O.: Memories and Tributes of Relatives,*

Colleagues and Students, with Some Autobiographical Writings, which was compiled by Ogston's son Walter. Most interesting to me were the recollections written by Ogston's daughters, Helen and Constance, and those written by his colleagues. The stat about Boston City Hospital in 1941 came from a 2010 *Journal of the Association of Basic Medical Sciences* article, "Methicillin-Resistant Staphylococcus Aureus (MRSA) as a Cause of Nosocomial Wound Infections," by Maida Šiširak, Amra Zvizdić, and Mirsada Hukić, which also helped me understand the contemporary disease burden of staph infections. I learned about Albert Alexander and his daughter Sheila (now Sheila LeBlanc) from a 2012 *Press-Enterprise* newspaper article by Penny Schwartz, "Local Artists Share Childhood Bond," which is also how I came to see some of LeBlanc's paintings. Much of the information about the synthesis of penicillin comes from Robert Gaynes's 2012 article in *Emerging Infectious Diseases*, "The Discovery of Penicillin—New Insights After More Than 75 Years of Clinical Use." I also learned a lot about staph and Ogston's role in discovering it from S. W. B. Newsom's article in *The Journal of Hospital Infection*, "Ogston's Coccus."

The Internet

The summer of CompuServe was made magical by the presence of my friends there—especially Dean, Marie, and Kevin.

Academic Decathlon

The Terry Tempest Williams quote is from her book *Red: Passion and Patience in the Desert*. The Maya Jasanoff quote about rivers is from her biography of Joseph Conrad, *The Dawn Watch*. Academic Decathlon still exists; you can learn more about it at usad.org. Todd, I love you. Thank you.

Sunsets

I learned about Claude glass from Sarah, who also introduced me to the Thomas Gray quote, which is from his journal of touring the Lake District in 1769. The Bolaño quote is from *2666* as translated by Natasha Wimmer;

the Anna Akhmatova quote is from "A land not mine, still," as translated by Jane Kenyon. The Eliot line about the Invisible Light is from *Choruses from "The Rock."* The Tacita Dean quote is from "The Magic Hour."

I have been thinking about the Son/Sun thing for a long time, ever since it was first introduced to me by Professor Royal Rhodes. The only short story I ever wrote about my time as a chaplain, which I finished when I was twenty-three, ended with an extremely on-the-nose scene where the chaplain is driving home after a long forty-eight hours in the hospital, "the risen Sun too bright in his losing eyes." I'd like to say I've learned to better resist the urge to put a button on the figurative points I'm trying to make, but *The Fault in Our Stars* ends with a wedding, so.

But back to the review! I was introduced to that e. e. cummings poem by Jenny Lawton, the brilliant producer who oversaw the podcast version of *The Anthropocene Reviewed* at WNYC. The Morrison quote about the world's beauty is from her 1981 novel, *Tar Baby*. I first read that book because of Professor Ellen Mankoff's Intro to Lit class at Kenyon College. The Alec Soth quote is from Michael Brown's 2015 profile of Soth in the *Telegraph*.

Jerzy Dudek's Performance on May 25, 2005

The vast majority of the information in this review—the quotes from Dudek and Mirabella, the outline of Dudek's career, the descriptions of the death of Pope John Paul II—come from Jerzy Dudek's book *A Big Pole in Our Goal*. As a Liverpool fan I am admittedly biased, but the book is a fascinating look at a very unlikely career. (Dudek is now in a second unlikely career: He has taken up race car driving.) The Jamie Carragher quotes about his dream turning to dust, and his version of his pressuring Dudek to try the wobbly legs, came from *Carra: My Autobiography*, which is also a great read. The story of Dudek's mother visiting the coal mine is told in "Jerzy Dudek: My Secret Vice," a *FourFourTwo* article from July 28, 2009, as told to Nick Moore. And then there is the question of whether Pope JP II really said, "Of all the unimportant things, football is the most important." John Paul II did *love* football (and played goalie as a teenager!), but I could find no firm source for the quotation.

Penguins of Madagascar

I watched *Penguins of Madagascar* for the first time as a favor to my children; since then, they have watched it many times as a favor to me. I am such a fan of the unshakable earnestness of Werner Herzog's filmmaking, and also of his simultaneous ability to be self-aware enough to make a hilarious cameo in *Penguins of Madagascar*. As noted in the review, I learned about *White Wilderness* first from my dad, and then from watching the film itself, which is widely available. I learned much more about lemmings, including our bygone belief that they rained from the sky, from the *Encyclopedia Britannica* online article "Do Lemmings Really Commit Mass Suicide?" (Just to say it one more time: No. They don't.)

Piggly Wiggly

I first heard the astonishing story of Clarence Saunders and Piggly Wiggly from Sarah, who shared with me a passage about the grocery store chain in William Sitwell's *A History of Food in 100 Recipes*. Most of the Saunders quotes in this essay, and the quote from Ernie Pyle, come from Mike Freeman's 2011 book, *Clarence Saunders and the Founding of Piggly Wiggly: The Rise & Fall of a Memphis Maverick*. For information about my great-grandfather, I am grateful to my mom, Sydney Green, and my late grandmother, Billie Grace Goodrich, who was incidentally a loyal Piggly Wiggly shopper.

The Nathan's Famous Hot Dog Eating Contest

The George Shea quotations cited here are all from televised introductions to the annual Nathan's Famous Hot Dog Eating Contest. The Mortimer Matz quote comes from a 2010 *New York Times* interview by Sam Roberts. The documentary mentioned is *The Good, the Bad, the Hungry*, directed by Nicole Lucas Haimes. Two histories of Nathan's Famous also provided helpful background for this essay: *Famous Nathan* by Lloyd Handwerker and Gil

Reavill, and *Nathan's Famous: The First 100 Years* by William Handwerker and Jayne Pearl. I did not expect that in my life I would finish two entire books about a hot dog stand, but 2020 was full of surprises, and both the books are quite interesting.

CNN

The first CNN broadcast is available not at CNN.com but on YouTube. To learn more about trends in child mortality, I strongly recommend *Our World in Data* (ourworldindata.org). It contextualizes data on a wide variety of topics—from Covid to poverty to carbon emissions—with the kind of clarity and thoughtfulness that helps you remember that everyone has birthdays. The statistic about 74 percent of Americans thinking child mortality is getting worse comes from a 2017 Ipsos report called "Perils of Perception." I learned about it from *Our World in Data*. Shannon, Katie, Hassan: I love you all. Thank you. Long live the cult of Claremont.

Harvey

The Sontag quote about depression is from *Illness as Metaphor*. The William Styron quote is from *Darkness Visible*. Both those books have been hugely important to me as I live with mental illness. The complete Emily Dickinson poem, sometimes known as Poem 314, is available in most collections of Dickinson's work. Bill Ott and Ilene Cooper have guided me to *Harvey* and so much else in the last twenty years; this essay is my attempt to thank Bill.

The Yips

Rick Ankiel's memoir about his time in baseball, written with Tim Brown, is called *The Phenomenon: Pressure, the Yips, and the Pitch that Changed My Life*. I first learned about Ana Ivanovic's yips from Louisa Thomas's 2011 *Grantland* article, "Lovable Headcases," which contains the Ivanovic quote about overanalyzing. Katie Baker's *Grantland* piece "The Yips Plague and the Battle of Mind Over Matter" was also helpful, as was Tom Perrotta's piece in the September 2010 issue of the *Atlantic* called "High Strung: The

Inexplicable Collapse of a Tennis Phenom." There have been many academic studies of the yips; the one I referred to most is titled "The 'Yips' in Golf: A Continuum Between a Focal Dystonia and Choking," lead author Aynsley M. Smith. (All hail continuums over dichotomies.) The golfing coach referred to is Hank Haney, whose story is told in David Owen's 2014 *New Yorker* piece "The Yips."

Auld Lang Syne

The Robert Burns online encyclopedia (robertburns.org) is a wonderful resource for those looking to learn more about Burns, "Auld Lang Syne," or Burns's fascinating friendship with Frances Dunlop. Most of the quotes from Burns's letters come from the encyclopedia. The Morgan Library and Museum (themorgan.org) has an extensive archive about the song, including Burns's letter to George Thomson describing the original melody as "mediocre." Scans of Henry Williamson's letter to his mother about the Christmas Truce of 1914 are also available online at the Henry Williamson archive; I first learned of the other quotes about the Christmas Truce (and several other details in the essay) from a 2013 BBC article by Steven Brocklehurst, "How Auld Lang Syne Took Over the World." The Robert Hughes quote is from his book *The Shock of the New*. After Amy died, McSweeney's reprinted her columns from *Might* magazine, so they are now archived online. Amy's books quoted here are *Encyclopedia of an Ordinary Life* and *Textbook Amy Krouse Rosenthal*. The Amy Krouse Rosenthal Foundation funds ovarian cancer research and childhood literacy initiatives. You can learn more at amykrouserosenthalfoundation.org.

Googling Strangers

Years after writing this review, I had a chance to talk with the kid in question, who is now a young man—older, in fact, than I was when I was a chaplain. That conversation—which provided me with consolation and hope that I can't possibly find language for—was made possible by the podcast *Heavyweight*. Thanks to everyone at *Heavyweight* for making that happen, especially Jonathan Goldstein, Kalila Holt, Mona Madgavkar, and Stevie Lane. And thanks most of all to Nick, who evinces the love and kindheartedness that lights the way.

Indianapolis

The data about Indianapolis's size and population are taken from 2017 U.S. Census estimates. The *Indianapolis Star*'s 2019 series about the White River and its water quality was very helpful to me. (It's also the kind of journalism that cities like Indianapolis desperately need.) The parts of the series I relied upon were written and reported by Sarah Bowman and Emily Hopkins. In 2016, WalletHub ranked Indianapolis as America's #1 microcosm city. The Vonnegut quote about maintenance comes from his book *Hocus Pocus*; the quote about not being able to get home again comes from Simon Hough's 2005 profile of Vonnegut in the *Globe and Mail*, "The World According to Kurt." The line about the terrible disease of loneliness is reprinted in the book *Palm Sunday*, a wonderful collage of Vonnegut's memories, essays, and speeches.

Kentucky Bluegrass

I first learned about America's turfgrass problem from Diana Balmori and Fritz Haeg's book, *Edible Estates: Attack on the Front Lawn*. The book, a companion to Haeg's ongoing art project involving replacing front lawns with vegetable gardens, changed both my lawn and my life. I also recommend *The Lawn: A History of an American Obsession* by Virginia Scott Jenkins and Ted Steinberg's *American Green: The Obsessive Quest for the Perfect Lawn*. Oregon State University's "BeaverTurf" web portal helped me understand which turfgrass is Kentucky bluegrass and where it is widely cultivated. The estimate on the percentage of American land devoted to the growth of turfgrass comes from a study in *Environmental Management* called "Mapping and Modeling the Biogeochemical Cycling of Turf Grasses in the United States," lead author Cristina Milesi. The statistic about almost a third of U.S. residential water use going to watering lawns comes from the EPA's "Outdoor Water Use in the United States."

The Indianapolis 500

My favorite book about the Indy 500 explores its formation and the first race at the Speedway: Charles Leerhsen's *Blood and Smoke: A True Tale of Mystery, Mayhem, and the Birth of the Indy 500*. I owe my interest in IndyCar to my best friend, Chris Waters, and to other members of our race crew, especially Marina Waters, Shaun Souers, Kevin Schoville, Nate Miller, and Tom Edwards. Our branch of the annual bike-to-the-race tradition was founded by Kevin Daly. Thanks also to IndyCar drivers James Hinchcliffe and Alexander Rossi for giving me an idea of how racing works for the drivers, and how they live with the risks inherent to the sport.

Monopoly

Mary Pilon's book *The Monopolists* is a comprehensive history of Monopoly's early days and especially illuminating in its portrayal of Elizabeth Magie. I was introduced to the video game *Universal Paperclips* by Elyse Marshall and her husband, Josef Pfeiffer. I learned of Hasbro's response to Elizabeth Magie from Antonia Noori Farzan's 2019 *Washington Post* piece, "The New Monopoly 'Celebrates Women Trailblazers.' But the Game's Female Inventor Still Isn't Getting Credit." That piece also contains the most concise and comprehensible summary of Georgism I've come across.

Super Mario Kart

The Super Mario wiki (mariowiki.com) is so astonishingly exhaustive and carefully sourced that it might be the best wiki I've ever encountered. Its article about *Super Mario Kart* gave me much of the background I needed for this review. The interview with Shigeru Miyamoto I quote comes from a Nintendo roundtable; it's available online under the headline "It Started with a Guy in Overalls."

Bonneville Salt Flats

Donald Hall's essay "The Third Thing" was first published in *Poetry* magazine in 2005; I was introduced to it by Kaveh Akbar and Ellen Grafton.

Much of the information about the Bonneville Salt Flats came from the Utah Geological Survey; I am particularly indebted to Christine Wilkerson's article "GeoSights: Bonnevile Salt Flats, Utah." I learned about the history of the *Enola Gay* and Wendover from the artist William Lamson and the Center for Land Use Interpretation in Wendover. The Melville quote is from *Moby-Dick*, which I read only thanks to the dogged efforts of Professor Perry Lentz. We were joined on that trip to Wendover by Mark Olsen and Stuart Hyatt, both of whom deeply enriched my understanding of the salt flats.

Hiroyuki Doi's Circle Drawings

I first saw Hiroyuki Doi's artwork in 2006 at the American Folk Art Museum's exhibition *Obsessive Drawing*. The untitled drawing I refer to can be seen at its digitized collection at folkartmuseum.org. The Doi quotes and his biographical background come from a 2013 *Japan Times* article by Edward Gómez, "Outsider Drawn to the Circle of Life," from a 2017 *Wall Street International* review of a Doi exhibition at Ricco/Maresca Gallery, and from a 2016 review in *Brut Force* by Carrie McGath called "The Inscape in Escape Routes: Five Works by Hiroyuki Doi." The study "What Does Doodling Do?" was published by Jackie Andrade in *Applied Cognitive Psychology* in 2009.

Whispering

The idea for this review came from a conversation with my friends Enrico Lo Gatto, Craig Lee, and Alex Jimenez. I don't remember how I learned that cotton-top tamarins whisper, but a 2013 paper in *Zoo Biology* by Rachel Morrison and Diana Reiss details "Whisper-like behavior in a non-human primate." The authors noted that a group of cotton-top tamarins whispered (or, technically, engaged in whisper-like vocalizations) when in the presence of a human they didn't like, which is the sort of detail that reminds me that humans are just primates trying to make the best of a very strange situation.

Viral Meningitis

No book has helped me understand my own pain like Elaine Scarry's *The Body in Pain*, which was recommended to me by Mike Rugnetta. The Susan Sontag line about giving illness a meaning comes from *Illness as Metaphor*. I learned about meningitis, and recovered from it, thanks to excellent care by the neurologist Dr. Jay Bhatt. I know about catastrophizing thanks to a lifetime of doing it. I learned about the scope of viruses from Philipp Dettmer's brilliant book *Immune*. If you are interested in the relationship between microbes and their hosts (especially their human hosts), I recommend *Immune* and also Ed Yong's book *I Contain Multitudes*. The Nicola Twilley quote comes from her 2020 *New Yorker* piece "When a Virus Is the Cure."

Plague

Most of the quotes from witness accounts of the Black Death in this review are from Rosemary Horrox's book *The Black Death*. The book was recommended to me by my friend and colleague Stan Muller, and I've gone back to it many times in the last few years. It's unlike anything I've ever read, and deeply moving. I'm also indebted to Barbara Tuchman's *A Distant Mirror: The Calamitous 14th Century*. I learned of al-Maqrizi and Ibn Khaldūn's accounts of the Black Death first from Joseph Byrne's *Encyclopedia of the Black Death*. The information about cholera's history comes from Charles Rosenberg's *The Cholera Years*, Amanda Thomas's *Cholera: The Victorian Plague*, Steven Johnson's *The Ghost Map*, and Christopher Hamlin's *Cholera: The Biography*. The more recent information about cholera and tuberculosis, including their annual death toll, comes from the WHO. For help understanding what drives contemporary cholera outbreaks, I am indebted to John Lascher and Dr. Bailor Barrie at Partners in Health Sierra Leone. Dr. Joia Mukherjee's *An Introduction to Global Health Delivery* explores in detail the many ways in which poverty is humanity's biggest health problem. The Tina Rosenberg quote about malaria is from her 2004 essay first published in the *New York Times*, "What the World Needs Now Is DDT"; I learned of it via Eula Biss's book *On Immunity*. The Margaret Atwood quote is from *The Testaments*. Ibn Battuta's story of Damascus is from *The Travels of Ibn Battuta*, as translated by H.A.R. Gibb.

Wintry Mix

I first read Kaveh Akbar's poem "Wild Pear Tree" in his book *Calling a Wolf a Wolf*. The Mountain Goats song is "The Mess Inside" from their album *All Hail West Texas*. I first learned the phrase "wintry mix" from my friend Shannon James. Some of Wilson Bentley's snowflake photographs are archived at the Smithsonian Institute; I know about them because of a 2017 *Washington Post* article by Sarah Kaplan called "The Man Who Uncovered the Secret Lives of Snowflakes." The Ruskin quotes are from *Modern Painters*, Volume 3; the Walter Scott quote is from *Lord of the Isles*. The cummings quotes about the soft white damn is from a poem that begins "i will cultivate within." I am a little hard on the poem in this review, even though actually it is one of my very favorite poems. Speaking of very favorite poems, the Paige Lewis quote is from their book *Space Struck*. The Anne Carson lines are from the verse novel *Autobiography of Red*.

In addition to being the first person to spacewalk, Alexei Leonov was probably the first person to make art in space—he brought colored pencils and paper with him into orbit. He recounts his first space walk, and the truly harrowing story of how their spacecraft landed hundreds of miles off-course, in "The Nightmare of Voskhod 2," an essay published in *Air and Space* in 2005. I heard Leonov's story thanks to a video made by Sarah called "Art We Launched into Space."

The Hot Dogs of Bæjarins Beztu Pylsur

Laura, Ryan, and Sarah all agree that some of the events I describe in this essay took place on a different day from the Olympic Medal Day, and I continue to believe that they are all wrong and that my memory is unimpeachably accurate. We all agree that was a great hot dog, though.

The Notes App

I learned about skeuomorphic design from a conversation with Ann-Marie and Stuart Hyatt. The 2012 *Wired* essay "Clive Thompson on Analog Designs in the Digital Age" gave me more examples of the phenomenon. The Mountain Goats' song "Jenny" is from the album *All Hail West Texas*. Sarah Manguso's astonishing and wrenching book *The Two Kinds of Decay* was first published in 2008. (I also love love love Manguso's book *Ongoingness*. In fact, I need to make a note to ask Sarah to read it.)

The Mountain Goats

Thanks to John Darnielle, Peter Hughes, Jon Wurster, Matt Douglas, and all the other Mountain Goats through the years. Thanks also to the extraordinary Mountain Goats fandom, which responds to the songs with all kinds of magnificence—from fan art to flowcharts. Valerie Barr and Arka Pain are among the many people who've deepened my love for the band; thanks also to KT O'Conor for setting me straight on the meaning of "Jenny."

The QWERTY Keyboard

I began this review after coming across a *Smithsonian* magazine article by Jimmy Stamp, "Fact or Fiction? The Legend of the QWERTY Keyboard." "The Fable of the Keys," an article by Stan J. Liebowitz and Stephen E. Margolis first published in the April 1990 issue of *The Journal of Law and Economics*, makes a convincing case that QWERTY is actually a pretty good keyboard layout, and that the studies finding DVORAK superior are deeply flawed. Thorin Klosowski's 2013 Lifehacker piece, "Should I Use an Alternative Keyboard Layout Like Dvorak?" is a great summary of the (admittedly limited!) research into that question, and makes a case that QWERTY is only slightly worse than optimized key layouts. I learned of Sholes's battle against the death penalty from the Wisconsin Historical Society. I also benefited from Bruce Bliven's 1954 book, *The Wonderful Writing Machine*, and from Graham Lawton's *New Scientist: The Origin of (almost) Everything*.

The World's Largest Ball of Paint

Mike Carmichael is still caring for (and helping paint) the world's largest ball of paint in Alexandria, Indiana. It is very much worth a trip just for the joy of meeting him and adding your own layer to the ball. You can email Mike at worldslargestbop@yahoo.com. Thanks to Emily for joining me on many trips to visit roadside attractions, and to Ransom Riggs and Kathy Hickner, who took a cross-country road trip with me where we discovered much about roadside America. Speaking of which, Roadside America (roadsideamerica.com) has for decades been a wonderful guide to the world's largests and smallests. We used it in college, and I use it still, infuriating my kids with side trips to, say, the office building shaped like a picnic basket. More recently, Atlas Obscura (atlasobscura.com and, in book form, *Atlas Obscura: An Explorer's Guide to the World's Hidden Wonders*) has become an indispensable resource. Eric Grundhauser's Atlas Obscura article on the ball of paint was very helpful to me. Finally, a special word of thanks to ArcGIS StoryMaps article "Big Balls," by Ella Axelrod, which contains many wonderful pictures and also some magnificent subheadings, like "Big Balls: An Overview" and "Balls of Various Composition."

Sycamore Trees

This review references two of my all-time favorite books: Jacqueline Woodson's devastating and perfectly wrought *If You Come Softly* and Annie Dillard's *Pilgrim at Tinker Creek*. Among its many gifts to me, *Pilgrim at Tinker Creek* introduced me to Herodotus's story of Xerxes and the sycamore. I learned of the so-called Pringle Tree on a visit to Pringle Tree Park in Buckhannon, West Virginia. I first read the Edna St. Vincent Millay poem "Not So Far as the Forest" in her 1939 book, *Huntsman, What Quarry?*

"New Partner"

"New Partner" appears on the Palace Music album *Viva Last Blues*. I first heard the song because of Ransom Riggs and Kathy Hickner, who heard it because of Jacob and Nathaniel Otting. Kaveh Akbar's "The Palace" was first published in the *New Yorker* in April of 2019.

Three Farmers on Their Way to a Dance

This review would've been utterly impossible without help from the on-line community Tuataria, especially Ketie Saner, who translated a lot of German for me and tracked down all kinds of leads. I would never have learned the story of the young farmers without the dogged reporting of Reinhard Pabst in the *Frankfurter Allgemeine* newspaper. In a 2014 article, Pabst collected other research about the young farmers as well as accounts of the men from their surviving descendants. I am also immensely grateful for Richard Powers's novel *Three Farmers on Their Way to a Dance*. Powers's books have been with me for twenty years, and they always seem to find me where and when I need them. A 2014 conversation (archived online at srf.ch) between Christa Miranda and Sander researcher Gabriele Conrath-Scholl was also helpful to me in learning about the photograph. The John Berger quote is from his book *About Looking*. I'm also indebted to Susanne Lange's book *August Sander* in the Photofile series, to the Sander collection *August Sander: Face of Our Time*, and to the 2013 collection *August Sander: People of the 20th Century*, edited by Susanne Lange and Gabriele Conrath-Scholl.

Postscript

I've had the same German editor (Saskia Heintz at Hanser) and translator (Sophie Zeitz) since my first book was published in 2005. One of the joys of having my books translated is seeing the titles change. In German, *The Fault in Our Stars* became *Das Schicksal ist ein mieser Verräter*, which translates to something like *Fate Is a Lousy Traitor*. Fate really is a lousy traitor, and I love that title, as I love the German title of this book. But the best title of any of my books in any language is the Norwegian translation of *The Fault in Our Stars*. It's called *Faen ta skjebnen*—or *Fuck Fate*.

The Orbital Sunrise

This review began with an assignment from Sarah Urist Green's book *You Are an Artist*, but I first learned of Alexei Leonov's artwork from a different project by Sarah, a YouTube video called "Art We Launched Into Space." The Faulkner quote is from his Nobel Prize acceptance speech. The Victor Glover quote comes from his Instagram, which features some phenomenally beautiful images of orbital sunrises, while the Mae Jemison quote is from a 1994 interview with the *Chicago Tribune*. All the quotations from Alexei Leonov come from *Two Sides of the Moon*, a dual memoir written with American astronaut David Scott. The Mary Oliver quote is from "Poem of the One World," and Eudora Welty made her observation that all serious daring starts from within in *One Writer's Beginnings*.

The Ginkgo Tree

I first came across that Gertrude Stein essay in a book called *The Best American Essays of the Century*. (The century in question was the twentieth.) I don't know if it actually contains the best American essays of the twentieth century, but that Gertrude Stein essay changed the way I think about writing. I learned about the history of this patch of Indianapolis from Kurt Vonnegut's *Palm Sunday*, and from research done by the landscape architect Chris Merritt and his firm, Merritt Chase. Neighbors told me about Edith Lieber Vonnegut's time living in the cottage near the ginkgo. I'm very grateful to Gordon Wishard for sharing his love of the land with me. If you want to learn more about ginkgo trees, I highly recommend Peter Crane's *Ginkgo: The Tree That Time Forgot*.

DISCOVER
JOHN GREEN'S
CRITICALLY ACCLAIMED FICTION

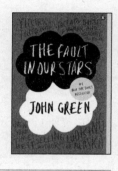

I find ads inside of books a bit gauche, but then again, my publisher tells me they're effective. The hope ~
made it all the way to the back page of this book, you might be interested to learn that I have written ~
And I would like for you to read those books. Have you ever played the game "Marco Polo"? One ~
and the other players answer "Polo." Writing is like that for me. For years I'm in my basement, ~
"Marco, Marco, Marco, Marco." And then one day, a reader says, "Polo." Hearing that response ne~
is the real thrill of both reading and writing. The connections forged by books make me feel les~
deep. So if this ad leads to a few more "Polo" moments, I can't begrudge its presence. I give back page~